Here, There are Dragons

A MEMOIR BY WITNESS J

Published in Australia in 2020

10 9 8 7 6 5 4 3 2 1

Enquiries to reach the author should be made through the Attorney-General's Department on (02) 6141 3888 (+61261413888), quoting reference number 19/1112. Alternatively, a request can be made to typhon2@protonmail.com.

A catalogue record for this book is available from the National Library of Australia.

ISBN: 978 0 646 81739 2 (paperback)

Cover artwork by Marija Stojkovic
Book formatting by www.bookclaw.com

Dedicated to victims everywhere.

Forgive me for colouring in your monsters.

FOREWORD

By Robert Macklin and Julian Burnside.

Robert Macklin
Tuross Head, January 2020.

In late 2019 I was completing a book on an organisation with close ties to Australia's defence establishment. So when an email arrived – circuitously – from a prisoner who had been secretly incarcerated in Canberra's Alexander Maconochie Centre (AMC) and given a government alias, 'Alan Johns' to hide his identity, I was intrigued but wary.

This 'Alan Johns', said the email, had been in the AMC long enough to have written a memoir of his time there of some 80,000 words. He'd read one of my books – *Warrior Elite* - a history of our Special Forces and Intelligence services - and asked very politely if I would meet him in the prison to advise on getting his work published.

Red lights were flashing wherever I looked. However, I had begun my writing life as a journalist, and if true, this was a story that demanded to be told. This was Australia, after all, and we don't have secret trials. Nor do we send the accused secretly to jail...and in the National Capital of all places.

So, before I acted, I met with some highly placed friends in the Defence and Intelligence game; and to a man they were as bemused as myself. I also told the principals of the organisation I was writing about and they naturally urged caution. So, with not a little trepidation, I telephoned the jail and sought an appointment. They sent me a form which I filled out and returned.

The questions were simple enough. The only one that gave me pause asked whether my visit was private or professional. I took 'professional' to be directed at prisoners' legal counsel; and since I wasn't a lawyer and was not about to charge for my advice – which I often gave to hopeful authors – I ticked 'private'. My visit was approved for the following week.

However, the day before came a call from the jail to say the unnamed general manager had now disapproved my visit. And when I asked the reason, none was forthcoming. In the interim, according to a later judicial judgement, the general manager had seen my request and had 'suspected that he was an author'. She alerted the Australian Federal Police who seem to have confirmed her suspicions. They then raided the prisoner's cell and the home of his brother in Melbourne.

I remained in the dark about this until another email arrived – from the prisoner's brother - to say that a judgement would be handed down in Court 4 of the ACT Supreme Court and I was welcome to attend. It was scheduled for a Friday afternoon when, deliberately or not, the building would be pretty much deserted.

My wife Wendy and I took our places at the back of the Court and the prisoner arrived to represent himself. By then he had served his sentence and been released from AMC. We'd had a brief meeting at our Canberra home the day before. He seemed a pleasant, if emotionally fragile, young man in his mid-thirties, highly intelligent and with the deferential manners of the Duntroon graduate and DFAT officer he had been for the last fifteen years.

He had taken a civil action against the AMC authorities over their refusal to allow my visit and the raids that followed. And on the day, Justice John Burns delivered his judgement, finding for the AMC authorities and awarding costs against 'Alan Johns'. He pleaded with the judge from the bar table to reverse the costs ruling, but Burns

J declined and suggested he approach the ACT Justice Department lawyers.

At the end of the short hearing, Witness J passed me the long judgement, and at last I had the material to write the story of the secret prisoner. In the judgement, I was amused to discover, I was referred to by the coded initials 'SN'. Since my real initials are RM, if you just use the next letters of the alphabet…it did not need the expertise of Bletchley Park to crack the code.

Since 'Alan Johns' hated the government-imposed alias – his real name being *verboten* for other reasons – I cast about for a suitable *nom de plume*.

As it happened, I'd recently written a column for the Canberra newsmagazine *CityNews* on the appalling decision to charge Bernard Collaery and his client, Witness K with offences related to the bugging of the East Timorese during negotiations over the Timor Gap oil and gas agreement. So I reversed the judgement's code and my subject became Witness J.

When I filed the story the following day, *CityNews* editor Ian Meikle was ready to give it the treatment it deserved. Perhaps not surprisingly, it became *CityNews*'s biggest story of the year. And because my by-line was used, the phone soon rang hot with reporters wanting to follow it up.

There was very little I could add since it seemed – though I was never told – that the troubles that sent Witness J to prison for 15 months were themselves secret. And gradually the story faded into the mist.

But that left Witness J without a job and with a prison record. So a life dedicated to his country in the front lines of East Timor, Afghanistan and Iraq - and in government service thereafter – was tenuous at best. He returned to the book he'd written in prison and sought a publisher.

At last I was permitted to help, but there was not much more I could do than introduce him to my regular publisher and to some literary agents. I was pleased to do so, because the subject was fascinating one. Not only had he been secretly imprisoned but once inside the AMC they housed him with the vile sexual perverts – rapists and paedophiles – who are isolated for their own protection.

Absolutely nothing in Witness J's background, or in the troubles that caused him to be imprisoned, involved sexual deviance. On the contrary, he was and remains very much a conventional bloke and has, from her photographs, a lovely fiancée. He was housed with them simply because they were set apart from the ruffians and yobbos of the general prison population.

While others might well have surrendered to a depressive malaise and drifted, Witness J responded very differently. He began observing then writing about these deeply flawed creatures, analysing their deceptions and their self-delusions. Then he took the next brave step and explored the morality of his own responses to them, not just as monsters, but as damaged human beings.

Now, for the first time in Australian literary history, he has opened that window to a world not just within a prison but one barred even to the prisoners. And he brings to it the perception of a decent man and a thoughtful one.

It is a disturbing exposition, one which deserves to take its place in both the academic and the socio-sexual libraries of our nation. And, unlike the commercial publishers who feared it, I strongly suspect that it will find a market within the intelligent general readership, first of our country then of the wider world.

Witness J has distinguished himself by his courage on the front lines of the conflicts of our time. He is now battling to rebuild his life, this time as a writer. He has chosen a vocation that requires exactly the kind of moral courage that shines through this book.

He deserves to win the battle.

I hope and believe he will.

Robert Macklin is one of Australia's most respected and popular authors of Australian history and biography.

* * *

Julian Burnside AO QC
Melbourne, February 2020

Not enough people know the case of Witness J. I do not know what he was charged with, and he is not allowed to say.

His trial in the Supreme Court of the A.C.T, in Canberra, was held in secret, and he was sent to jail at the Alexander Maconochie Centre in the A.C.T.. He served his time in that part of the prison which is allocated for sex offenders and paedophiles, although it becomes plain that he was not charged with, or suspected of, sex or paedophilia offences. Before his trial, he was held without bail. When the facts emerged in November 2019, even the ACT Attorney-General was unaware of the case. Witness J later brought a civil action against the general manager of the prison in which he served his (secret) sentence.

The general manager of the prison at the time was Corinne Justason. Justason was aware of the fact that certain Commonwealth orders applied to Witness J, although she was not aware of the terms of the orders. She was aware that the disclosure of information relating to Witness J (and the offences of which he had been convicted) was prohibited. Justason learned that Witness J had written a novel, and she informed the Federal police. J's privileges were subsequently revoked. His access to email was terminated. His brother's house was raided: just 9 days after Justason had told the AFP that Witness J had written a novel. Two days later the AFP executed a search warrant raid on Witness J's cell.

This book tells the story of his time in prison.

The book makes it increasingly clear that J was housed in that part of the jail so that any public protest by him would be seen as coming from an inmate of the sex offenders and paedophiles wing.

I assume, without knowing, that this is the book the manuscript of which was the subject of the search warrant raids. If that assumption is right, the people who authorised the search warrant raids must have been disappointed: the wing of the Alexander Maconochie Centre in which J was held comes across as a truly enlightened place, and the people J was imprisoned with appear, for the most part, to be quite ordinary people: when they are seen as complete human beings in three dimensions, rather than simply one-dimensional sex offenders or paedophiles, so despised by the tabloid press.

During his time in jail J, who was a former army officer and diplomat in his thirties with no prior criminal history, formed relationships, and even friendships in some cases, with prisoners who included senior public servants, a catholic priest, a university law professor, a scout master, a senior UN officer, teachers and many others: all of them sexual-predators.

From the time of his arrest to the time of his release, J spent about 15 months in prison.

I read the book because I was eager to find out what J had done which deserved a secret charge, secret trial and secret imprisonment. But soon that question took second place to genuine surprise that so many people – people who have been convicted of some of the worst crimes, people who are loathed by the tabloid press – turn out to be interesting and engaging characters. Only a small minority seem to justify the contempt with which they are all generally treated.

The book considers the philosophical question J has struggled with: can you accept the humanity of people like these and not lose yourself in the process? Having read the book, and having had a number of discussions with J, I think the answer is Yes: you can accept the humanity of people like these and not lose yourself in the process. But the circumstances which led me to reading the book left me with a larger question concerning the circumstances which led to J's imprisonment. When the AFP raided the home of Witness J's brother, and when they raided his prison cell, they were looking for the manuscript of the novel. While AFP raids for sensitive documents have become common in recent months (recent striking examples are the raid on the Sydney headquarters of the ABC and on journalist Annika Smethurst), this is a departure from the norm even tested against that worrying standard. And that question is: can you accept the humanity of the people who prosecuted, tried and sentenced J? Forget about whether you lose yourself in the process. Can you accept their humanity at all?

That question is impossible to answer as long as we are not allowed to know who they are.

Julian Burnside AO QC is an esteemed Australian barrister. He is also a prominent human rights and refugee advocate, and author.

PREFACE

I began writing this memoir while I was embarked on the unenjoyable journey of being our nation's first ever secret prisoner. In 2018 I was arrested, remanded, indicted and sentenced, in total and unprecedented secrecy (for Australia I should note: we now join the ranks of other nations we tend to turn our noses up to), and, save for the curiosity of esteemed author Robert Macklin, my case may never have become known to the Australian public.

After secretly serving 455 days in prison, I was released on recognizance in August 2019 and quietly re-entered society. Since then it has become a matter of public record that I worked over two careers as an intelligence officer, serving in flashpoints like East Timor, Afghanistan, Iraq, and elsewhere abroad, often under diplomatic cover, and always serving Australia's national interest in both war and peace.

For those that begin these pages hoping for insightful and scandalous operational details of the military, or the secret intelligence agency I worked for (and still cannot legally name), you will be bitterly disappointed. The contents of this book – editing and contributions not withstanding – were written while I was in prison. I wrote openly and with the permission of the then prison warden in my cell, knowing that dozens of invisible eyes peered over my shoulder as I typed every word. Given these constraints, I hope the reader will excuse the fact I have not expanded on the true rottenness and corruption of the prison, or the scandalous circumstances that brought me there. Perhaps one day soon…

In February 2019, a new prison warden was appointed. On learning I had written this memoir, she panicked, and notified the police I had sent it on to a family member via my prison email account. The federal police then executed, infuriatingly, secret warranted raids on my family. Because of this I sued the prison, and went so far as to subpoena the warden and question her on the stand, much to the amazement of senior and long serving corrections officers who told me they had never seen such a sight.

I lost my civil case, mind you, to the very same judge who now has the inglorious distinction of having established the precedent of secret trials in this country. However the delightful irony was this: my situation was unmasked through the clumsy actions of the prison and the police, and the murkiness of this unprecedented scandal is still settling as this book is being published. Thus, while I may have lost the battle in court, I feel I've won the wider war. My victory is the hope that no other Australian citizen will ever again be subjected to a secret trial like I was.

* * *

This writing project was born through the advice of the compassionate and caring prison mental health staff, who suggested I write to focus my mind and process the difficult situation I found myself in.

This book is a rolling memoir of the trouble I had processing my feelings of living alongside forty-odd repulsive paedophiles and rapists in my prison wing. I am not a sexual offender, so I wrote in an attempt to reconcile these feelings of being personable with people who had committed the gravest acts of depravity against the most vulnerable in our society. I *had* to live with these people; I *had* to be personable, and so I chose to explore this daily inner conflict through writing, and did so with a consciousness that certain victims or their advocates would have little sympathy for my labours. However, should you outright reject the premise of this book, I make no apologies to you. I have a voice, and having suffered enough censorship and suppression to last ten lifetimes, I will be heard. I encourage these early dissenters to at least read the epilogue and understand my own conclusions; in doing so, your criticisms will at least have some authority. For others that consume and find this content difficult, I am sympathetic, and the book's dedication was always clear to me from the moment I started writing.

In some cases, it was only after my release that I could read about some of my fellow detainee's heinous crimes. I have made a deliberate decision not to make edits along the way clarifying this, and believe the reader will be better served by experiencing the interactions as I did at the time.

Lastly, where a fellow prisoner described in this book has been convicted of committing a sexual offence against a family member, I have appended a pseudonym to protect the victim(s) from being identified.

Otherwise I have told it as it is.

Witness J

March 2020

PART I

HIC SUNT DRACONES

Here, there are dragons

Oft written for uncharted territories
on old maps and globes; first seen
engraved on two conjoined ostrich
egg halves dated to 1504.

CHAPTER 1

Cameron Tully is someone who just gets along with everyone instantly and effortlessly. It's that charisma. You know what I'm talking about; he's someone who just makes you smile and like them in a way that you don't fully appreciate, except to know that it's real and wonderful. Perhaps you even fool yourself into thinking it's *you* making the encounter so fluently natural. If you do recognise the skill, it can even make you envious to see that disarming and even enchanting personality at work, easily parrying away awkwardness and tearing down personal boundaries.

That's what I felt wash over me when I arrived at my new accommodation and was introduced to Cameron as the delegate for this part of the prison. A former senior public servant, he's a tall guy, and never minds providing his exact measurements when the topic comes up. "Six-three," he'll say, typically when describing a physical altercation he's had in the past four years of his own stay here as a prisoner. I've heard this measurement enough now to know it with certainty, despite the different weights and heights some of the others throw around during the inescapable idle chats of incarcerated life.

The backbone of maintaining your sanity when imprisoned is finding the right kind of relationship where an idle chat can go around and around without becoming tiresome, and it took me a while to understand this properly. You talk with mostly everyone about anything, and the same topics form the foundation of the half-relationships you develop with your incarcerated peers, and by the time you swing around to your fifth, tenth or twentieth chat about Formula One, a specific legal case, or the latest gossip about someone else or their recent actions, you really start to wear down, at which point it's essential to avoid that topic to maintain your own sanity. I'm currently avoiding chats on Arthur Hoyle's imminent legal appeal decision, Adam Carrington's explicit and thoroughly unwanted descriptions of the evidence in his ongoing trial, catching and skinning rabbits (as half-recalled by the eighty-year-old Cyril), and anything to do with the card game *Magic: The Gathering*. I'm also dodging anything from my own neighbour who never properly hears me when all I reply to his greeting is: "Fine thanks, how are you going?" The reflexive answer from Dave, sixty-eight years old, is "What?" and it just annoys me these days. It's a shame because he's a nice guy, and he just happens to live in the room adjacent mine, so I'm forced through our polite dance twice (on average) every day.

I haven't yet pulled apart all of the acronyms and lingo of jail, so strict protection, remand side one or two, cottage this and cottage that, the women's yard, and the dreaded solitary confinement where I started my own journey are all mostly foreign concepts right now. They all have tight acronyms that make sense to the corrections officers, civilian staff and prisoners – seemingly everyone here but me – like SCU, SU1, SU2, RU1, CSU, TRC, etc. Mingling among all of these acronyms are 400 prisoners with their own sense of normality and different power dynamics. Rebels outlaw motorcycle gang members here, Comanchero members there; men, women, 'spinners' (crazies), this ethnicity, that ethnicity, drugs, no drugs . . . That the corrections staff can make sense of all of this seems improbable, and I suspect they don't really know what's happening until a violent incident occurs.

Cameron is one of the few people I can really talk to, and it's nice to live closely with the delegate for the forty-odd prisoners in this part of the jail. That first day in the wing when I was introduced to Cam,

I wasn't sure how I was supposed to feel. Relieved, concerned or even worried about the stigma? I'd already been in the jail for a month and had split my time roughly between solitary confinement, which is where they put me until they could work out what to do with me, and then the close observation part of the jail where all the 'spinners' are. Spinners – as in around the bend; crazy; insane. It's my first piece of jail lingo, though I haven't yet substantively added to my lexicon.

The morning I moved to this new wing I was met by the general manager of the jail, a Scot named Ian Robb, who is short, dark-haired and very recently arrived from Western Australia, and the UK before that. I'm assuming I'm afforded this sort of one-on-one meeting because I'm a sort of anomaly here. You could say I'm kind of special, although I can't really tell you why. I don't mean to annoy you this early on, but it's really out of my hands, and for what it's worth I wish I could be a little more upfront. No one seems to know what to do with me, except to put me in the quietest and most remote part of the jail in the hope that I won't draw much unwanted attention.

Ian warned me about my new wing when we met: there was a stigma attached to the Women's Correctional Centre, or WCC, and he asked if it was something that would bother me. I'm a male in his early thirties, and I certainly wasn't being housed with any women, although it was an idea that might have appealed to me before I learned how difficult the women here actually are. Ian explained that the WCC has kept its original name, even though the thirty-odd women who used to be housed here were moved to another part of the jail to free up beds. I nodded and told Mr Robb, or Ian, as he politely insisted I call him, that this new part of the facility sounded appealing, and no, I wasn't concerned about the stigma, although it was something I was required to discuss with a mental health professional before I could eventually follow Ian across the jail. On this walk, heads turned.

Usually, the escorting of other prisoners around the jail is done by the most junior of the corrections staff, who try to avoid the dreaded and never-ending rover duties that require them to criss-cross the facility every fifteen to twenty minutes – if not constantly. You see, this jail is unique in the region, because within its walls it houses every category of prisoner from the most minimal of security – those who depart unsupervised during daylight hours to attend approved work duties in the community – to the high-risk, high-security killers and enforcers who have twenty plus years to serve, and respect little else but brute force. Men, women, mains, protection, strict protection, different gangs, feuds, he-said-she-said . . . It's high school with – no joke – drugs and violence, and moving different prisoners around the jail, often in close proximity to each other, is a never-ending Rubik's cube that the corrections staff must solve.

It's a part of my own experience: through a door or fence I'll spot someone who comes from a more dangerous part of the jail than I do (which is everywhere else, I'm sorry to admit), and these mostly twenty-something roughnecks are usually identified by tattoos, bad haircuts and the hunched-over look of a jackal. This, I've noticed, is the entry level into predation – they are only dangerous in numbers and when their prey is vulnerable and isolated.

I'm a polite and confident get-along-fellow, and I always take it somewhat personally when I'm quickly shuffled into an adjacent cell or room as one of these jackals passes by. Very few of these people strike me as physically threatening by themselves, but then the odd bruiser will appear who does indeed look like trouble. Wanton violence is not the norm here; typically, one must accrue a drug debt and then lapse on the payments. But the law of the jungle is not something I'm fully across yet, so I try and keep my wits about me, noting the prisoners in my wing are especially targeted for the nature of their offences. I give a wry and chipper smile in passing to the jackals and brutes, but in a place where boiling jam is flung as improvised napalm, and tins of tuna are dropped into socks and swung into a target's face, much is possible.

Cameron warmly shakes my hand when I first meet him, and the general manager instructs him to make sure I'm comfortable. I'll later learn that before my arrival Cameron was told explicitly that I was to be looked after and not harassed in any way, and this explains my placement in the same pod as him.

My arrival even involved the eviction of Cameron's best friend – a highly competent cook and Russian-speaking former Indian diplomat by the name of Navin Edwin – to another pod. Navin's new residence is within the same wing, but as it's a different pod he can only visit between eight am and five pm. The five pod members have now lost Navin's cooking, which is simply superb (so I'm told – I'm yet to try any myself). I have little awareness of all of this as I arrive, but later I compliment my new neighbours on not having made me feel bad about my arrival, and I pass my apologies to the good-natured Navin for having him quite unknowingly evicted.

Cameron gives me the run down and explains the pod layout as my senior escort taps my shoulder and leaves with a nod and final handshake. My room is amazing; amazing for a jail, that is, and certainly a step up from my earlier accommodation of cold brick-built boxes. I have my own room, shower, toilet, computer, television and a lovely window that teasingly looks out at a busy heliport just across the perimeter fence. It surprises me that this proximity to the logistics heliport is not more often a point of humour for the rest of the wing, but a few grumbles about noise are issued by other less-enthused detainees from time to time.

Aside from being six-foot-three, Cameron has a thick Clooney-esque head of salt and pepper hair that's combed straight back, and he talks with a barely present lisp from a minor under-bite. Cam's favourite reply to most things is "Fantastic!" and he's unceasingly positive in a way that makes him rather confidence-boosting to be around, often finding glamour in another's mediocrity, which contrasts well against many others who strive continually for the negative. My African-American neighbour Kenny Johnson is plucked bald on top but with a spattering of half-curly black hair around the back and sides. He claims you can see Cameron's thick hair growing if you watch just long enough.

Cameron walks through the common area we all share in the pod of six and shows me the kitchen and lounge room. I'm surprised to see that Cam has partitioned off a portion of the tiled common area with a few bed sheets where he has an ad hoc room set up. There are five rooms in the pod, and two are supposed to share a room, although bunk beds for that room haven't yet turned up, and so Cam sleeps in the common area to the satisfaction of all concerned. His single mattress sits above a half dozen or so milk-crates forming a bed base, and his computer and television are on an adjacent desk. It's a room only a charismatic extrovert like Cameron could occupy. In contrast, I slump with relief when I can swing my own heavy metal door shut and escape my pod and wing at will; solitude has always been my medicine.

That first dinner everyone is polite, but they are trying to feel me out, probing for a snippet of information here or there. I'm special, which I say with absolutely no hint of egotism or pride, and it seems obvious to my new neighbours. I'm later to learn that they understand the rhythm of monotony and procedure so completely that anything different is glaringly apparent. I had arrived at a different time, place and with no background information in a way that no other detainee had ever done before, though I suspect that having the general manager evict someone and then personally escort a new detainee in is unlikely to be considered normal. For detainees who, in nine years, have not had a single conversation with the general manager, being escorted in by him and on first-name basis is odd to the extreme. Kenny is the first at dinner to investigate.

"So, what's the story?"

"Well, I guess I'm living here now," I offer with a shrug, "and everything is pretty new still." It's clearly not what he wants, though at the time I fail to see that his response is framed around the absurdity of my special treatment. Of course I understand my own story and how I got to be where I am, just not how obvious it is that I'm different.

Kenny nods his head and doesn't make eye contact – it's something he will rarely do, and fleeting eye contact seems to scold him in a way that's interesting to observe. It's not a lack of confidence – not completely, as Kenny is in his element in jail, but it's perhaps a fleetingness that's more built on shame and a fear of being judged. It's only far later when I learn what Kenny is doing here in jail for his second stint of incarceration that I realise why he feels this shame. His charges are heinous in a way that I can't fully grasp, and only Alwyn Baume – the odd Howard Hughes-esque hermit also living in our pod – supersedes Kenny's crimes in severity and by a significant factor. Kenny is an expert on the United States, very much self-claimed from his mixed ancestry (he is born to an African-American father and Caucasian-American mother) and he spent the first few years of his life in Washington State. He's culturally Australian in accent, slang and most manners, and he makes claims to his American heritage that, while very real, appear forced at times. In short: he's perhaps a lazy five-foot-eight or nine, he's heavy in the stomach and very much loves the NFL, Thanksgiving Day, and commenting on anything remotely approaching American politics or culture. He has an undeniable intellect but is handicapped by his access to *Time* magazine and the quasi-current affairs and comedy show *Planet America*, which gives him a thin veneer of real knowledge that's at times parried away quite quickly. I don't claim to be an expert on international affairs, but his grandiose and well-delivered insights sit uncomfortably on a thinness that's rarely backed by any true substance. Unfortunately, his rebuttals of "You wouldn't understand, you're not American" are met with a raised eyebrow and ultimately make any further argumentative pursuit too tiresome. He spends his days playing the card game *Magic: The Gathering* with his friends Adam Carrington and Glen Vandavord, both from differing adjacent pods, and often critiques me for not getting out enough during the day and being more social. I sometimes don't have the heart to tell him that I'm actively avoiding social contact with a few people in our wing.

All told, Kenny and I get along quite well, and he's a mellow-enough person with experience in many jails across New South Wales. He can be something of a gatekeeper: "You haven't been to/experienced jail until you've been to [insert facility]," is a tiresome position of incarceration authority, but he's institutionalised to the letter and has spent much of his thirty-four years of adulthood locked up, with only a few years here or there of freedom. He tells Jason, who has been incarcerated far longer, of the iPhone's magic: the last piece of ground-breaking technology Kenny had his hands on before returning to jail. Encrypted applications, Snapchat, Flickr and Instagram are more foreign to him than typewriters and fax machines, which I find amazing, though it makes me worry if I'll fall behind myself.

I asked Kenny what he found odd when he was released last time, back in 2010, and his answers were fascinating. For example, anything above Kenny's head, such as highly placed groceries in a supermarket, badly unnerves him because it's not something he deals with in prison. He also finds watching large televisions and using metal cutlery so uncomfortable that he avoids both. Incarcerated, Kenny is at home, and he has clearly come to rely on the state for his physical and social sustenance; I sometimes wonder whether his second range of convictions were a welcome relief from a world that is foreign to him. Cam and Kenny talk regularly and clearly share an ease, having been around each other for four years now, though it is Kenny and Jason who I see as the twins in our pod.

Jason, in his mid-forties, is, and I offer this not rudely but for accuracy, a fattish ogre-like man with a stomach that protrudes out distinctly and a matching ogre face. He has short, shaved hair and is covered in half-finished tattoos: a scorpion on his forearm, a flaming skull and the outline of a dragon on his back, and a love heart with 'Tracey' and an accompanying arrow on his upper right arm. Jason has also spent his life in and out of jail and seems to have relied more heavily on drugs and alcohol than anyone else in our group of six. He has a black sense of humour and draws from the unspeakable well of his and others' similar crimes for a catchy punch line or opportune comment. He's a cliché of racism too, yet I don't feel that his hatred runs through to his heart in any serious way. Asian, Lebanese, Aboriginal . . . they are all fair game for his simple punchline jokes (what do you call a

[race] who [action], etc), and others just smile or give him the outraged reaction he was striving for.

It's clear Jason has been dealt bad cards his entire life; he seems to acknowledge this but also admit to the fact that he's never really tried to make a better life for himself as he's fallen foul of the law again and again. And again. But there he is, hunched over his homework and completing answers on some management theory he's just learned about, trying to better himself, with his small reading glasses perched on the end of a face that would genuinely scare children. He'll allow himself to be tutored by Navin, who comes around during the day to teach him, and asks plenty of questions of Cam. Occasionally, I'll catch that look of frustration he hides badly, and wander over myself to read the question he's stopped on and try and nudge him in the right direction if I can. I want to like Jason because of his efforts to improve himself, and underneath the tattoos and bad humour you can almost see the good person there, but he sabotages himself so consistently. People no doubt look at him, look at his crimes, and dismiss him – throw him away in the garbage and give it a loud ringing kick for good measure. Even when Jason slinks off when it's time to do the dishes or smokes in his room and not outside, I want to believe there's good still there, but the more I learn about him the less I'm really sure. One day I'll find out who the Tracey tattooed on him is – I'm already reliably informed it's a long story.

If Jason's tattoos are a warning on 'how not to do it', then David, our pod elder at sixty-eight, is a canvas of genuine art. Dave is in this part of the jail for his own physical protection, and not for the nature of his offending. He's spent a lifetime collecting drug debts for outlaw motorcycle gangs, and he wears a scorching white mohawk down the centre of his tattooed head. Spiders, skulls, snakes, geisha and playing cards wrap the full length of his arms and legs in bright brilliantly done strokes that the artist must have been paid exorbitantly for. Crippled by gout, he hobbles around in pain to meet with some of the other elders in the wing, and he is received warmly each Thursday and Saturday, much like Cam, with his large family. He has five girls who all seem aghast that their elderly father has finally been 'got' by the law and is doing his first stint in jail for six to ten years (although an appeal and reduction of sentence is likely). Dave is a fine example of an honest crook, if I could be so bold and put it that way. Among a life of honest hard work as a cleaner, a role he proudly claims he never took a day off from, he exudes a sense of hard-man justice, and he says with a real pride that he never hurt anyone who didn't deserve it. Some of his stories are extraordinary for a civic-minded person to hear, but you can't help feeling a sense of awe at the different world he's lived in over the long years of his life, self-managed with an honour code – of sorts. Dave and I arrived at nearly the same time (he had just settled into the room next to me when I arrived) and shares with me one commonality: we are both here because we are anomalies in the jail, although how we both arrived here couldn't differ more.

And then there is Alwyn Baume, our sixth member in the pod. Alwyn is a recluse who lives and eats privately, only ever popping his head out for our multitude of daily musters or stealing through the common area for a cigarette or gasp of fresh air. He's possibly older than Dave and in the range of late sixties to early seventies, and is a curiously thin man of medium height, with a full salt and pepper head of hair in equal proportions to Cam's, but unlike Cam's natural handsomeness, Alwyn wears a bowl haircut that unwittingly adds to his menace. Curiously, he has either an Aboriginal or Arab/Persian ancestry (I could be convinced of both), although I suspect the former based on his anglicised name. He's also unique in that he's incarcerated with his wife and son Kane (who is in his late thirties), both of whom reside in other parts of the jail.

Alwyn's eccentricities at times cause him to fall into unfortunate spirals of imaginary conspiracy (of which I have been the unwitting and unknowing centre on a few occasions) causing strife for himself and others around him. Aside from those situations, a typical interaction with Alwyn (perhaps about sourcing toiletries, or food, or some other innocuous matter) involves a 48-hour period where he will return to one's room frequently either with slight corrections on what he said, or to confirm the hidden non-existent meaning behind what you said.

"Ah, hello," he'll say while looking down. "I just wanted to confirm that you weren't putting your laundry on right after me to have a go at me?"

"Sorry? I was just doing my laundry . . ."

"Oh, okay, no problems then; just wanted to make sure we didn't have a problem or a misunderstanding."

"Nope. Literally just doing my laundry, Alwyn. I wouldn't read anything into it beyond that."

Two hours later, presumably after dissecting this briefest of interactions, there'll be another knock on my door.

"Hi again. Sorry to disturb you; I just wanted to confirm that when you said, 'don't read into it' that you didn't mean I was missing something that could be read into?"

"Ah, no, Alwyn. There are no issues at all," I'll say as precisely as I can manage. The next day Alwyn returns and asks if I was being aggressive. It's a no-win situation, and so he descends into imaginary conspiracy from a point of nothing.

It's curious, and he's so off the mark of reason in the conclusions that he comes to that it's often better to just ignore and not try to explain anything. My own non-existent conspiracy against him started when I began closing my door too loudly, and he allowed the matter to explode (much to my genuine surprise) across the whole wing. Cam, with his patient manner, sat Alwyn down and spoke methodically to him, pricking the tension from the imaginary matter like a caring father speaking to a child who has learning disabilities. After one such episode, Cam confessed to me it was a role he had played with Alwyn for four long years, and he was frankly tiring of it and looking for a reason to have him moved to a more appropriate place to continue serving his long sentence.

Something I find hard to reconcile, despite the obvious mental health challenges that Alwyn faces, is the heinous nature of Alwyn and his family's crimes. In a wing of some truly repulsive people, Alwyn sits in a league all on his own, and it makes my skin crawl to know he sleeps only two rooms away from me. Cam, Kenny, Jason and Dave are very human, in their failings as much as their personalities, but Alwyn scares me in a way that isn't physical but is perhaps more moral. He has deep, unfocussed black eyes, almost like a shark's, and I feel that the predation and coldness of a shark sit behind them as well. He honestly chills me.

So, that's the six of us who live in our pod, known cryptically as 'WR2' (formerly Women's Remand Two), in the forty-person wing known as the 'WCC'. Oh, I probably haven't explained why all of these characters are detained together in the WCC. Those convicted of sexual crimes are targeted in jails as the lowest form of life in the pecking order, and they are housed together for their own protection against violence.

You see, I live with paedophiles and rapists.

CHAPTER 2

I've never raped anyone. It's a strange thing to have to admit, but it's true. I've also never looked at 'CEM', the tidy acronym that many of the people I live with use to describe child exploitation material; child pornography.

I've also never sexually abused a child.

Thirty-six of the forty people who live in this wing of the jail cannot make the same claims. Some profess their innocence; some admit their crimes; many are guilty of some of the above, and many are guilty of all. We have a priest. A university professor. A senior United Nations officer. A scoutmaster. A cricket coach. Teachers, bus drivers, public servants . . . Fathers and grandfathers.

Trusted men.

We have them all here in the WCC. There is a long, tired joke that the WCC really stands for Women and Child Chasers, which is a title I've laughed at while also shaking my head at its inappropriateness. I shouldn't laugh, I know that.

There is someone in here, a serial burglar and rapist named Shaun Burke who has already served twelve years, having been famously sentenced to more than thirty-six years in prison (which is referenced in court as an example of a crushing sentence), who raped and battered a girl in a share house my sister lived in. She heard Burke enter the house, thought it was a roommate returning late, and went back to sleep. When my sister woke up the next day and heard what had happened to her friend, she gave a stunned statement to the police.

Shaun Burke lives in the pod next to mine and is a friendly guy. We stand in line together waiting for medication and chatting away the afternoon. It's the polite chatter of people thrown together by circumstance who don't know anything about each other and pass the time as best they can. Shaun Burke. A monster who raped and beat someone while my sister slept next door. But that's where the evil abstract of a ruthless serial rapist stops for my sister, and probably most of his victims, including the poor girl who unforgivably had her world turned upside down that night. Until I became someone who lived in the same wing as Burke, his crimes, had I known about them, would exist as an abstract I could easily put away and not consider further. That's changed, and I can't avoid that fact no matter how hard I try; it's a feeling that I'm rolling around in my head trying to process.

I saw he was having a bad time of it on what I'd been told was his birthday, pacing around the yard trying to burn his frustrations off, so I shook his hand and wished him a happy birthday. Shook his hand. *A serial rapist.*

Standing in line, he told me about reading Leo Tolstoy's *War and Peace*, and how much of a grind it was, but also how he enjoyed the hell out of it once it had grabbed him. Another time he told me about making his own sunglasses from discarded bits and pieces around the jail, and when I asked him how long he had to go on his sentence, he told me he had nine years left before he could even apply for parole. Nine years left, and he's been here twelve.

What I cannot reconcile is the meaning of shaking his hand and wishing him a happy birthday, of acknowledging the humanity of someone who has so violently ripped that same humanity away from innocent people. I don't know any more about his crimes and I feel content with that, but what kind of person am I to see the humanity in someone who has been sentenced to be locked in a detention facility for more than thirty-six years? It's why I have to write this down, to acknowledge both sides of what this experience will have to be for me as I live here.

* * *

The brother of a friend of mine, and I understand other siblings too, were badly mistreated as children. Badly mistreated: a polite euphemism for sexually abused, by a person of authority, in a position of trust. By a priest.

John Aitchison is a convicted paedophile priest, and he's someone I often chat to around the facility here as well, similar to Shaun Burke. We have long chats about our favourite authors, recommend books to each other, and pass the time together talking about everything and nothing. We smile when we see each other. John Aitchison has already served two years in jail for sexually abusing young children in his Catholic Parish, and a month ago as of writing this, he was sentenced to another five years for sexually penetrating a thirteen-year-old girl, again through his role as a priest. "Oh, but it was a historical crime," they say in his defence, as if the passage of time is poured out like some healing elixir that cleans the wounds of his victims. Does my friend's brother feel better with the passage of time?

John is undoubtedly a lovely fellow, yet I feel, really *feel*, he is someone I should detest. I do privately, but is that right and fair? How far is too far in our society's perception of punishing these heinous crimes of violating – and sexually, no less – the most vulnerable among us: our own children? With some quick arithmetic, I put myself at the right age in the right year for Father Aitchison's historical crimes. *I* was his victim's age in 1990, but they look me in the eye and say the words: "Oh, but it's historical," in a way I simply don't comprehend.

John Aitchison, the paedophile priest, the human being; he has a grey afro of unkempt curly hair and walks around with his hands in his jacket pockets and head down, often finding a chair in the sun and leaning back to absorb its full warmth. Arthur, his former roommate (his pod sleeps two to a room in a bunk bed arrangement) often tells me about nights where John is screaming himself awake in nightmares and then sobbing himself back to sleep. He speaks with a light British accent, pleasantly paced and rural, like someone with a few errands in the Shire and the whole day to complete them. It's a voice of trust and comfort, and a voice that has allowed him to achieve much good, no doubt, and also much evil, which is certain through his convictions. When I first met him, the very first day when his story of being a former priest seemed too clichéd, he told me he used to scribble down names and descriptions (often not flattering, he joked) of his Parish members so he could better remember them next time. It's a hard thing to hear how a priest used certain tricks to remember people and build trust and then violated that trust in one of the worst ways possible. But was he a good priest when he remembered the names of the people he cared for and helped? Those whose trust he didn't violate?

Shaun Burke and John Aitchison make me think nearly more than anyone else in this wing, although there is one other that gives me pause. I won't write about him until the end of this stream of consciousness, perhaps another day, week or month – maybe in a year.

You would walk past these people in the street, see them leading normal lives with their families and friends, and easily surrender your own trust without thinking critically about it.

You would see Adam Carrington, the former senior Foreign Affairs and United Nations officer having lunch with his family, showing them how to play the game he loves more than anything else: *Magic: The Gathering*. He plays *Magic* competitively and has introduced it to some of the other detainees here, including my neighbour Kenny the American. They aren't allowed to actually bring the cards into the jail, as they are worth quite a bit of money and can be used as currency –

so the guards claim – so instead, Adam has ingeniously downloaded photos of the cards with the help of the librarian, and then stuck the cut-out photos onto playing cards for rigidity. They spend all afternoon sitting in the recreation room at the top of the wing. Hours and hours, just discussing cards and playing the game. Like me, Adam is on remand and not yet convicted of any offences, and he has already had a terrible time in his eight or so months in jail. On arrival, he was threatened and subsequently attacked on a number of occasions by other detainees who learned he was here for child pornography. His case, like others who are fighting accusations or still justifying convictions, is a grey area, and he tells me about the evidence the police have on him. Before I can politely slip away, Adam, a fortyish man of medium build and with a full head of grey and black hair, not unlike Cameron's, and a square face with glasses, talks me through the evidence.

"They [the AFP] are over-exaggerating the photos of my daughter," he starts. There's not much I can add as he bails me up by the little garden in front of his pod where they grow dill and other aromatic herbs and continues to describe the case.

"Sure, the angle is up her skirt, but her legs are closed." Another justification: "Her shirt is off in some photos, but she's not bosomy in them. She's bosomy now, but not then," he says, describing his own young daughter.

I stand there, complicit, and nod, agreeing with him that everything will be okay, that the Australian Federal Police are corrupt and not doing things the right way. I nod, and smile; I'm personable – not confrontational, as I listen to a man describe and justify how he photographed his own daughter naked, violating her trust in him as a parent in the worst possible way. Will she ever process this abuse? Now, or later as a teen, or as a young woman in her twenties, or perhaps never? Perhaps she will just push it deep down and pretend it's not there as she goes about living her life – with that evil knowledge still waiting. I cannot fathom his actions.

Age has served Adam well, and you can tell that his poor complexion and love of *Magic: The Gathering* perhaps speaks to an awkward period of adolescence. His maturity now hides the traumatic past of sexual abuse he claims to have suffered, and I have no reason to doubt that this experience influenced his own offending. He discusses working as a UN officer in Rwanda in 1995 when the Hutus undertook their genocidal massacres against the Tutsis, and he tries to explain how this traumatic experience influenced his own sexual offending in some way that doesn't seem clear to me. This, of all his excuses and justifications, makes me raise my eyebrows the most and causes me to reflect on my own confronting experiences in a similar environment. It's something I don't share with him, but I think back to Afghanistan where I served as a young officer and once experienced the confronting shock of seeing bodies ripped apart by a suicide bombing; the bodies of women and children – like Adam no doubt witnessed in Rwanda. But it doesn't make me think I could do anything like he's accused of having done to his own children, and that's where the comparison ends between us. Sure, people process different confronting experiences individually, yet in some ways, it almost has the opposite effect on me and makes me more angry that he uses an experience that I can in some ways relate with to justify his offences.

Ray Layton is like Adam, having photographed his own children sexually, and he is an incorrigible racist to boot, but he's also a warm-hearted man who cares about his friends. Ray is one of life's extroverts, similar to Cameron, but in a more roll-a-cigarette-with-you kind of way, whereas Cam is intellectually engaging and social to many different kinds of people. Ray is somewhere in his sixties, has a neatly cropped ponytail (fifteen centimetres higher it would qualify as a man bun), and has an uncanny resemblance to Anthony Hopkins' portrayal of Hannibal Lecter. There is no psychological or intellectual comparison between the two; only the face and pulled-back hair. He also has an injured eye from a motorbike accident a few years back, which he suffers a good deal of pain from. Ray is good friends with David Will, my debt-collecting tattooed neighbour, and often prepares him a lot of food for lunch, typically arriving with an ice cream container filled to the brim with his chicken soup concoction, which he's shared with me at least twice, regardless that I've never asked. Despite the fact that our own pod has plenty of food and poor Dave, hobbled with his gout (we lost him for a fortnight to hospital recently) eats well, Ray is always on hand to help. I think I could almost like Ray; he's a straight shooter, but where the oafish Jason's racist jokes are flung carelessly but without real malice, Ray truly condemns others with a venom I cannot stand. Arabs, Asians, Aboriginals and others are mercilessly attacked by Ray as he sits down with a cup of tea and a cigarette. He's the target audience of talk-back radio and their shock jocks, and any other pigheaded bigot who labels people for *what* they are, and not who they are. He's another conflicted character in this place: an exceedingly caring racist who uses his own children to produce child pornography and takes holidays consistently and opaquely to Thailand.

Michael-John 'MJ' Stratford is a musician and the spitting image of Ernest Hemingway from every possible angle and is in here convicted of sexual crimes I don't yet know about. Others infer that his deep psychological problems cause him to dream of visiting extreme violence on other people, including routinely (and horrifically) dreaming of decapitating his own family. Yet MJ is an otherwise thoroughly pleasant person, and we smile and chat whenever our paths cross, although we never dive into topics beyond polite nattering over when I'm next going to use the bath in their pod. While the five people in my pod have their own shower (Cam, who sleeps in our common area annexe, uses either Jason's, Kenny's or mine when he needs to), MJ's pod shares a communal toilet, shower and bath. The bath is a heavenly luxury, and a few months back I used it with the permission of MJ and his fellow pod members. A jail shower, initiated with the press of a metal button, lasts six adequate minutes with two warning cuts coming in the last thirty seconds, but the bath they have can be enjoyed for as long as one can manage between musters when you must then return to your own pod to be counted.

"When are you coming back over to have another bath?" MJ will ask me, making light conversation.

21

"I'll have to book another appointment shortly; don't worry, I'll be back." It's a tired routine but the only piece of common ground the affable-enough MJ and I have to discuss, and it's a few repetitive months before I enlist his help to mediate a dispute with the reclusive Alwyn Baume, giving us the chance to chat about something more than bathing schedules.

Continuing on the sliding scale of detainees within the Women and Child Chasers' wing, there is a collection of the normal grubs you would more obviously assume to be paedophiles, and we pass each other in the yard with just a polite nod, or sometimes ignore each other altogether. There's Tom Johnstone, the middle-aged, short and fat former public servant who is perpetually filthy and omits a foul odour. He stands in the line for medication and argues with the nurses, barking at them and criticising some tiny mistake that all of us would otherwise tolerate without the same overreaction and indignation he dishes out. Once, standing in line, he nibbled roasted coffee beans, and when I told him I missed coffee (we're understandably subjected to instant coffee only – although barista courses are run in the jail as a sort of vocational qualification: hence the coffee beans), he handed two or three beans from his dirty fingers into my hand while simultaneously revealing his long yellow and brown fingernails. I smiled and thanked him – I suppose it *was* a nice gesture – and as he turned back towards the medication window, I flung them behind me onto the grass. Tom's fatness is crowned with a squished face and a red button nose, and his glasses seem to get lost in the folds of his face. His mop of hair is unruly and has the odd appearance of a cheap wig; almost as if he's a classically trained actor playing the part of an oafish and squatly paedophile. Tom fits the profile for me of being the grubby and manipulative paedophile you could (and should) spot at one hundred paces, and he's generally despised and avoided by all others in the wing. Despite this repellent personality, Tom is always intertwined with others and at the centre of some new controversy or discord, clearly enjoying the drama that unfolds from concocting rumours or conjecture from thin air.

CHAPTER 3

I was arrested in May of 2018, and that was when my own prison journey began. I wasn't *sure* it was coming, but I suspected it and immediately knew what was happening and why. The police were good, professional, and I went through the process and arrived in my current location about twenty-four hours after being remanded. I was a flight risk: too much experience living overseas, and too many passports. I would never have slipped out of Australia as it would mean never coming home again, but I knew I could if I had to. I wasn't ready to leave my family and other Australian connections, so I settled myself into facing the music.

As I've said, I'm not your ordinary prisoner, and while I wish I could tell you about myself, I can't. Suffice to say the first four weeks of my incarcerated life began in solitary confinement – the dreaded 'management unit' – as the General Manager was worried about how to deal with me in a way that would prevent the guards and other prisoners learning why I was there, and who I was. It caused me a great degree of stress to be isolated, but I kept myself busy with planning ahead, reading and watching television. I suffered through the red-headed royal wedding during that month.

To be honest, I was so curious about everything that it was quite the adventure in some ways, which no doubt sounds odd coming from someone starting a period in jail. I'd only ever known about prison from American television, and that was a poor guide when compared to my own experiences. Many guards, knowing I was different and not understanding why, asked me openly what I was doing there and tried to elicit some small detail that would confirm one of the many hypotheses that were springing into being. Was it espionage? Was I a former police officer? Some horrible serial killer perhaps? No, no and no – not even close, and the guesses made me smile as they came. In the management unit, I was allowed out for one hour a day, which I spent in a large metal cage outside that received sunlight. During these moments, I would sip coffee and read my hour away, often chatting with the guards who without fail took the opportunity to enjoy a cigarette and pry as much of my story from me as they could. Some were subtle; others less so, but you could tell they all wanted to know. I wish I could have put them out of their misery and just told them, but that wasn't an option.

My room there had a shower and toilet, a small desk, and a television in a protective casing high in the corner of the room. I had a remote, and I watched television and ate the meals that were slipped through the letterbox slot on my door. The others around me, during their own hour out, would pace around and often come to my door, staring through at the new guy and attempting to gauge what crimes had brought him in here. One of the jackals managed to make himself heard through the crack of my door and forcefully demanded to know why I was there. I shrugged back and gave him my best 'I don't know what's happening smile' as I deflected his questions. He assured me that as long as I wasn't in there for sexual crimes, I would be okay, which was comforting to know as that certainly wasn't the case. Only later, when settled into my current wing, would that become a prescient comment, as I heard those hated sexual offenders tell their stories of threats and violence.

I then met one of the jails most infamous detainees – Dennis the Menace – whose infamy relates to the trouble he causes the staff, as opposed to what brought him in there. He, too, occupied an individual cell within the management area, and he spent much of his time kicking the door loudly and screaming, during the day and all night too, until he presumably collapsed with the exertion.

I have now learnt that there is a technique to properly kicking a cell door so that maximum noise and endurance is achieved. One must put their back to the door, and then cow kick behind oneself into the bottom half of the metal. This can be done for hours, as I can personally attest to, being Dennis's neighbour. It amazed me that he was able to elicit such explosive replies from the others locked up around him. One particular neighbour of Dennis's screamed for silence until he broke down and loudly cried. Dennis, too, would scream – usually barely decipherable requests for cigarettes, lighters or time out of his small cell. "I'm gunna skitz out you farking cunttttttzzzz!" he would bellow with regularity.

I'd never previously heard the word 'cunt' screamed so intensely and so often, and Dennis was unstoppable in his demands. Some of the most patient and professional performances from the often-maligned guards have been their calm and reasoned discussions with Dennis to hear him out and de-escalate his angry tantrums.

On the third night in the management unit, I was provided earplugs, which I didn't use, and the female guard who gave them to me suggested Dennis would have been better euthanised at birth for all the trouble he caused. One thing I couldn't work out was how the guards allowed him to misbehave so much.

American Kenny, my neighbour in the new wing, is employed to clean up spills across the jail and is called once every few days to mop and sanitise the hepatitis-laden and HIV-stained blood from the latest bashing or self-harm incident. He also deals with the excrement that has been hurled or used as body paint and scrapes the odd rabbit or duck off the jail walkways that the foxes like to chase during the long nights we are all locked in our pods. Kenny is also regularly called to help clean up Dennis's torched cell. He manages to set fire to it with alarming consistency, running up an enormous cost to the jail and therefore the taxpayer every time the fire brigade arrives.

Fires that threaten a detained population are extremely serious – no protocols exist to simply open the doors if a building is threatened. Indeed, one guard was infamously disciplined when he allowed a detainee to leave his cell instead of die of smoke inhalation. It's one of the scarily inhumane aspects to being a ward of the state. Despite Dennis's pattern of torching his cells, guards continue to give him his lighter; I don't understand how they justify this given the destruction and cost that he inflicts, and it's one of the aspects of this jail's operation that I suspect would fail the 'news headline' test of public scrutiny. One ambitious reporter seeking a freedom of information request on how many fires Dennis has caused and the total cost of the responses would create instant community outrage, especially as the guards enable his habit in this manner. Given the long list of contraband items not allowed in here, the fact that Dennis is easily and often able to set fire to his cell confuses me. Surely they should just deny him the use of a lighter? When I raise it with Cam, Kenny or Jason, they all seem to think the guards give him lighters to keep him quiet during their own shifts.

It's been a fascinating journey to learn what constitutes contraband in the jail, and on the scale of sensible to ridiculous, the list varies widely. Sugar is out – one can make alcohol with it, and so is anything spicy like chilli or pepper, which can be weaponised by detainees and thrown on someone's eyes. Covert quantities of pepper and a secretly grown chilli plant in the garden is the limit to the contraband items I'm aware of. It's absurd that we cannot have these items when drugs, syringes and tattoo guns seem to flow unimpeded through the jail. We also cannot grow potatoes for the same reason we can't possess sugar, but we can and do buy them in large quantities for cooking. It's a crazy contradiction, but one of many that exists. Of course, as we cook for ourselves, a knife is needed, and our kitchen comes equipped with a large butcher's knife chained to the counter with about a one-metre reach in all directions. Only the cottages, otherwise known as pods, have these kitchen facilities and access to knives and other utensils, and most of those in the rest of the jail live on meals that are delivered in cardboard containers and eaten with plastic cutlery.

But not us; we get to sit down to our own cooked meals, although the plastic cutlery is also a feature of our nightly dining experience. Having just attempted to cut a few pork schnitzels, cooked by Cameron, my plastic knife was polished clean of any serration after a cumulative sixty seconds sawing away on an ever-so-slightly overcooked meal. A cold beer and decent steak knife are on my mind. One day.

Cameron and I play chess most days, though he usually pips me two games to my one, and as a result, we slowly drift apart from playing as I hate to lose. I'm too competitive, and ill-balanced games bring out the worst in me, unfortunately, so I concede to Cam as our resident grandmaster. We have a small board that we play on, and also have a chess program on our computers. Cam and I switch our attentions to attempting to beat the computerised game on the hard setting. It quickly escalates from the blundering easy setting to the difficult normal level, until it finally reaches a deep blue assassin-like intensity at the highest level of hard. We read about chess, talk about chess – the immortal game is a favourite – and Cam even submits a Fischer and Spassky game to the librarian to include in her newsletter, which she does. When the annotated game arrives I quickly find Cam and implore him to check it out, but he only smiles at me and tells me it was him who submitted it in the first place. Both of us are yet to win on hard, but we chip away slowly and with great frustration.

Cameron's out in the kitchen now dusting breadcrumbs over pork fillets, making a coleslaw and preparing apple crumbles for the five of us in the pod. He's a magnificent cook and we eat like kings in our area; far better than the other pods (I suspect) and certainly better than some people at home. The guards in particular, during their last six pm muster and pod lock-in, typically arrive as the five of us sit down for dinner. (Alwyn never joins us for meals, and lives on soy milk, yoghurt and god knows what else from his room.) The guards look longingly at the burgers, steaks, roast pork and other treats we eat each night. Of course, they can leave the jail, open a beer and enjoy their freedom, but I see the longing in their eyes, and I often ask them if they'd like something from our smorgasbord, but never ever is anything taken or tried. I think rules must exist that guards cannot, under any circumstances, take food from detainees. It makes sense, less we try to poison and incapacitate them, although the guards share so much of our lives, I wish one would enjoy an offered morsel one day.

The guards are a fascinating and varied group of individuals, and in many ways, they are just as foreign to me as the rapists and paedophiles that I live among. As a general rule, the guards, or corrections staff as they are formally known, are a decent bunch of people doing a tremendously monotonous job, and one that is sometimes punctuated by bursts of violence or misbehaviour from the detainees. Many people hate the guards with an unbridled passion and see them as the front line of a society that has rejected them as worthy human beings. I certainly don't hate the guards and have the opinion that many of them are simply fallible humans like ourselves doing a job and earning a salary. I've had one minor run-in with a senior female guard, which is now a popular anecdote among the detainees and guards of the wing, but otherwise, I have what I would consider is a functional relationship with them here. They have a job to do, and I don't stand in the way of their duties at all; I even try to make their days easier as they do for us. A smile, a hello, a quick chat to see how they are . . . honesty and respect seems to keep everyone on side. The guards seem to almost ubiquitously smoke cigarettes and follow rugby league (two things that don't interest me), and I don't think many would hold tertiary qualifications, though a few have a real spark of intelligence. Of course, while they might not have tertiary qualifications and higher intellects, they certainly have a practicality about them and what I would describe as savvy street-smarts here in prison. It's a necessity, no doubt, to understand the tricks and deceptions that ninety-five per cent of the detainees exhibit to the guards on a constant basis, as drugs come into and are spread around the jail, vendettas are settled, and gang affiliations are built on. The intelligence staff in the prison (which I understand is two people) must have a fantastically exciting anthropological mission of deciphering relationships and affiliations in this complex web of 400 detainees, including visitors, online and phone contacts, former detainees and guards that know detainees outside of the gates. It is a core responsibility of the guards to declare any possible conflicts of interest, although it's a well-known fact that certain guards around here can be bribed to bring in a mobile phone, drugs or even alcohol. As human beings, the guards aren't above corrupt behaviour, and the stories the twins – Kenny and Jason – tell amaze me in how brazenly some of them break the rules.

The loudspeaker crackles, "Afternoon muster, afternoon muster." Nearly three pm. One of the better guards shows up five minutes later with his large book of photos and names, quickly ticking us off as being present.

"Mr Wilson, I've heard you're somewhat of a car fan," I say. He looks over to me with a smile. Cam is in the kitchen, and Kenny, Jason, Dave and even Alwyn are hovering in their doorways.

I go on. "I used to own a terribly fast sports car, and I miss it a lot."

"Yeah, I've got one in the garage, but I need to watch it," he says. "I've lost a few points recently."

Cameron jumps in and says, "Well then, make it a good one, and you can come join us in here!" He gives a wry smile. The guard has a polite laugh and then disappears back to the office to report that all detainees are accounted for. It's the kind of lightning contact we have daily with the corrections staff. Superficially polite and pleasant.

The guards are a part of our life, no doubt, but of course, an inseparable distance remains between us that can never be crossed. Still, it's nice to speak with the guards about what books we're reading, projects we're embarking on, previous cars or motorcycles owned, countries visited, or anything else that normal people might discuss. A trust can more easily develop when one doesn't have anything to hide from them, as we typically don't. Aside from the reason I'm in jail, which no one except one person understands, I don't desire drugs, money or influence, and so can happily follow the rules with a smile.

CHAPTER 4

The detainee delegates from all of the different wings gather at least once a month to discuss matters that affect the jail through the correctional leadership. It's a very civilised way for the prisoners to have some kind of representation with the management staff, and it's another thing that has surprised me since I arrived in jail. Cameron is incredibly organised and attends these monthly meetings to lobby for the detainees in our wing, raising concerns around parole criteria, living conditions and other matters important enough for someone to seek him out and share their concerns. One example is Kenny Johnson's denied request for an extended two-hour visit with his father, who will be travelling from the United States to see him. The request was denied without a reason, and Cameron tells him there's some logical explanation for this: an administrative foul-up or a guard just getting it wrong. Kenny is sure it's a deliberate attempt to punish him, as that's all the corrections staff care about in their day-to-day job as far as he's concerned: making life hard for detainees. Cameron disagrees, raises the issue, and the visit goes ahead.

Cam even comes back from the delegate meetings with typed minutes and a notebook full of scribblings, swinging into the five pods that make up our wing of the jail and passing on the relevant information that someone needs to know or has asked about. Without even knowing all of the other delegates, I'm sure no other wing receives the same level of service Cam provides us.

I have met one of the other delegates, who is a young kid named Taylor Schmidt. He slipped me my first covert prison note a month back, and I won't lie and tell you I wasn't intrigued. Three or four hands had moved the note from his section of the jail to mine, and while the act of passing a note like this isn't in itself an offence, it avoids providing a steady stream of prisoner intelligence for the corrections staff to draw false conclusions from and is quicker than using the formal detainee request system. Taylor had heard from the librarian that I speak a second language fluently, which he just happens to be in the process of learning, and he asked if I would be willing to meet up and help him. Taylor is a convicted murderer and a shade either side of twenty-seven or twenty-eight, with a hint of real brains but no formal education. He represents his wing at the delegate's meetings, and I simply don't see the same level of maturity and patience that Cameron brings to those meetings on our behalf. We're certainly lucky to have Cam in our wing of forty. I'm luckier still to live in his pod of six.

* * *

Tomorrow I'm heading to court, my fourth appearance if my counting is correct, and for the first time I'm going to attend in the comfortable clothing that we wear in jail. Unfortunately, it's not the clichéd orange one-piece jumpsuits, but simply cotton track pants, shirts and jumpers. Blue for remand; grey for sentenced; and purple for the women. I was issued my blue clothing on arrival: two sets with white socks, and the cheapest functional shoes that are sold in Australia. The brand is PureSport, and I heartedly recommend you steer clear of them should you ever see them in a store. I wear these cheap shoes inside my room around the carpeted floor, and then use the black hiking shoes I arrived in jail with for all outside activity. Despite being on remand and owning the appropriate blue clothing, I also have some worn-in grey outfits, which not only feel more comfortable but also prevent me having to cycle my two sets of clothing through the washing machines every day. I could wear my tailored navy-blue suit tomorrow; tie a half-Windsor knot, slip my late grandfather's cufflinks on and tie up my leather shoes, but I'm not going to bother. Frankly, I don't think it will make a difference when I make my brief appearance, and if anything, the jail-issued clothing will be more comfortable for the long hours I'll have to wait at the courthouse until my four-thirty pm hearing begins. There's nothing worse than being that guy who has to enter the side of the courtroom once everyone else is seated. It's when your own alleged criminality rears its head to create maximum contrast, and the glances from those in attendance make you feel the most self-conscious; everyone has to take a peek and make their own judgements. Nasty to endure, for sure; especially in my situation – as unique as it is. Because of the nature of my case, the corrections staff, who would normally sit behind the detainee in the courtroom, are not allowed to attend, and I can tell that it frustrates them that they aren't worthy of knowing what is happening behind those closed doors. The guards don't like this because their attendance is an important source of gossip that they either take back to chat about or, in the case of Adam Carrington's hearing, simply transmit on a private channel through their radios for all of their guard buddies to listen in. Unprofessional and unethical, but it happens.

The drive from the jail to the court is a short one, and it's an opportunity to slip into handcuffs and see a little of the countryside, and watch people going about their lives in freedom; rushing to work or meetings or attending errands, just like I am. My barrister is Jewish, and tomorrow is Yom Kippur, two things I learned in our last meeting, so I'll have to whisper something appropriate after I take my seat, but I don't really know what I should say. Maybe I'll just tell him it's a shame he has to work on an important holiday, but I know he'll have plans and will no doubt race from our hearing to some social gathering. A good guy, my barrister; expensive, but he's competent, compassionate and, as Arthur assures me, "eats raw meat for breakfast" (which I'm told is the mark of a good criminal lawyer). I've got a good solicitor as well, but he appears a little bedazzled by my situation, and seems to have trouble focussing to the same level as my barrister. I can't say I blame him though: my case *is* totally unprecedented. You must be pretty annoyed by now that I still can't let you into it, and all I can do is apologise and assure you it's out of my hands.

Whenever you leave the prison – say to go to court, like I did today – you have the joy of wearing handcuffs. The first time I ever had them put on, which was mercifully not when I was arrested at an international airport, I was slightly amazed that I had never worn a pair before, despite a few interactions with police officers as a kid (friends of the family or at school visits, let me add – never as a juvenile delinquent). It's what you expect: a snap over the wrist, though the lock isn't the little simple key you see in the movies, but something understandably more elaborate. They do make a pleasantly loud ratchet sound as they go on and off, if that's something that you're curious about, and once on they do a good job of keeping you immobilised, as I found out while trying to navigate around between two guards while managing a stack of magazines (waiting cells in courts are dreadfully boring). I've never had my hands cuffed behind my back as you often see in the movies, so I'm as yet unable to report on the practicalities of swinging one's arms under one's legs during a high-speed departure from a corrections officer escort.

The court appearance is routine, and I am out within ten minutes and back into the correction facility's bus that has specially built-in transportation cells. Mine, for this return journey, faces backwards, so I have a lovely view of the route back to the jail and witness the reasoning for a decidedly heavy brake pumping episode along the highway as a speed camera comes into view from my window. Two jackals are out of sight behind me, carrying on one of those inane little conversations about weight gain, cigarette smoking – the comment: "Yeah, I'm off the ciggies, bruz – only five a day now," was a tad confusing – and pithy jail gossip that you can't escape no matter where you are.

Sitting anywhere on the bus: forward, sidewards or rearward facing, one is always fighting a tedious battle of staying on your seat, as the loose seat belt (sometimes not applied at all) does nothing to hold you firmly down, and every accelerating or braking motion as well as every corner causes a commensurate slide in the opposite direction, which forces some quick lower-leg muscular work to avoid contact with the grubby and graffitied walls all around you. The Aboriginal flag seems to be a real favourite for penning or engraving into the walls, as well as the predictable amount of 'he-loves-she-loves', 'he-sucks-she-sucks', 'fuck-the-cops/police', 'and so-and-so-is-a-dog-cunt' (the last being surprisingly consistent around the place).

Back in my comfortable single room, I notice high above my computer and television, close to the ceiling, a large capitalised and grammatically incorrect 'DOG'S' has been penned (I'll stand corrected on the grammar if the possessive form was intended). I'll admit that it took me a good two months to notice it up there. Given this wing was previously occupied by women, I'll have to assume it was one of them who felt the moment of artistic (and gymnastic – quite the climb up!) inspiration. 'MellyMel loves Will Fields 4 ever XO' is also present in a few differing versions around my room. Aside from this minor graffiti, my room is a pleasant cinder block painted duck-egg blue, with dark grey carpets (heated floors – do they have these everywhere?) and a green metal door where a white sheet is draped either side for additional privacy. The window, immediately to my right, is grilled but otherwise fantastically opens out to an empty yard, past the perimeter fence to where the aforementioned heliport is located. I can open and close it with two buttons, which allows a breeze to come in. The room isn't too bad, I must confess, though of course the rest of the jail differs heavily, with some detainees living two to a featureless room in the dreaded blocks.

* * *

The following day, poor Cameron cracks it and proclaims to Kenny and Jason, our incorrigible twins, that "there will be no more prison talk when we're locked into our pods." This has the effect of immediately silencing Kenny, whose entire repertoire of conversational interests involves (in order): jail gossip or insights, the NFL and anything related to the United States of America, no matter how wide of his expertise it is, and *Transport Tycoon Deluxe* (a game on our prison computers). Jason is a little less impacted as he has his university study or ongoing battle to quit smoking as topics of conversation, but even he has spent so much of his life in prison that he finds it hard to steer himself clear, and occasionally draws Cameron's ire. I appreciate Cameron's desire to avoid the same banal conversations circulating ceaselessly, but it's more about the civility inherent in *not* discussing someone's murder charges, for example, while we're sitting down for dinner. Something like this happens every other night, it seems, and I've rolled my eyes often enough and tried to blatantly change the topic of conversation (today's weather, anyone?) that Cameron has picked up on it and is also realising how much banality he's subjected to. Of course, it all happens innocently enough and usually starts with someone getting some news about a friend in the jail or hearing of the arrival of a new person. They discuss this, naturally enough, and sometimes more than one person will know the person in question, which is what initiates the detailed inquisitions.

"I heard so-and-so's back in the prison," Dave Will might say.

"Oh, is that so-and-so from that-other-prison?" Jason might add.

"Yeah, he got picked up for icing (killing) so-and-so bikie, and just got sentenced to fifteen years."

"*He* killed so-and-so? Oh, I heard about that. Wasn't it in response to so-and-so killing so-and-so from that other-place?" Now Kenny.

"Yeah, that's him. There's a couple blokes trying to stick (knife) so-and-so now he's arrived here," says Dave.

"He better watch out for so-and-so in case he jumps him too."

You can appreciate how common conversations like this would be, and how inappropriate a topic it is when you're trying to sit down and enjoy a civil meal.

As much as this annoys both Cameron and me, I also seem to be agitated by the constant chat around legal appeals, parole and other judiciary-related matters, which I find as banal as the discussions about the criminal acts. Cameron is heavily involved in these legal matters, and often puts a person's appeal together with assistance from Arthur (it's handy having a professor of law available!) His strike-rate is remarkable, truth be told, but it's the same kind of conversations and I'll often excuse myself from a table when Cameron and Arthur launch into the latest case or appeal, although typically they both ask me to sit back down and change the conversation to something else. This lasts five or ten minutes before it swings around again.

So, what to discuss? It's a good question with no fixed rule, but take anything and spend months – *literally months* – discussing it, with the same two or three people, and you'll be surprised how quickly your stress and boredom flare into a potency that forces you to pull away from the conversation in question. As I said to you in the beginning: the secret to incarcerated sanity is finding the *right* kinds of idle conversations that can spin around and around without becoming deathly tiresome. I'm finding it hard work being idle.

CHAPTER 5

While watching Sarah Ferguson's television series (*Hitting Home with Sarah Ferguson*), I was intrigued to hear one particular story of a brutalised woman and her incarcerated husband describe in parallel the event that led to the latter's incarceration. The jailed husband is wearing a Sherwood-green shirt and baseball cap while attempting to explain how he is, in fact, not that intimidating. Despite his protests, he has that dangerously menacing combination of both size and dim wit that you can just tell explodes into horrendous violence, as indeed he's convicted of perpetrating against his 60-kilogram wife. He's certainly a scary-looking kind of guy. It's timely to watch this, as it's been one of those interesting days in jail, and it might give you an appreciation of the kinds of things that tend to roll through a day – the things that illuminate the real humanity of the sexual offenders in this wing.

This week is also unusual as it's the first time I've seen someone I live with paraded on the local news. Along with Cameron, this person – former University of Canberra Professor (of law, no less) Arthur Hoyle – has kept me sane with his friendship and even council and advice regarding my own situation. From the day I arrived here in the WCC (Women and Child Chasers, in case you need a reminder), Arthur made an effort to befriend me, and I suspect he also took a degree of personal satisfaction that he of all others quickly built a relationship with the mysterious detainee. (A detainee who, as you know, was unprecedentedly parachuted into the best-possible accommodation without having to do time in the hated blocks before matriculating to a cottage.) From my side, Arthur was kept at arm's length (perhaps elbow; I did seek his counsel on a few technical matters in my own opaque case), but Arthur had no concerns in bringing me up to speed on every salacious detail of his own pending appeal, which had already been through court before my arrival, and only needed to be formally delivered by the presiding judges. As Arthur and I circled the wing chatting idly away, I was kept abreast of the slipping weeks as his pending judicial answer, clearly stalled, tortured him and his sanity endlessly. It was incidentally convenient that Arthur's accumulating count of weeks paralleled my own time in the wing, and I was somewhat surprised at the quick overall passage, although it's an incarcerated truth that days crawl and weeks fly. (Months tend to tick through normally and I can't yet comment [and hope never to] on the passing of years.) He would outline all of the possible outcomes, the relevant points of law he was challenging, and what he felt were both good and bad reasons that would affect the appellant judge's decision.

Arthur was convicted of raping and sexually assaulting a number of foreign female university students under his tutelage, which is a conviction he strenuously denies, I should include here for completeness. There is, if one listens to his reasoning, a malicious and mendacious campaign to besmirch him and his character, with students who were failing courses being coerced into making allegations to improve their marks, satisfying the agenda of some Machiavellian university colleague who has it in for him. As a neutral party, I can only take both the Crown and Arthur at their respective words, and I appreciate that I'm not sufficiently informed to have a strong opinion either way. I reserve the same approach for a select few others in the wing who deny their crimes (a notable example being Cameron Tully) but cast my own appraisal on others when my own overriding feeling is that guilt is the more likely reality. I do find it curious that I unconsciously apply this contradictory approach, but it's a reality of how I perceive the other sexual offenders in this wing. That established, I feel for my own sanity no need to condemn any relationship based on the severity of a person's crimes, and simply feel obligated to associate or not associate with a person on the facts that are in front of me. Foul odours are at times enough, as are personalities that grate for any range of reasons; Tom Johnstone, the former bus driver, public servant and a very manipulative paedophile being one such malodorous grub I avoid. I do make a significant exception for the curious Alwyn Baume, the hermit of my pod, who has crimes of such severity that I find it hard to even be polite to him, no matter how hard I try, but then his odd and rancorous personality is enough to be outright repellent.

So, I listen to Arthur, the convicted (and later upheld on appeal) rapist who also tells me stories about his daughter and her recent promotion to senior partner in her international legal firm. I track her business trip to Europe through Arthur, and her most recent holiday to Hawaii where Arthur proudly uses a photo of her relaxing on a bench, with a setting sun behind her, as his computer desktop background. I know his daughter's partner through Arthur's stories: the former police officer coping with post-traumatic stress disorder who Arthur accepts, even though he feels his daughter could do far better. I hear about Arthur's early model Ferrari, a garish 1970s or 1980s model that seems to fill a design gap between classic early lines and modern sleek performance. Not owning a Ferrari myself, though this shouldn't surprise you, I'm loath to be so critical over a car I would still love to have, but it very much fits Arthur's half-quirky personality. I also know all about Arthur's sailing boat, moored in Sydney Harbour somewhere, and his journeys ferrying it up the coast, and how he was caught in a tremendous storm when he first bought it. I'm familiar with the renovations to the house, his friends, family and life. I've met Elaine, his patient and dutiful wife, who smiles at me during visits and keeps up-to-date on all the wing's news. I know Arthur very well.

I like Arthur; however, do admit that at times his desire to talk about the law and cases around the compound (while natural, given his expertise) often wears me down. We share a great passion for classical history, but his knowledge and his visits to different sites far exceed my own. His real passion is Alexander the Great, and I enjoy telling him about my own tribute of carrying a copy of Homer's *Iliad* to Afghanistan. Alexander had it read to him as he campaigned across Persia and modern-day Afghanistan 2,500 years earlier, and I couldn't resist taking my own copy, although I have to shamefully confess I never had time to finish the book until I found myself incarcerated. Arthur and I smile as we share our experiences of walking on the cobblestone floor of the Roman forum, retracing the steps of Emperors Augustus, Nero or Aurelius; standing in the Colosseum or gawking at some ruined aqueduct. Our classical passions substantively overlap with Julius Caesar, and we chat back and forth gleefully over his Gaelic campaign and ascension to eventual Roman dictator. We argue over the pronunciations ('Vercingetorix' being a point of contention) and other quarrelsome details, but sit and smile with coffee and tea or pace around on our counter-clockwise laps. He's a good friend, a trusted confidant and a fierce intellect.

And a rapist.

I've never heard it said out loud, but seeing Arthur on the news this afternoon, which showed old footage of him walking to and from court, and labelled him so, was an odd experience. He was clean-shaven in the footage (now he has a tastefully short white beard) and looked odd, like someone I didn't know so well. Arthur is about the same height as I am, at a shade under six foot, but he has a slight slump to his figure that is one-part his sixty-eight years of age, one-part academic, and one-part fatigue and boredom. He still has his hair, although like his beard it is white, which grows long in the unkempt way jail ensures. Good haircuts are rare here, but a few styles persevere. He speaks in a very deliberate way, as you would expect from an intelligent professor of law, and he often shoots up a finger to make his point or explain the clever nuance he's landed on, which happens with pleasant regularity.

We shoot basketballs at the forgivingly rebounding hoop between our two pods, and Arthur claims it's important for his mental agility to maintain activity, on advice from his brother, who is head of the Royal Melbourne Hospital (and apparently a very accomplished orchestra musician – what a family!) Arthur and I shoot hoops for thirty minutes every other day, and while he sinks his fair share of baskets, his physical abilities and overall coordination are most certainly not equal to his academic abilities. I still find it discretely hilarious to watch poor Arthur track the trajectory of a basketball bouncing towards him and invariably over his head. He simply doesn't seem to be able to predict the thing's journey and stands full of trepidation with his arms held out in front of him, elbows nearly touching, awaiting the inbound rubber missile. I often plan my passes to rebound towards him forgivingly, but at times a yorker or short bounce catches him cold. Cameron and I share a polite smile over it. Arthur wears his black shorts and blue fleece jumper religiously, and his tanned legs stick down and into his badly worn PureSport prison shoes. Professor Arthur Hoyle: a ten-second one-dimensional rapist for the local news. For me, a fully formed person with complexity and humanity and fault. I promise Arthur that one day we will sit down and share a bottle of red wine, and he smiles at the thought. In return, I'm promised a drive of his Ferrari and a sail on his boat, and I also want to take him up on these things.

* * *

I meet Beatrice for the first time today. She's a Scot who now lives in Australia and works as an occupational psychologist for the jail. The poor state of my mental health helped to land me in my current predicament, and I've focussed on a therapeutic journey that includes these regular meetings. I'd been seeing another Briton named Sonny Ward, until management promoted her (albeit temporarily), forcing her to relinquish control of my case for the next few months. We'd built a fantastic rapport, Sonny and I, and while she – like the others – didn't know my background or the reasons that brought me to prison, she suspected enough to help me take my mind to more useful places, avoiding the unchanging past or potentially unrealised future calamities. The here and now; 'thisness', as the quacks repeat and emphasise. Importantly, she helped me with my current non-legal dilemma, as I struggle to reconcile the right to develop cordial relationships with the rapists and paedophiles I live with.

I could tell Sonny felt bad that she was stopping our chats for a while, but Beatrice is pleasant to meet, and I feel she handles our initial effort to build rapport well. She explains a little of her own background, which includes an academic interest in castle and fortification history in her British Isles home, with a particular fondness for Eleanor of Aquitaine and Hugh de Puiset, the Bishop of Durham. In turn, I explain that I am reading a little about Henry VIII and his six wives, which incidentally is a topic my mother finds endlessly fascinating (I feel my own curiosity will conclude happily when the book does). As I've said, I enjoy many aspects of history but can't claim any reading about the Dark Ages through to the Renaissance, where much (all?) medieval history seems to lay.

Beatrice is warm and also tells me about her children and life in Australia compared to her home in London and before that in Scotland. At times it's a little hard to concentrate, as her use of hand movements when she talks (which draws my eye) occurs in the foreground of large and nearly exposed breasts. Don't call me a hypocrite (yet) with everything I've claimed and said about my detained colleagues, but as a red-blooded male denied a woman's touch for near on six months, it's a sight that I do my utmost to not be drawn to impolitely. I hope and assume that the reader will have a healthy and normal relationship with sex, and can sympathise with me.

Interestingly, the mention of anything sexual around here tends to result in awkward interactions with people in which sex is very much taboo and negative. It's curious, and something I learned quite by accident. Once, a comment I made at dinner (which I thought was restrained and complimentary) about a cute female guard at the library caused a reaction that amazed me. Kenny and Jason, though more particularly Kenny, reacted dismissively – as one would if I had said I thought a *child* was attractive. Kenny oddly said something along the lines of, "Ah, so inappropriate," and awkwardly stared into his plate of food. It was then that I realised how dysfunctional their relationship with sex was, and in some ways, I really pitied them for it. I don't know the detail of Kenny's crimes, though I understand from Cameron that his 'hands-on paedophilia' (which I acknowledge is a terrible way to put it) was with young boys and that Kenny's homosexual repression played a significant factor. It's Kenny who so quickly dismisses anything gay as being bad, and sees it as a valid insult or slight against someone, who crawls up inside himself at the mere mention of anything sexual. Kenny once tried slipping a gay magazine into a newspaper I was taking from the library, thinking I would be shocked or find it funny. I wasn't shocked, of course, and while a happy heterosexual, I had to tell Kenny (not for the last time, mind you) that there was absolutely nothing wrong with being gay. I hope to make a slight impression on Kenny that there is nothing wrong with homosexuality, if indeed that's something he hasn't reconciled with himself, and that most people aren't judgemental and actually don't really care out in the real world. I don't expect him to ever say anything to me about it, but I want him to know inside him that if he did, it wouldn't be a problem. Kenneth Johnson: the African-American repressed homosexual paedophile, who makes his own ice cream (which is outrageously amazing – seriously), teaches me about the rules in the NFL, reminisces about Nintendo and his favourite games and works in the library to keep himself occupied.

After speaking with my busty mental health psychologist Beatrice, I went off to the library with Kenny and his *Magic* card-playing friend Glen Vandavord. Belinda, who is a shining and patient angelic figure in a sea of grim detainees and corrections staff, runs our fantastic library. In her fifties or sixties, her dark grey hair and reading glasses are almost clichéd, but she is simply amazing at her job, which is evidenced in the various things she does for detainees like organising book clubs, getting in new books each and every week, running writing competitions and ensuring items requested over email are put aside for that person's next visit. I often enjoy sitting near her door and listening to people go in and chat with her, and it's a rare opportunity (the only other being visits) where some of the tattooed or menacing jackals soften their personas and ask for a book, or for Belinda to print off a particular design for a tattoo. Watching Belinda interact with murderers, rapists, paedophiles, drug addicts and the others who come to the library is to glimpse the best of humanity, and it reminds me that a good and caring world still exists outside of the locked gates and high fences. Without doubt, the most touching thing I have yet seen since being incarcerated was an interaction between Belinda and a young but large tattooed bruiser. He was illiterate, and she was providing him some printed drawings so he could colour them in in the privacy of his cell later that evening. It's the colliding worlds that give dimension and depth to people.

Kenny works in the library, and when he's not doing chores around the place like returning books to the shelves, he's sitting in a chair in Belinda's office just chatting away. Again, watching the ease in which Kenny and Belinda just natter away is lovely for me, and it's seeing these two people from very different worlds interact together so easily that makes me smile. In some ways, Belinda is also the closest to figuring me out: I once asked her to discretely provide something for me, and when I next visited she had printed something else off and had it waiting. It amuses me that with all the intrigue, it's Belinda who is the closest to peeling back the onion.

CHAPTER *6*

Ah, Fridays. I just love them. No one minds working, really, when they know that sweet double-day of rest is just around the corner. A few whiskeys after work (or perhaps before the end of the day), and that weekend feeling just pleasantly arrives and you can stretch out and log off. You wave goodbye to the co-workers you can stand and silently walk past the ones you can't. It's a feeling I love. And it's a feeling totally absent in jail.

Every day in jail feels like a bizarre combination of a weekday and a weekend: you're not quite working or busy, but you're certainly not left to your own devices and able to spend the day as you would on a normal Saturday or a Sunday. That's what jail feels like. Good jail, I should emphasise. I think being in the blocks would be hellish, but I can't really comment on it – don't get arrested and wind up in the blocks thinking it's going to be the experience that I'm having. That was highlighted today by Kenny being called out to clean up a blood spill after there was a bashing somewhere else in the jail around lunchtime.

Fridays are the days we are provided our 'buy-ups', a weekly purchase of special food and sundry items like chocolate, chips, biscuits and all the junk food and crap you could ever want. Soap, shampoo and other personal items are available, but we are already provided with the basics. When the buy-up items are delivered on Friday, debts are settled, or typically not, which results in violence. One thing I've learned since being in jail is that most violence occurs because people don't pay drug and other debts. It's the cause of ninety per cent of the violence (I'm told), and the rest is through disrespecting someone, arguments or one of the young jackals trying to make a name for themselves.

So, when Kenny is called out, he prepares his bleach and other chemicals, takes his bright yellow hazard-labelled buckets and mops, and walks up through the yard. Having him in this role is actually quite fortuitous for him (for the pay) and us (for the gossip) as it allows us to track violence and other incidents throughout the jail with the surety of a primary account, although admittedly Kenny is forced to play forensics detective at times to make sense of the blood-splatter patterns or clumps of ripped-out hair. Those around him usually tell the story, or if not, he makes his own judgements based on the part of the jail he's in, the individual cell configuration and its occupant, and the amount of blood. Kenny's likely attended to more crime scenes than many busy detectives and probably has an eye that would make him useful in a future law enforcement role, as impossible as that is. I'm told that violence happens in the common areas relatively regularly, and the most common way is when someone gets a few taps across the face for missing a payment. When they swarm you with three to five jackals in one of the cells, that's when the real damage is done. The stories of people being jumped by that many people with the intention of *really* hurting you is chilling. To hell with the blocks.

As Kenny disappears towards the blood, we're left to sit on one of our wooden park benches placed among some bottlebrush and rose bushes in a garden area outside. It's a lovely, sunny spring day and we all sit and chat, sipping coffee from our dark-green plastic mugs and listening to stories and gossip. Adam Carrington, the senior United Nations officer who described in great detail the photographing of his naked daughter, is at court applying for bail, and it's not long before we hear news that it's been granted and he won't be coming back (at least for now). Everyone is happy for him and wishes him well, and it's welcome news after Arthur's failed appeal from the day before. With

Adam leaving the prison, the *Magic* card game he played with Kenny and Glen is likely to fall away, as Kenny and Adam formed the core of the interest. Kenny seems a bit bummed out about this as he returns from mopping up his latest blood spill, and I can tell he'll have to find something else to fill the long days here.

I'm happy that Carrington is released on bail, and that he's out and back in society (although not with his kids, who have a protective court order in place), which includes being able to visit with his elderly mother who is having a hard time with dementia, but I have a sneaking suspicion that we might see him again. Arthur, both aware of Adam's case and reaching into his own deep repertoire of legal knowledge, explains to us that Adam had already served the sentence he was likely to get here on remand, and so doesn't expect him back at all. Adam's also pursuing a civil action to seek damages from the abuse he received as a younger child and had been busy contacting willing co-victims to join the class action before he was bailed. It's a sad and strange state of affairs, and one I don't think is unique to Adam: defending yourself for abusing your own children, while seeking justice for the abuse you yourself received as a child. What a horrible cycle.

Arthur comes into our kitchen area as I'm making a coffee, so I start the process of putting together his preferred cup of tea. Half a packet of sweetener (remember no sugar) noting Arthur's insistence that the provided sweetener, rather than his purchased alternative, is an inferior product (frankly I don't mind either way). I ask him how he's slept, and he tells me he took a pill (one of his Mirtazapine anti-depressants) and slept alright, though he looks haggard and more hunched than usual. I feel genuinely sorry for Arthur, and I think this is based on the publicity he received through the humiliation of losing his appeal. Apparently, when he went to court the explanation wasn't even read out – the judge merely explained that his appeal was denied and that the reasons could be found listed publicly. What a horrible experience, to have this personal and vulnerable experience exposed to the world, and I tell our little picnic table just that. Sitting and chatting with Dave, my tattooed, mohawked and former debt-collecting neighbour, he relays that a particular police officer has received a bravery award of some kind and that the article in the news mentions this officer's efforts in "bringing down the mastermind of the Mawson Club armed robbery, Dave Will". Dave seems unperturbed by this, but he and the others launch into their usual spiel about the incompetence and corruption of the police, and what they would do if they got their hands on them. Dave tells us how he flattened a media photographer who was accosting him and his family during his trial, and no one including myself minds that someone who aggressively pushed a camera into his face copped a physical reaction. We all agree the media sucks, and I feel appreciative that I get to avoid their scrutiny.

I take Arthur and we go for a half-dozen of our counter-clockwise laps, and I let him debrief whatever he wants with me. There's a lot there. He maintains with fiery conviction that he's innocent and that he was mistreated during the appeal. He outlines the points of law the judges failed to address and also outlines how he intends to go forward from here with a desire to pursue an obscure and rarely employed judicial review (a process whereby the judge's decision is questioned for its technical accuracy). Arthur is desperate to clear his name. In the meantime, he's back with us and settles himself into his routine again, but he'll need to decompress this emotion in a way that works for him, and I'll keep him walking around the yard and yapping about whatever he wants until that occurs. I feel conflicted on his appeal: does his crime seem more or less confirmed now that the decision has come down against him? Arthur's explanations on the points of law make sense to me as a layman and his claims that the false allegations of rape and sexual assault are centred on a conspiracy to destroy him reputationally (if not financially – he explains he's already spent a whopping half a million dollars on lawyers, and this is likely to keep going up) which seems possible if not slightly far-fetched. Then again, his appeal is rejected, making his convictions stand in the face of the best legal representation he could bring to bear. He uses the same barrister he recommended to me, Kieran Ginges, and has also sat in jail thinking of nothing but his case. He's a professor of law, for heaven's sake, and perhaps my confidence in a functioning legal system makes me think that he's had a fair hearing (two now) and that he is indeed a rapist. Arthur the rapist. *My friend Arthur the rapist.* We end our walk by shooting a few basketballs and then I rejoin the picnic table.

* * *

Earlier in the day when the 'buy-ups' arrived, I received a pair of forty-dollar sneakers in a size nine. We are issued the surprisingly horrible PureSports, as I've mentioned, but one can also order two kinds of sneakers on the monthly activities buy-up, which is a less frequent list of more practical items like fans, radios and clothing. I pull on the size nine white and red sneakers and instantly realise they don't fit. I'm annoyed with myself, but only in so much that I should have found someone in the compound with the same size and asked to try them on. Having bought too many shoes around the world I'm everything from a size eight to eleven, a handful of European sizes and god knows what else too. I figured nine was a safe bet, and I bet wrong.

At the picnic table, I explain my recent misfortune and offer the new shoes to anyone with a size nine foot and a pressing need for shoes. One of the younger detainees in the WCC, Craig Stevens, is sitting with us (he's younger than most but still older than I am, probably being in his mid-thirties). He's an interesting character and someone I would consider more on the traditional grub/jackal side of things, although clearly, he's detained here for some kind of sexual crime. He's like a young George Costanza from the hit show *Seinfeld*, except he wears a black anti-smoking baseball cap above his frameless glasses and has severe scarring up his legs from some kind of motor vehicle accident a few years back. Interestingly (or perhaps not because it is jail), he perpetually wears a long-sleeved white thermal top under his blue short-sleeved polo shirt. One of my first interactions with Craig was playing soccer with him on our concrete tennis court (this was a few months back during the world cup) and he fell over and was generally very uncoordinated. I later learned that his lack of coordination was a result of him having drunk a good deal of hand-pump sanitiser before our game. I'm not sure how; typically, the alcohol-based sanitisers are banned unless someone has some kind of gastrointestinal issue, and even then, they're carefully watched. I'm tickled silly that someone could be so damned desperate and idiotic to drink that stuff, but before me sits Craig.

Yet, I'm too quick to judge, and the gifting of shoes to Craig sends me on one of those little journeys of inner conflict that stops me easily assigning someone to a category, and I'm forced to acknowledge and then deal with the multi-dimensional complexity that is inherent in every person here, including those who are tossed into jail and forgotten about. Those who are so close to the end of their own dignity that they drink hand sanitiser and fall down publicly. I've already agreed to give Craig the shoes, and no, I don't want anything for them. It's forty dollars of mine, but I can't wear them and there is nothing else that I need, so I don't mind them being reassigned in this way. We're shooting a few more basketballs when I tell Craig he's welcome to go and grab the shoes from my room, and I explain that they're located in a box in the left-hand compartment under my bed. He looks at me with a little bit of surprise, that I would send him into my room without accompanying him, given we don't really know each other and that he's certainly never been in there before. There are two detainees in the WCC I wouldn't extend this offer to, but I take a little bit of pride in letting Craig go in knowing that I trust him, and he comes back out a minute later, shakes my hand firmly and thanks me. I guess that's the payment I was seeking: a recognition of generosity without anything physical or monetarily desired in return, and he walks away quite chuffed. But then Craig arrives back in my room an hour later with a folder; he wants to show me something, but I have no idea what it is. He proceeds to open the folder and show me photos of a matchstick model car, with an attached trailer, and even a little bicycle that he's put together for his son (he has a few children, but I can't track the family breakdown he flies through). The little model car he's made, that's been safely sent out of the jail for safekeeping, is masterfully superb and a real surprise. He's made little working leaf suspension bars for it, an engine, an exhaust system and many other fine details. The tiny bicycle, which attaches to the back of the caravan, actually works, and I'm genuinely taken aback with his skill and the detail in what he's created. One of the other detainees, an older man named Willem 'Bill' Scheeren, makes wooden popsicle stick structures like tables and lampshades, but Craig's little car is a marvel. Craig tells me it's a 1962 Ford Anglia, and he owns the actual vehicle itself, which is his pride and joy (presumably with his children) and he has taken it to many car shows previously. He even admits to having the tattoo of the car across his back, and Cameron later tells me it's a horribly crooked rendition that will make me smile if I see it one day.

* * *

The day ends with me discussing with the others my foreign language student, Taylor Schmidt: the young murderer I meet in the library for chats and impromptu lessons. Kenny tells me over dinner that he's crazy, and when I reply that he's just a little immature and perhaps juvenile, but not crazy, I'm corrected and learn more about his crime. I understood that Taylor was jailed for killing someone during a botched robbery and that he was with some accomplices at the time, who are also somewhere in the jail. Kenny informs me that, in fact, Taylor and his buddies went out and killed someone – a young Asian male – out of curiosity, and only robbed him as an afterthought. Misinformation circulates around the jail with regularity, but I'm privately perturbed about this new piece of information on Taylor, and particularly that his victim was targeted for his race. I seemed reconciled that he had murdered someone, which occurred as a horrible but not strictly premeditated act, but to think that he went out and deliberately murdered someone for its own sake; killing with knives and swords, Kenny informs me, makes me wonder if I want to meet with him again. Should I make some excuse and just let him carry on with his studies privately?

Arthur the rapist. The professor, and my friend. Kenny the paedophile. My friend and neighbour. I hear him snoring through the wall behind me. Craig the hand-sanitiser drinking master craftsman. The sexual assaulter. Wearing his new shoes. Taylor the murderer. Taking a business degree, learning a new language. Killed because he was curious.

Do I have the right to judge these people? To throw these labels at them and also to let you make judgements based on society's perceptions that they're some of the worst people you could ever meet; that they should be locked up and have the key thrown away. Every day, week and month here adds colour to both the good and bad and gives me pause when I think of these people who I live with. It's probably tiring reading as I unwrap this continuous moral dichotomy, but I can't see an easy answer in front of me; nothing that makes any of this fall into place and become sensible, like I feel it should. And I can't turn my back on this experience either, because I'm also a detainee, deprived of my liberty and choice. I'm forced to live with and interact with these people. It's a journey I haven't chosen to be on, but I'm here; I must set a course to somewhere.

CHAPTER 7

In a blur of days that seem to follow a standard recipe of musters, meals and mediocre television, a day like today will occasionally come along and surprise. And it started fairly late – I woke up at eleven am, which so far seems the only silver lining to being incarcerated: an ability to sleep and lounge about as much as you'd like. I take quite the pleasure in returning to bed once woken for the eight am morning muster.

As I head into the kitchen to make the first of a few mandatory coffees, Cameron is mopping the tiled area and I apologise as I stumble over the still-damp floors to reach the kettle and stir my morning elixir. Walking on damp floors is absurd, as the heated tiles make mopping a quick process that dries in about thirty seconds, and Kenny accuses me of being 'morning drunk' for not waiting. It's an apt description of my cognitive and motor abilities in this first hour of consciousness, and I've been notorious with family, girlfriends and colleagues (and now fellow inmates) for having this slovenly trait; I wish I could just flick some switch and became a morning person. But alas, I think I'm destined for a long life of being a night owl. Frankly, I love the evenings and enjoy the quiet and stillness with my own thoughts, but I certainly understand what I'm missing out on. Mornings. Yuck.

Kenny is frantically preparing an obscure meal that involves most of our not-inconsiderable number of pumpkins, and he's cutting and chopping and mixing his concoction with great enthusiasm. I stand just outside the kitchen with my hair sticking up everywhere and get through my third cup of coffee, about what I need to move onto the next phase of my routine in a timed six-minute prison shower. No dropping of the soap jokes please, although the first time it happened to me back in solitary confinement I caught the moment's irony. Cameron's finished mopping and starts chatting to Kenny about his dad's visit for the coming evening, and it suddenly hits me why Kenny is doing all of this preparation. His dad has flown in from the United States, a huge African-American man Kenny hasn't seen in six years, so today is a happy but somewhat anxious time, I quickly realise. Kenny is baking his pumpkin-pie recipe so he can take one to the visit and enjoy it over the two hours (the duration of an extended visit) he has with his father.

Cam shares with me more of Kenny's back story and lifts some of the veil. While I know his crimes are extreme and heinous (and 'hands-on', to use that unavoidably terrible euphemism), I have to piece his and most of the other inmate's stories together fragment by fragment, as I'm disinclined to directly ask in most cases. Kenny is anxious about this meet with his father, as his first six-year stint in jail saw his family come together and support him through the ordeal, helping him to re-enter society, which he did back in 2010. Then, sadly for him and his family, but more-so his victims, he re-offended, and the family saw this as a betrayal of their own efforts and thus became more distant from him. It's one of the many little tragedies here in the WCC, and no doubt across the wider jail population, and yet Kenny's Australian-based mother dutifully visits him from interstate most weeks and bucks his spirits. Cameron goes on: Kenny also plans to live with another detainee once they are both released. This detainee, someone who Kenny sheepishly refers to as his "little love muffin" is another child predator who was incarcerated alongside Kenny before being moved to a different jail. They plan to live together and support themselves and each other, and I nod as Cam explains this all to me.

"So, living together as friends," I say. "Smart – cheaper rent and they know they can live together."

"Oh, they'll be living together as partners; *lovers*," Cameron corrects me.

I'm aware of some of Kenny's problems in expressing his homosexuality, and his journey of self-acceptance, but I'm caught a little unawares that these references to his "little love muffin" are indeed an overt statement of his intentions and sexual orientation – something I had thought to date was some dirty secret (of course, only in Kenny's own eyes) that we weren't supposed to know. The subtle hints I make around him that homosexuality is no big deal, and that 'gay people' are fine (to even have to make these comments in the artificial environment of jail is odd, but a reality) seem like a soft touch now. I'll have to up my amperage and maybe even have a little direct chat with him about owning this gay thing because no one who matters thinks it's a big deal. He's so oddly self-conscious for someone who is 'out', but it's hard to make judgements about his situation, which is obviously complicated and deeply personal. Sex is, of course, an incredibly dysfunctional thing for people who have molested children, and in Kenny's case enough to do two heavy stints in jail, so I shouldn't assume too much. Cameron concludes his discreet revelation by saying the parole board sees paedophiles who can maintain healthy adult relationships as less likely to re-offend. It makes sense, I guess, and I hope Kenny and his love muffin can find solace in each other once they rejoin society.

An hour passes and Kenny comes back into the kitchen, cursing Jason who's apparently failed to turn off the oven (which lately is annoyingly loud with an ill-fitted extraction fan) and his pumpkin pies are quickly examined for damage. I offer my own opinion that the pies will be fine no matter what, but you can tell Kenny is stressed and unhappy with Jason's failure to pay attention. Luckily the pies are salvageable and Kenny seems to have averted disaster. I listen to him recount some old calamitous story about catching trains from stations that are too close to schools (a 'no go' for him and his brethren) before he heads off nervously to meet his dad with his over-baked pumpkin pie.

* * *

I'm taken to see Doctor Joey Lee, one of the psychiatrists here at the jail. It's a regular check-up after two months and it feels like a meeting that doesn't need to occur. I'm probed for appetite, sleep and mood and we swap a few comments back and forth before it's obvious that everything is fine. I appreciate the system that's in place to make sure I and others are okay, but the young and well-dressed Doctor Lee would be better focussed elsewhere.

We shake hands and I make my way back to the Women and Child Chasers, where I have a curious experience with one of the other non-sexual offenders (if you recall there are four of us) who is caught doing something mischievous.

I'll get back to that, but first let me add some context here. Aside from me and the elderly tattooed mohawk-wearing Dave, the other two non-sexual offenders, 'Crafty' and 'Thomo', complete the four. Daniel Craft and Jason Thomas are an interesting pair, perhaps in their early thirties, and are easily pigeon-holed into the category the guards and I like to call 'gronks'. Gronks are your petty thieves and drug addicts: young stupid hooligans who think that because they've stolen a half-dozen cars it makes them notorious, like Danny Ocean or Bugsy Malone (help me out here; my repertoire of infamous criminals is still quite small), when in fact they are just worthless petty criminals. Every time you turn on the news and hear of some ninety-year-old war veteran or grandmother getting a black eye during a horrible home invasion, you can be sure that a Crafty or Thomo-like gronk is behind it. The gronk is similar but still different to the jackal; a jackal, by comparison (I should also warn you once more this is my take alone and not some established language), is violent and will fight when safety in numbers is present; however, a gronk is primarily a non-violent scuttling lizard. Both Crafty and Thomo are in this part of the jail for their own protection, and very much fit the profile of a scuttling pair of gronks. They are despised by the rest of the wings for running up unpaid drug debts and "grassing" (informing on) others to derive a benefit themselves, and because of that, they're guaranteed a severe bashing on contact from many other begrudged inmates. They'll never go to the library where we mix with other wings and mostly keep to themselves. The pair are known derisively as Beavis and Butthead by all and sundry, and it fits the rather lowly status that they hold. It's quite the feat to be looked down on by the thirty-six rapists and paedophiles in the jail, but Crafty and Thomo would put themselves above the dreaded "pests," which is what sex offenders are derisively known as. Bruisers, jackals, gronks and pests. The last and perhaps most feared category is the female "banshee", and without exception the guards I ask recount horrid stories of how these aggressive and unreasonable female detainees maim each other and hold grudges for literally decades. One savage beating that occurred before I arrived in the prison was undertaken to settle a dispute that started over twelve years ago.

Crafty the gronk is quite overweight, with a sideways hat and a piercing in his lip, and he has the normal smattering of badly drawn prison tattoos all over him. On his right rear calf, a large cross presents dates of birth and death for some deceased friend or relative. Crafty (and presumably Thomo as his only friend) doesn't like me, as I once barked at him for pushing into the medication line shortly after I arrived. Ten of us were standing there patiently as Crafty walked up to the person in front of me, the hugely overweight and very sad case Glen Vandavord (Kenny's *Magic: The Gathering* friend), and asked to go ahead of him. Glen is Crafty's roommate (some here share a room) and he is bullied by Crafty, whose approval (or anyone else's) he desperately craves. As Crafty walked up to the front of the office where the nurse sits behind a small square window, I pulled out of line and demanded to know why Crafty thought his time was more valuable than ours, sweeping my arm along the ten patient souls waiting behind him. He dutifully went to the back of the line grumbling the whole way, and I knew from then on, he would be someone to keep at arm's length. Over the next couple of days, Crafty whispered to the guards that I might have drugs or other contraband, and he sought to have me 'tipped': the dreaded departure from a comfortable cottage to the blocks. Unfortunately, Crafty wasn't aware that my case was different and he had as much chance of getting me 'tipped' as he did of getting himself released that afternoon.

As I return from my meeting with Doctor Lee, Thomo, who wears a short blond ponytail over a medium-sized build (chubby without being fat) is way down in the corner of the yard with the second corrections officer on duty. As I stand with the other, we wait until the pair walk up to us and learn that Thomo has been caught either throwing something over the fence or receiving an item from the other side. It's a standard trick of the detainees to move drugs and other contraband between the yards, even potentially introducing items from outside the jail. Thomo has been caught at a sort of cross-section of fencing that includes both the adjacent yard as well as the perimeter fence (beyond which are pleasantly rolling hills and fields that fill with kangaroos every day without exception) so anything is a possibility. The corrections officer is searching Thomo and running his fingers through his ratty ponytail. He knows something has occurred, but exactly what it is will remain a mystery, as nothing is found on him. Rumours abound later of a homemade tattoo gun, and it's eventually confirmed by large fresh tattoos up and down Thomo's legs. He has the infamous Kelly quote 'Such is life' on the shin of his right leg, and on the other, he has a list of attributes he seems to think are important: 'honour', 'loyalty' and 'family' are written on top of each other, and it's a curiosity that he's penned at least two in direct contravention to how he's lived his life or indeed what his reputation is. A dishonest gronk with 'honesty' penned illicitly on his leg.

Later, Cameron shakes his head at the stupidity of Thomo to be passing things over the jail fences, and that he's jeopardising his place in one of the few areas of the jail where his safety is not threatened on a daily basis. Cam thinks the guards will go back to the camera footage to unravel the whole thing, discerning the direction of the contraband at a minimum, and identifying who the other party was. Goodness knows how they manage in the wings that are *full* of gronks and other troublemakers.

After the visits, Kenny returns with a smile and shares stories from his dad's journey to Australia, and his confusion over the various football codes (he assures Kenny that from his American home he can stream 'Rugby Union League', which seems unlikely). The pumpkin pie was eaten and enjoyed, and we now slice apart the second pie and share it among ourselves. It's a credit to Kenny – his pie is delicious, despite Jason's best efforts to overcook it, and we chatter away about the day's events. The famed (but overrated) *Shawshank Redemption* is on tonight, and I somewhat excitedly tell Kenny that we are just like the movie's protagonists: Red and Andy Dufraine. I go so far as to scrawl these new names and slide them into the plastic containers that attach to the walls outside every room (we each have a gloomy prison photo, our names and dates of birth) though I feel the optimism is a little one-sided. I'm still somewhat fascinated by the clash of prison culture between fiction and my reality, though the others are worn out after years of incarceration. The movie is good, and I relate to the concepts of slipping time (a dreadful reality), institutionalisation and the necessity for one to have a project in prison to help pass the time.

CHAPTER 8

The local news announced that a paedophile had been arrested and jailed. He was exposing himself, so the pretty news anchor said, to children through the gates of their school, and went on to pull a child's hand into "an indecent act", which I assume means that means he forced the child's hand to touch his genitals. He apparently asked the children if they wanted to see a magic trick.

I've heard friends joke and use that very line, often mimicking dodgy van owners and repeating that predatory approach in an attempt at black humour. It's funny, if I recall it from a former life not incarcerated, but here it is being used by a real-life predator to conduct his heinous and disgusting act. He's in the jail tonight, in a faraway block or protection area, no doubt contemplating his fate and nervously recalculating his life against the reality unfolding in front of him now. They named him and showed a police sketch, and the jail's other detainees will know exactly who he is, with many jackals and bruisers calling him names and tormenting him; promising him extreme violence and punishment in parallel to his remanding. This violence may find him soon; even tonight. I don't feel sorry for him in the slightest. I don't know him.

He's a one-dimensional monster to me, and someone I only know from the announcement via the local news. Even the young pretty anchor allowed herself to editorialise, stating that "he was where he belonged, behind bars." She's right, of course, and I have the same feeling of anger over this predator abusing children in this way. It's completely abhorrent. If he works his way through the jail into our wing, I suspect I will view him differently than I do the others here, some of whom are convicted of much more heinous crimes. Sitting here right now, I do not feel even the slightest inclination of wanting to meet him and hope that if he indeed arrives he will live in another pod and never interact with me. I won't shake his hand; the same one which undid his trousers in front of those children; the same hand which pulled a child's arm into his crotch.

Or maybe I'll have to shake his hand and say hello to him, introduce myself and be courteous. How could I refuse to? He's not greatly different to the others I live with. He'll become multi-dimensional to me once he arrives, and become glaringly human in his full complexity. Thinking about him, I feel like you do: disgusted and even angry at his acts. It's easier to package these single dimensions and place them on the shelf out of sight.

* * *

On Tuesdays, we are locked in during the afternoons, which simply means we can move about in our pod of six but can't leave and mix with the other thirty-four detainees in the wing. I split my time between reading and watching television in my room and sitting out in the common area chatting away with Kenny, Jason and Cameron. Dave sometimes joins us but usually spends the afternoons quietly napping in his own room, and our recluse Alwyn Baume doesn't stir at all. We've actually started wondering if Alwyn is eating properly, as he seems to be living off soy milk and yoghurt in his room, only occasionally emerging for a cigarette or to use the laundry right next to his door. He's a vapour to me; always just there but never *really* present.

Jason is describing to me how the intra-jail 'shops' work, as I'm confused about some of the mechanics in this underground economic system. While detainees can buy items from an official weekly and monthly list, these other unofficial shops exist all across the jail (with the singular exception of our wing) and are run by the detainees for profit. While not strictly allowed, the guards seem to tolerate these improper shops, and this confounds me even further as the shops tend to lead to a lot of violence when debt is accrued and unpaid. In a system where detainees can legitimately buy items such as tobacco, junk food and sundry items, you might be curious about what would motivate a detainee to go to one of these underground shops and buy something on a 'two-to-one cost'. What you take now, you must pay back twice at the next opportunity. It seems a huge number of detainees simply cannot control their impulses and buy all sorts of products on this absurd usury system, then quickly fall behind in the payments. Weakness is unacceptable in jail, and the shopkeepers must chase debt or be seen as someone who can be exploited. This, then, results in bashings and other feats of violence that perpetuate the spiral of unrest the guards would surely be better off without. But they turn a blind eye. Jail is confusing.

Kenny is ranting about trade relations between the United States and Canada and making grand sweeping statements about something he presumably heard on the news. He's wearing his blue polo shirt and black shorts and has his crossed feet resting on our dining table. It's one of my little pet hates in the pod: when people sit on or put their feet on the table we also eat on. I'm less passive when it comes to Jason trying to sneakily smoke in his room near the window, and I popped my head into his room last night to tell him off like a child caught in a school bathroom.

As I've mentioned, Kenny makes quite broadly sweeping statements about the United States and seems to mistakenly think that his American heritage somehow imbues his argument with more credibility.

"Canada doesn't realise that Americans do not care about them." Kenny starts to warm himself up.

"Uh-huh."

"Canada is just a joke to Americans. Many people don't realise that Trump is only allowing the new trade deal because he feels sorry for them."

"Sure."

"Yeah, and the American President never goes to Canada. Canada is nothing to America and Americans," Kenny goes on.

"Well," I try, "the US and Canada are sort of like Australia and New Zealand: two friendly and culturally similar neighbours who don't need to do a lot of diplomacy with each other."

"Nah," Kenny corrects me on behalf of more than 300 million people. "Trust me, Americans don't think *anything* of Canada."

These circular discussions tend to taper off within the first few minutes as I fall silent. It's boring to try and wrangle a point through, and so we return to some piece of prison gossip or await Kenny's next confrontation with the news on anything related to his distant and unfamiliar country of origin.

Nilander 'Neil' Sirowi, our short stocky Indian rapist (one of a group of five or six – the subcontinent is grossly over-represented in the wing) is causing trouble in the pod next to ours and is making his cellmate, the paedophile priest John Aitchison, move from the bottom to the top bunk. I thought from my background of absorbing theatrical prison culture through movies and television that the top bunk was the good one, but perhaps I've got that the wrong way around. Neil, who I get along with without any issue, seems to have a long and sordid history of violence and non-sociability that makes everyone wary of him, but I can't see that from the short jovial Indian who is perhaps a few years older than me and seems a bit punch drunk from previous professional fighting bouts. He has a long plaited rats-tail and a Sanskrit character tattooed behind his ear. He's convicted of rape, but he vigorously denies it and claims the Australian legal system unfairly treated him on racial grounds. He and John are certainly the odd couple, and our professor Arthur, who sleeps in another cell in the same pod, also claims that Neil has been consuming too many eggs and flour. Cameron and I laugh and agree that we're lucky to live in the only pod that seems to function without any real issues, though of course, we are lucky to have Cameron's leadership and maturity as our delegate. Indeed, Cameron is often forced to intervene on behalf of others who cannot reconcile their minor living squabbles. With Kenny routinely departing to clean all parts of the jail, and Cameron's intervention among our wing, our pod is never without the latest piece of intrigue or gossip.

Shortly before five pm, we are let out by the guards to stretch our legs for forty minutes before getting locked in for the night. We sit on the wooden park bench and lazily watch the afternoon flights criss-cross the sky with long contrails, and occasionally fly close to the jail as they come into land. As we relax, we see a commotion at the guards' station and watch as five corrections officers depart their office heading to the opposite side of the wing to 'ramp' someone, which refers to the conducting of a detailed search seeking to find some contraband. The gronks (Crafty and Thomo) and other disreputables all live on the other side, and so the focus is often there. Six months in, and I'm yet to see one of these focussed searches occur in our own pod, although the guards do token and routine light searches once a fortnight at evening muster periods.

One of the guards that's on today is an old hand, though it's the first time he's worked in this wing since I've been here, and so I ask the other's opinions about him. I'm told he was a former military man; an ex-paratrooper, and so I take this news at face value and ask this guard about it during the final lock-in. He seems a little caught off guard when I ask him about it, and it takes him a second to blurt out he was formerly special forces. When I then ask him which unit, even offering him the name of the one I thought he might have served in, it becomes quite clear he's not telling the truth and he makes up some rubbish about serving in the United Kingdom before coming to Australia. He speaks with a very established Australian accent. Goodness knows why he would lie about it (but there are thousands of fabricators out there claiming similar accolades), and I mention it to one of the other guards who rolls his eyes and recounts a similar story from the same untruthful guard. It's an interesting moment where one guard sides with a detainee (and in front of four others) against one of his peers, but I like that he shows some independence in his assessment. The guards are both fallible and human, as these two have shown me in their own ways today.

* * *

The latest gossip seems to be a disagreement between Cyril and Ali, two elderly characters who are both in their own ways locked into the very different worldly perceptions they both have. Cyril is eighty years old and doing a relatively short stint of six months, so is looking to re-enter society in November. He's a former racing car event director who is here for historical crimes (if you'll recall, those crimes in which the perpetrator and his colleagues dismiss out of hand as if time is an excuse) and is a nice enough fellow, often stopping to chat and tell you about the latest book he's read or how to catch and skin rabbits; something he presumably did a lot of as a child. He's fine to interact with, and he tends to call me "young man" as we idly chat about some sort of nothingness, and I can't help but feel sorry for him that he's here so late in life. If you met him, it would be like meeting any other eighty-year-old you have no familial or other close connection with, but he could easily be your grandfather too. Cyril has the hunch of an elderly man and looks at you with his one good eye (the other being blind from some unknown ailment), although I can never work out which one the good one is, and I find myself tracking down the line of sight of an eye that's focussed nowhere. When you do get that good eye, and despite Cyril talking to you at an odd angle that leads you into a false sense of security that he's not paying attention, it is typically locked onto your soul and is penetrative in an uncomfortable way. I'm halfway struck between empathising with this old man and feeling curiously unsettled that he's committed the sexual crimes he has, wondering if he's lived a good life and has somehow atoned for the damage he was convicted of inflicting. It's a well-joked-about maxim here that everyone is innocent of their crimes, but that they still deserve to be locked up for the things they *got away with*. I wonder if the raping or molesting Cyril once did was isolated, or if he's spent a lifetime perpetrating maniacal abuse on others and has gotten away with the majority of it. It's hard to tell; it could be somewhere in the middle, perhaps, but it's odd to me that he's as possible of being the lifetime perpetrator as he is of being the grandfather who stumbled once.

I know less about Ali, whose actual name is Ayman Hassan. He's a recent arrival of a fortnight ago, though has spent years in the other parts of the jail and is well known by the others who have been around. Ali is an elderly Lebanese-Australian with a long beard who is here for paedophilia, and claims to have been a senior officer in the Lebanese military; a Lieutenant Colonel or Colonel perhaps. Jason describes him not inaccurately as the "Lebanese Papa Smurf", which should give you a clear idea of the short shuffling child sex offender who does laps of the yard. As he walks past me on one of his circuitous laps, we exchange quick greetings and wish each other well.

"Salaam-alaykum, Ali."

"Alaykum-salaam, friend," he'll reply.

"How are you, well?"

"Very well, the sun is shining!"

"Ah, Alhamdulillah!" I'll conclude, getting a beaming smile in return. At this stage, Ali is typically walking out of earshot, but I think he likes these little interactions, and I enjoy opening a small window and hinting at my experiences in the Middle East and South Asia.

Cyril and Ali live together in the adjacent pod and have been bickering over kitchen use. As I sit and listen to Professor Arthur Hoyle, who also lives in the same area, Cameron and I smile and shake our heads that these adults cannot find an amicable way to live with each other without resorting to petty squabbles. Ali spends far too much time in the kitchen, Arthur informs us, and Cyril has become ticked off, resulting in a geriatric scuffle that spreads like wildfire through the other pods, with interested people siding with one or the other (though it seems they tend to side with Cyril – Ali finds himself with few friends here). I'm almost annoyed that I'm interested in listening to this crappy gossip to break the monotony of the day, however, Cam contemplates the situation a little longer and then heads over to talk to the two senior citizens. Cameron is pulled into the pods as the WCC delegate and de facto leader to mediate and resolve the disputes that adults shouldn't require external support to resolve. He's tired of it, he tells me often, but still dutifully gets up and speaks patiently with whomever needs it, playing arbitrator to someone using too many eggs, disputes over remote controls, or – god forbid – should someone be closing their door too loudly. Clearly, there are those who thrive on developing conflict to mitigate boredom, but mostly it's irritable older men learning for the first times in their lives that they must share.

CHAPTER 9

It so happens that while in the library with the professor, I came across the newspaper article describing Arthur's failed appeal. He was sitting next to me bringing me up to speed on his application to secure work release at a new legal firm his friend had opened, despite the fact that I was quite content to quietly read by myself. I did pause for a second; I was curious if I should show Arthur the article, which admittedly was only a small piece buried a half-dozen pages in. In the end, I thought it too oddly serendipitous not to and flashed him the page with a sardonic little smile. He didn't seem to care that much and quickly went back to explaining his application to me.

Convicted minimum security detainees with less than twelve months on their sentences can apply for transitional work release, which in effect is a strictly regulated release to attend work during approved hours. Arthur, with his academic qualifications, is desperate to secure this application, which would see him depart the jail during working hours on Monday through to Friday. It's a tricky program: one that requires absolute trust from corrections to ensure that someone doesn't take the opportunity to escape or commit other crimes while away from the jail.

It's a program that Cameron is also pursuing, although he is still more than two years from release; he will be making an application on his good behaviour to date. Cameron's parents' property is a short drive from the jail, and so he's interested in attending their place for the purposes of conducting maintenance and clearing away flammable debris that could put the house at risk during the forthcoming summer. Cameron also includes me in his application, and I feel flattered that he's included me in this plan to help his parents, which would allow me to join him there. Personally, I would love the chance to depart the jail each day and use my time productively, in this case helping an elderly couple with some basic maintenance and other chores, although I cannot see how the corrections leadership will approve the request. Cam makes no secret of the fact that he wants to leverage my relationship with general manager Ian Robb in this application, and I'll have to wait to see how it goes. All fingers are crossed, but I am sceptical about the decision; it still requires the certainty of my sentencing, which is months away.

* * *

In the evening, four or five guards head down to the pod Crafty and Thomo live in and conduct another 'ramping', which is the conduct of surprise and detailed searching that includes strip-searching and the removal of desks and other fixed items to identify any contraband. It's obvious what they're hoping to find: the tattoo equipment that is responsible for the fresh black lettering across Thomo's legs and goodness knows where else. Our pod is never bothered with these detailed searches, and it's very much for the others to tolerate as they invite the ire of the guards through flagrant rule violations. We don't get the full story but do learn that some tattoo paraphernalia such as ink is found and confiscated. Thomo was being rather clever by hiding some of it in the bins outside all of the other pods (all except his own), volunteering to empty bins while no doubt either recovering or planting his equipment concurrently. There truly is never an innocent act undertaken by our two resident gronks.

The tattoo gun is a fine way to transmit bloodborne viral infections, which are littered throughout the occupants in the jail. Hepatitis this and Hepatitis that; HIV and AIDS and god knows what else are hidden within gronks, jackals and bruisers, and overtly on display in the myriad of pamphlets and posters that cover the jail walls. Friendly Aboriginal cartoon characters espouse the dangers of sharing needles and not sanitising hairdressing equipment and tattoo guns. With the amount of blood spilt across the jail, it's something I feel very conscious of, including the risk that Jason and Kenny may be carrying an infectious disease. They both have long tenure in jail that makes contact possible, and Kenny's near-daily interaction with blood spills, despite the strict hygiene precautions he follows, makes him a risk. Jason has been an intravenous drug user and is covered in shoddy tattoos (I still haven't learned who Tracey is) so it's possible he has something too. If indeed Jason or Kenny do carry an infectious bloodborne disease, it makes their sexual crimes all the more depraved. I have no way of knowing if the sixteen-year-old girl Jason raped or the young boys Kenny molested now carry a lifetime infection. It adds a fresh dimension of horror to crimes where horror is well represented.

I'll have to ask them if they carry anything; if their blood or secretions are dangerous – but what's the best way to do it? It could be a straightforward question or perhaps something I need to elicit more carefully; more delicately. But I wonder: do I have a right to know? It's not something I would expect with a friend outside of jail, but here our lives are so unwillingly brought together that it almost seems like a sensible thing to know, in the event that one detainee is exposed to the blood of another (a common enough occurrence in a prison).

Kenny seems amused at the question and simply tells me he doesn't have anything and takes his hygiene seriously when responding to spills, so that he often refuses flatly if the right chemicals or protective items aren't available. I press him further for an anecdote, and he tells me of a guard threatening to 'tip' him into the block if he didn't respond to a particular blood spill after Kenny had run out of face masks. The guard told him "to improvise and make his mind up quickly, or start packing his things." Now, Kenny is a very compliant and easy-going detainee, but in this case, he asked for the senior corrections officer who was on duty to come down and tell him to do it, knowing full well that he wouldn't make himself liable for a decision that might see Kenny exposed to an infectious disease. Kenny was right and was even asked if he wanted to put a complaint in against the junior guard, although he declined and simply requested the guard be better informed about such matters for future reference.

Jason also tells me he doesn't have anything, but I feel a degree of caution noting his long years of intravenous drug use, shoddy prison tattoos and generally poor lifestyle. I imagine anyone reading this, and living with an infectious disease like hepatitis or HIV, might think ill of my caution and desire to know the status of my neighbours, and I'll beg your pardon in my naiveté in this regard, but it's not a conversational topic I've been introduced to in a way where I feel informed – thus my cautious and perhaps insensitive approach here. Of all the pamphlets and flyers around the jail warning me of this and that infectious disease, not one cartoon strip is lightly portraying how a tit like me might go about asking (or indeed not) if someone has something.

Over dinner, Kenny and Jason both laugh at my earlier queries and explain that most people here are quite sensible when it comes to infectious diseases, and tattooing, haircutting, intravenous drug use and the cleaning of body-fluid spills are all undertaken with caution. Jason in particular talks about the trust that develops between intravenous drug users, being a former user himself, and that needles are cleaned with bleach or only shared among people that know they don't have an infectious disease, or conversely know they have a particular hepatitis strand (Jason doesn't mention HIV). Jason explains how a quick squirt of bleach and water will clean a needle pretty well, but the bleach risks affecting the quality of the drugs, so some don't bother at all if their supply is running low and they need to get the most out of it. It seems like an unacceptably high risk to accept a syringe from someone who has a disease that you don't, and simply squirting some diluted bleach through it and using that same syringe seems dangerous.

"Why?" Jason asks. He seems artificially perplexed, not dissimilar to how a teacher making a point might be.

"Well, how effective is the bleach? It's playing Russian roulette with three barrels full of ammunition," I offer back.

"Well, they can cure hepatitis now."

"Can they?" I ask. "Don't they just have a way of treating it? Or is it a cure for only one particular stand of hepatitis?" I ask, not really knowing, and it seems that Jason doesn't have a great handle on it as well.

"Well, if you don't all have the same diseases, you will eventually when you start regularly sharing fits," Jason says.

"Fits?"

"Fits," Jason repeats as if it should be obvious. "Syringes, needles. *Fits.*"

"Oh, so a hypodermic needle is a *fit?* Got it," I say and go on: "So, you're actually saying people *will* catch various things?" I'm genuinely confused at Jason's logic, but he seems to have a confident kind of fatalism: users will probably get something, but if they do it's curable. It sounds absurd to me.

"Anyway, better to share a dirty fit than get a good scotching," Jason says while looking at Kenny and smiling. Kenny looks at me, wondering if I've successfully translated Jason's new jail slang: I haven't.

"Ok, so what's a scotching?" I ask Jason. He looks again at Kenny and tells him to explain it to me, but Kenny isn't impressed.

"*You* tell him; you're the convicted scotcher here," Kenny says with some bite.

"Think about it: Scotch tape. Tape. Rape," Jason says.

"So 'a scotching' is a rape?" It seems I'm now getting a crash course on jail slang.

"That's it. So, get it? You can get hepatitis or whatever from a dirty fit, or from a scotching."

"Oh god! People with diseases do that to others?"

"Sure," Jason says drawing out the word. "It's the best way to fuck someone twice!" He bursts into hoarse laughter while Kenny admonishes him for the crassness. At this stage, Jason is trying to control himself while Kenny apologises on his behalf and goes on to tell me it's a pretty rare thing to have happen to a person in prison, but then tells me he's also heard of it happening to a few people in the blocks this year. Of all the horrific things that people do to each other in jail, a diseased 'scotching' takes the cake for being the most debased act of cruelty I've yet heard of. It takes a few minutes, but Jason eventually calms himself down enough to apologise for laughing and then tells me earnestly that it's a disgusting act. It's quite the statement for a convicted rapist, but then we all draw our own lines of morality somewhere.

As I dice cucumber slices and soak them in a briny solution with dill, Kenny makes pancakes for dessert further along the kitchen counter. After the cucumbers are placed in the fridge to mature and turn into tangy and tasty pickles, we sit down and smear plum jam, honey and cinnamon across our pancakes and eat and chat. We're already stuffed from a marvellous beef stroganoff Cam made earlier, and now the pancakes leave us completely full and contented. Kenny chats idly about the Nintendo emulators and how Sony wishes to now release one for the PlayStation, outlining all the technical challenges they will face as the rest of us politely nod. Cam shows me on his computer an American review for a new Ducati motorcycle and Jason skirts out of the washing up again (although Cam walks to his room and pulls him out, annoyed in the fatherly way that Cameron has). We are happy, locked up together in our little world, spending time as best we can and chatting idly away.

CHAPTER 10

There's a certain kind of perverse black humour that comes out of the detainees here from time to time. Jason, if feeling particularly humorous (or simply provided an unmissable opportunity) will occasionally come out with a joke that makes the others laugh and cringe, and often causes the audience to check me for my reaction as the resident non-sexual offender (although mohawked Dave is in the same category). It seems that if I find it funny, the others can then join in without feeling overly self-conscious. There is honour among thieves, and it's just as true that there is honour among paedophiles; simply being reminded of their crimes makes them shrink back into a shameful quietness, with only Jason's ruddy laughter and perhaps my own smirk allowing the rest to self-consciously join in with a well-timed joke.

Jason recounts an interaction he had in the kitchen where he works, while he was discussing his preference for nicotine patches – something he uses in his ongoing battle to try and reduce his smoking addiction. They come in seven-milligram and fourteen-milligram patches, and Jason swears that two seven-milligram patches – perhaps more strategically located around his body – are better than a single, larger fourteen-milligram patch. When one of the guards in the kitchen questioned this, Jason, seizing his opportunity, locked eyes with the official and said: "You know me chief – two sevens are always better than one fourteen," and held the gaze long enough for the implied deviancy to translate across. Jason recounts the story while demonstrating the glaring and predatory goblin-like stare he gave the guard: it's a face that would send chills through any person's body. Of course, Jason was joking, but he is here for raping an under-aged girl, and so his menace is more than theoretical. Still, it musters a chuckle and light admonishment from all of us.

Then there is Jason and Kenny; bantering as they do, when Jason stumbles on the familiarity between Kenny and 'The Rock', the latter otherwise known as Dwayne Johnstone. As Kenny's surname is the phonetically similar Johnson, Jason immediately nicknames our tubby African-American friend 'The Rock *Spider*' which leaves me initially dumbfounded as I need the term explained to me. I fail to realise that 'rock spider' is a common and derogatory term for a paedophile, it being one of the lowest forms of life, and so I have to listen to the others belly laughing at Jason's neat comparison, finally joining in later. Kenny is clearly deeply embarrassed by the joke and doesn't even seem up to defending himself in front of us; he waits until Cameron shows his levelled maturity to move everyone on from the verbal jab. Jason is so pleased with his joke it does the rounds of the wing and is heard here and there for days.

Jason receives some mail and excitedly opens up around a dozen pages of colour photographs of him and his family. It's a marvel to see Jason only ten years earlier, when his body still managed to hold some semblance of a shape other than round, and his skin was clearer and less splattered with half-finished tattoos. I stand over him as he looks at them and proudly points himself out, as well as his mother, grandmother and other relatives and friends. His mother has included a page explaining who is who and she's made little comments in the margins: "We love you," "Hang in there, love" and "We miss you every day." It's another of those touching moments and very human; showing the real side of Jason beyond his crimes and grisly outward appearance. Cameron comes over as well and Jason explains again who everyone is. He's happy, I sense, and when he lingers on one of the pages full of photographs of his mother, I take my cue and leave him be. I feel good for him.

While at the library I run into Taylor, my learned student and convicted murderer, and discuss some of the language he has done very well to teach himself in here. Graham Dillon, a large detainee with a squarish kind of build and haircut wanders around the library browsing self-help literature. Aside from the formidable appearance, he also has those unmistakable neck tattoos that make you hope you never find yourself on his bad side. Dillon is infamously here for quite horrendously murdering his eight-year-old son, and it's a story that makes it into the news again this week. Torturing your own child to death is a crime I just cannot fathom — much like all of the others in here I suppose — and he's settled into a very long stretch. As he shuffles down the narrow library aisle towards me, he dips his head and politely excuses himself as he slips through.

Also in the library is the older Italian man who killed his friend after a clearly serious falling out, even going so far as to amputate the genitals from the fresh corpse and stuff them into the mouth. An appalling crime, perpetrated by an old man who looks like he should be gaily hawking fresh fruit in a market somewhere, or happily tossing a grandchild into the air. Along with Taylor, it's a bit of a 'who's who of murderers' today in the library, and despite everyone's own crimes the two different groups mingle harmoniously and read newspapers or chat with Belinda the saintly librarian. There's little tension in these two groups, but as our own gathers for the return stroll to the wing, one of the younger jackals yells out to a few of our group: "Ya fuckin pest cunts!" They hate the paedophiles and must take every opportunity to harass and bash the members of the WCC to gain or maintain their own prestige. It's not anything I take personally, not being one, but one member of our wing, Dave Cashin, tells them off in reply: "Yes, righto, tough guy!" The others ignore the incoming barbs.

* * *

It's becoming warm enough to reach under my bed into one of the large cavities and pull out my new desk fan. It's been there for months, and Cameron recommended I buy one in the cold dead of winter before the demand caused the predictable sell-out as the days warmed up. It's noteworthy, and the design is specific for prison use, in that the container is made from translucent plastic. It's obvious when one considers it's designed to prevent detainees from storing contraband inside the device, given that guards can easily see through it, but it does have a somewhat sleek style, and I quite like it. Although in my room I have an ordinary black-cased computer (similar to those Apple computers that double as the screen) and a Samsung flat-screen television, the jail goes for clear items when possible, and this is most readily apparent in the range of clear watches and glasses that can be purchased on the monthly canteen forms. With Cameron's full-headed salt and pepper haircut, light grey prison shirt and pants, translucent watch and glasses, he looks like he's stepped away from the year 2100. We all look like futuristic citizens (although I have my stainless-steel Seiko diver's watch anchoring me to the last century) with our assortment of clear plastic items, and I can see a New York or Milan fashion show with a translucent grey prison vibe working quite well.

The fan whirs happily away, which is a relief, as I'm not sure they would believe me if I said it wasn't working after two months, and that today was the first time I'd tried it. ClearVue electronics is the brand, and the clunky three settings all appropriately escalate the fan's speed as it should. Some of the other pods are trialling humidity coolers which are simply fans with a water reservoir and misting capability, although the odorous Tom Johnstone (bus driver; paedophile) is giving everyone a headache with his constant and unwanted updates about the process. Despite the somewhat-aerated nature of my room and the pod, the thick bricks do threaten to hold the heat in and make life uncomfortable; something the others assure me is coming for a few weeks when it gets very hot.

* * *

There's trouble with our mental health-impaired pod resident Alwyn Baume, who has seemingly gone off another cliff of rationality, this time believing there is a conspiracy against him that relates to a new section of garden that has been taped off, preventing people walking on it. He visits Cameron up to five and six times a day outlining his concerns and asserting that no one will tell him where he can and cannot walk. The area he describes is probably ten square metres of grass that some of the others have planted delicate saplings in, putting up the string that forces people to inconveniently walk three additional metres around on the path to enter the games room. It's a pitiful thing to take issue with, but perhaps Alwyn sees it as an unauthorised encroachment on his already-encroached liberty. Cameron patiently hears him out each time, trying to talk Alwyn back down into reality. I'm amazed he has the patience at all to do this, and I wonder why he's tolerated it for four years. Cam, of course, tells me in quieter moments that he's quite sick and tired of it, and has raised objections with the guards that he's not equipped or even required to manage Alwyn's mental health issues, but the problems go on. Cam and I chat about it and agree to push it again, and Cameron sits down to pen a new email to senior management on the latest issue, also mentioning that Alwyn still finds my curious and mysterious case a problem, often raising this issue about me with the others in the pod and wider wing. I agree that I'll raise the issue as well, and speak with a caseworker about Alwyn's mental health, and the fact that he's eating less and less to the point that we are concerned for his physical wellbeing. I mention, carefully but deliberately, that he's approaching a point where I and the others believe there is a self-harm risk (Alwyn has previously tried to take his life on numerous occasions) and that triggers the caseworker to inform senior management. They arrive that evening to talk with Cameron and then Alwyn. The senior corrections officer, a level four (the top corrections rank; there are five substantive officers across the whole jail) explains to Alwyn that he will speak with him after the weekend on Tuesday to hear any concerns he has. Cam is pleased at this, as he thinks it will give Alwyn another outlet in which to vent his imaginary concerns, thereby relaxing some of the pressure on himself. It will also give the senior management an opportunity to see just how sick Alwyn is. It's a good result.

Alwyn's latest focus on me (in parallel to the garden issue) has Jason joking that Alwyn may burst into my room late at night with a knife, screaming, "Here's Johnny!" (Alwyn often goes by his middle name John to those in the wing), and it's a thought that doesn't sound too far from reality. As I've mentioned, despite having our own rooms around the pod, our doors aren't locked (only the external pod door is of an evening), and so it's quite possible to burst into someone's room late at night. Jason helpfully tests the large locking nut that secures the butcher's knife to its one metre chain in the kitchen. "He'd get it off if he wanted to," Jason unhelpfully informs me with his wry smile. Although Alwyn weighs 50-odd kilos, a man that has raped and tortured his own daughters and son must be capable of *anything*. His irrationality is the scariest aspect. There's no way to predict his thoughts and mood, and his descending and venomous opinion of me has occurred so insidiously that I don't know what's coming next.

Let's hope it's nothing like *The Shining*.

PART II

*"But it is one thing to read about
dragons and another to meet them."*

Ursula K. Le Guin, A Wizard of Earthsea

CHAPTER 11

Our pod lives in harmony. Cameron Tully, Kenneth Johnson, Jason Dodd, David Will and our recluse, Alwyn Baume. And myself. The other thirty-four residents of the Women and Child Chasers also hum along in a degree of harmony, and aside from the odd dispute about food, walking on the garden or random trivialities, there isn't any real trouble in our wing, and there's certainly no violence. Everyone here has much to lose: being 'tipped' back into another pod – or back to the dreaded blocks – ensures that behaviour is moderated and incidents are rare.

But, of course, some people push the boundaries and mostly get away with little indiscretions. Our cupboards are full of illicit pepper, cardamom pods and olive oil (I'm yet to understand why we can't have the latter two), but there are also drugs here, as I'm finding out. It's clear that our two gronks, Crafty and Thomo, are getting their hands on drugs, but it's also a few others as I'm coming to learn. I might be somewhat circumspect in describing the details here, but needless to say, some of those who interact with other detainees when working, visiting the library or doing other education programs are bringing stuff in, and paying a lot for it as well. I'm brought into the confidence of someone who claims they have paid upwards of five thousand dollars to sustain their habit, and I'm surprised to learn there is a corrections officer in a part of the process. Certain guards are complicit in the introduction of illicit items around the jail; as I've perhaps mentioned, it's quite common knowledge that one particular guard will get you a mobile phone for a thousand dollars, but the brazen nature of this activity causes my eyebrows to rise. Of course, it's all hearsay from my trusted source, and I feel they have named a different guard to monitor any indiscretion, should it come out, so it provides further impetus to write in generalities. I don't see this guard very often and wouldn't have had more than one or two quick conversations with them, so it's hard to say how surprised I feel either way. I'm certainly more surprised about the detainee consuming the narcotics (and the frequency) given that person's professional background and the risk of acquiring an extension to their sentence. I wonder if the corrections staff will obtain this fragment of intelligence and put me to task to disclose those involved? My suspicion is that they're already aware and are possibly monitoring it to see how far it spreads. With the rampant drugs and violence across the rest of the jail, I imagine it would require them to inordinately focus on this wing to the detriment of exposing other covert networks, which admittedly is possible given their hatred and disgust of the rapist and paedophiles who live here.

Interestingly, there exists an 'axis of evil' here in the Women and Child Chasers, and this ring of deviance includes three detainees that the corrections staff seem to believe have gotten away with breaking the rules in non-traditional ways. Specifically, Glen Vandavord, Tony Wyatt and Navin Edwards are three computer-literate residents who were caught a year ago hacking the PrisonPC system to gain access to the internet outside of the constraints we have. It was ingenious, frankly, and they merely used a RasberryPi, or small basic component computer, with a simple Linux-based operating system to bypass the PrisonPC controls. It was so ingenious that one of the members of the 'axis of evil' was offered total immunity to show the information technology staff how they did it so it could be better understood and prevented in the future. Rumours continue to stir that Tony, the detainee who seems to have invoked the fiercest resentment from senior management, is due to be charged by the federal police for a range of computer-based offences that risk further extending his already lengthy ten-year sentence. Tony is a skinny and tall man in his late forties, with a receding hairline, glasses and a prominent nose. He's a very pleasant fellow, and his tenure of more than eight detained years gives him a Zen-like calm that has clearly served him very well. I'm not aware of the nature of his offences but given his former occupation as a computer network engineer (and indeed illicit hacking here in jail) makes it likely his offences are of an online 'hands-off' nature and involving child pornography.

Tony visits our pod nearly every day to play a board game with Jason, and more recently Kenny as well. This game, *Catan*, is a trading game that Tony and Kenny spend hours and hours playing, flipping cards and invoking obscure rules such as 'harbour master' and building roads on the rare gold-fields terrain. They have a few expansion packs and also play with a number of 'house' rules that I don't pretend to know. I'll have to sit down one day and join in; Jason assures me it's straightforward to learn and has enough chance and luck to allow a beginner to be competitive. I'll have to see.

Tony, aside from being a rather Zen-like computer professional, also has a famous rage and explosive competitive edge, and on occasion (twice this week) will flip the board and scatter the pieces on the floor if he loses to Jason. Personally, I don't think I could stand for such behaviour, but Jason (and often Cameron who sits in his sheeted-off room in the common area) will laugh as it occurs. Tony, of course, picks up all of the pieces and bows in gracious defeat after that moment of rage, but it's an interesting quirk to see such impulsive behaviour take over his no doubt better senses. He's known to also scream at the television when his favourite football team the Sydney Swans are losing. It was once thought that his screaming was him assaulting his roommate.

Aside from Tony, this evil trio includes Navin, the incredibly accomplished Indian who as I understand from Cameron (who considers him a very close friend) was caught with "some silly photos," which again is one of those oft-heard euphemisms for child pornography, and in this case, was enough to detain Navin for six or seven years. Navin has worked as a diplomat and speaks Russian and a range of sub-continent languages. Indeed, so established is his language repertoire that he often translates between several of the other Indian detainees; some of whom do not share a common language beyond fractured English. Aside from his linguistic ability, he's also a somewhat accomplished cartoonist, and he's well deservedly famed across the wing for his clever, witty and highly skilled drawings. Further expanding on his Renaissance-man-like ability, Navin is also a skilled cook, and stories of his curries and other sub-continental cuisines are spoken of with awe whenever I produce one of my own competent (if I may say so) attempts at a curry (although not having chilli is a severe handicap here). Indeed, today on the way back from the library I asked Navin if he would visit our pod again (if you recall my arrival saw his departure) and prepare one of his chicken curries, in which he supposedly uses the marrow of the carcass to good effect. It's not the first time I've sought Navin's culinary assistance, and I can now produce a daal worthy of his own talents. As Cameron recounts, Navin never tends to overuse ingredients in the way I or others do, and this is highlighted in the daal recipe. My own, which I'll still happily gobble down, is an admittedly Frankenstein-like concoction with garlic, ginger, onions, tomato, turmeric, coriander powder, cumin powder, garam masala, curry powder, salt, lentils and oil. The first night I made it, Jason spooned it up and shook his head, telling me that "Whatever this was, it wasn't daal." It's become a bit of a joke for us whenever I make it, as I now follow Navin's simple recipe: lentils, a half-spoon of turmeric and some butter stirred through at the end. It's about managing the consistency and salt levels, I'm told, and what's produced is fantastic in how simple it is. I'm excited that soon I'll have Navin over to produce his chicken curry dish for us.

Navin always has a smile on his face, addresses his friends (which is everyone) as "brother," and walks around with his afro-like ponytail of long black hair and a big smile. In one of the private moments I share with Cameron, he happily tells me that Navin is one of only a couple of people he would maintain contact with outside of jail, and he worries that with Navin's release and deportation (he's not an Australian citizen) he may not be able to maintain that contact. I still feel privately dreadful for kicking Navin out of his room and into another pod: an event that took Cameron's closest friend away. They see each other through the day so the damage is minimal, and Cameron, and presumably Navin too, understands that I was not a master of my own circumstances on arrival.

The third member of the axis of evil is Glen Vandavord, or as Kenny calls him, "the 300-pound octopus." Glen is a former primary school teacher and a sad person who has clearly never fit in anywhere in his life. He's in his late thirties, but you would be mistaken to think he had the personality of someone in his early or mid-twenties, and his social awkwardness is so heavily impressed into him that even casual conversations about opinions on the weather are tough to endure. It's a shame, really, as he's someone who clearly has meant well in his life but has never found his internal confidence. He has a moplike and out-of-control greying haircut that sits on an awkward face. Without the large amount of extra weight that he carries, he could even be an attractive person, but his 120-kilogram frame is not only large for his medium height but sits and bulges across his hips in a most unfortunate way. I remember meeting Glen and him immediately telling me that he had hacked the prison computers (with Tony). I would have settled with a hello, welcome, or any other combination of the words that normal people exchange in the first few seconds of meeting each other. I understand Glen, being an accomplished computer programmer like Tony, is also here for online 'hands-off' crimes, but that they are extensive and perverse and could have extended into his role as a primary-level teacher. He's a good example of an adult who, in not forming healthy and productive adult relationships, has turned to minors for that comfort, and while he doesn't describe to me his crimes a few others do.

Glen has a solid and discreet stud piercing in his left ear and tends to stay on his side of the wing. This is due to one of Alwyn Baume's theories that Glen is a doer of evil (which is ironic, coming from the most evil person I have ever met in my life) and is therefore not welcomed in our pod. It goes a little further than that, and is even somewhat logical, as I later learn. After the RasberryPi hacking incident, all of the pods were stripped and searched intensively for any further contraband such as USB memory sticks and the like. There were even accusations that came from Crafty, always ready to grass on his fellow detainees to secure an advantage for himself, that the computer access that Tony, Navin and Glen had established was done so in order to "run a child pornography ring from jail". This apparently made the local papers, further inflaming the authorities and causing these searches to go ahead. That Glen never apologised is the basis of Alwyn's issue with him, and I can only presume that Tony has apologised, given he comes every afternoon to play *Catan* with Jason. While this incident pre-dated my arrival here, the idea that they were running a child pornography ring is clearly absurd, and probably started by Crafty, in some part maliciously.

I find this supposedly evil axis to be the stuff of fantasy and make-belief on account of the guards taking a personal dislike to Tony. Tony is indeed a fascinating person, but I'm at a loss as to why this animosity exists, though I do suspect it's in some way predicated on the fact they are scared of his computer abilities, and may even believe that he's gotten away with something in jail that they simply missed. The guards deal so often with the normal population of gronks, jackals and bruisers that violence, drugs and other petty issues are safe and known to them. Hacking the PrisonPC for external internet access clearly makes them uncomfortable.

* * *

Fortuitously, *Escape from Alcatraz* is on television and I watch with divided motivations. It's now an educational piece for me as well as entertainment, and I think about my own ability to mount some kind of sophisticated break from here. Fantasy, of course, given that I'll be a free man before too long (and besides, living in minimum security right next to the external fence hardly makes for a trying escape) but it's nice to wonder about the possibilities. I'm convinced that under the right circumstances I could simply talk my way out of the front door, but it's a plan I'll never put into practice. It's another five years for attempting to escape. Getting out of the country without official travel documents is also surprisingly straightforward under certain conditions, owing to lax maritime boundaries (there's your only hint). Clint Eastwood's efforts go in my bag of fantasy escape tricks right next to Tim Robbins's efforts from *Shawshank Redemption*. Next up is Henri Charrière's *Papillion*, followed by *The Count of Monte Cristo* by Alexandre Dumas.

CHAPTER 12

My curiosity around how people bring drugs into jail becomes a topic of conversation, and I further my education with Kenny, Jason and even Cameron contributing from their own experiences. It clearly speaks to my own naïveté that I find it so absurd that drugs in large quantities regularly make it past the guards, but then I've clearly underestimated how determined drug addiction, extreme boredom and profiteering can enhance ingenuity. Of course, visits are the traditional method of bringing in drugs, and I'm told that long kisses between lovers is the most common way to pass drugs across, as is the hug and quick drop of the package down the back of the detainees shirt, whereby they then attempt to catch the falling packet with their butt cheeks (true story). I've seen with my own eyes a more brazen drop and pick up during a visit, and it occurred when I was at an extended visit in the women's area. One female visitor walked past my small table and very obviously dropped a plastic bag in front of her, just as a banshee (female detainee) swooped in and picked it up. I was so shocked at how blatant it was that it stopped my conversation cold, and I excitedly told my visitor what I had just seen.

Of course, there are the far more sophisticated methods of bringing drugs in, including kicking drug-laden footballs over the fence to detainees, using drones to drop drugs (although this is rare), and secreting drugs into obscure books that are donated to the library, then simply borrowed by the detainee user at a later date. Thick and rarely read hard-cover books are said to be the best for this method, and I wonder how many books I may have already handled that were once inanimate mules.

But then, as tends to happen, an interesting contradiction of morals comes up when I hear of one of the more successful methods of bringing in drugs: the use of children, and particularly infants. Apparently, it's quite common for visitors to make their children carry drugs in through the security checks, and more than one child has (I'm told) innocently walked up to their father and produced the package in full view. Jason sits down at our table relaxing his girth onto the plastic handles either side of him, and tells me that nappies, even soiled nappies, are the best way to do it. A soiled nappy is a good way to put the drug-sniffing dogs off as well. Babies can't give the game away, and detainees do their fair share of handling bubs as they come in and are handed over by a partner. Naturally, the guards are hesitant to examine every single baby as if it was an unwitting drug mule, but then that's precisely the point being exploited. It reminds me of others around the world using woman and children in conflict for similar reasons, ultimately exploiting the humanity of their opponent for evil purposes.

Kenny, convicted for his second stint of quite serious paedophilia, is outraged that these drug mules stoop to using children and even babies to smuggle in drugs, and takes an interesting moral position against this exploitation of youth. I don't feel it's appropriate to point out his naked hypocrisy, and it's another fascinating insight into the compartmentalisation that these sexual offenders undertake regarding their own offences. I'm surprised at how often they tend to moralise their own crimes away from more mainstream offending, and I suspect that it's the same mentality that makes mainstream offenders look down on sexual offenders. Everyone here is ranked, ordered and judged for their worth based on how they arrived in prison. Although there is a degree of homogeneous community feeling in this wing, there certainly are those who pass judgement. Arthur, our professor who has just lost his appeal for raping a number of his students, seems especially poisonous in his dismissal of many others, always explaining that he's aware of this or that particular person's case (because they've gone to him for legal advice) but that he shouldn't go into the details. Needless to say, he'll offer the information that the person in question is a rotten scoundrel of the highest order.

Kenny carries on, his feet resting across the corner of the simple four-legged table in our common room, and explains more about drugs in this jail. Lawyers are also a regular source of drugs for certain detainees, and some even earn their fees directly from the deliveries they are facilitating through their legal privilege. I suspect that if guards are involved it makes sense for lawyers to be involved as well. Cameron adds to the conversation and talks about some of the serious criminal personalities in the jail and the kind of influence they can exert. Sitting on our dark brown leather chair and half-heartedly strumming an acoustic guitar (both he and Jason are quite good on it), he tells me about Matt Massey. He's a powerful and savvy mainstream detainee who runs the most lucrative drug ring inside this jail, and he is known to visit savage bashings on anyone foolish enough to challenge his monopoly. This kingpin bruiser even threatens the guards and their families to good effect, and I suspect that anyone with as much power as he has must clearly have a multitude of ways to reach people on the outside. It makes me sympathise with the guards who simply want to do their jobs and earn an honest wage, but of course, there would be some who are as greedy and willing to conduct illicit activities as these detainees. Cam says that a few guards were recruited simply based on their physicality and mixed martial arts backgrounds so as to control and stand up to some of these very lethal bruisers. Raucous detainees are contained and teargassed, but having to put hands on an uncooperative prisoner and exert force is the final resort.

Jason spends the day sitting on our little outdoor balcony smoking cigarettes and studying business management, and surprisingly does the dishes after Cam cooks a few pizzas for dinner (garlic and cheese being our regular favourite). Kenny is suitably impressed with his twin's performance during the day and decides to give Jason an A-grade in acknowledgement. Jason looks unimpressed as Kenny describes the impromptu decision to now award him a daily grade, which will depend on various factors including his sociability in the pod. Smoking in his room, avoiding the dishes and otherwise being too lazy for everyone's liking is something everyone is trying to get across to him as politely as possible. He complains that he works in the kitchen most days so he shouldn't have to do as much in the pod, but Dave, twenty years his elder, quickly puts him in his place and explains that his job has nothing to do with us. It's true, and it goes to the heart of detainees here thinking they have some enhanced social status based on things that are entirely irrelevant; time served, criminal history, associations, etc. In Jason's case, it is working a job that he alone earns money for. He doesn't pay rent or contribute extra services to the pod outside of regular cleaning or chores, and Dave tells him he could work twice as long and still be expected to do the dishes once in a while. It's particularly irritating to Jason who also doesn't cook, and so has very little room to manoeuvre on the issue, so as usual, he goes off to sulk in his room. He emerges thirty minutes later, as I listen to a thunderclap above us and a quickly arriving rainstorm. It's nice listening to the storm, and when I tell him how much I enjoy this, he agrees and tells me that he likes it too.

"It's one of the best times to rob someone," he says, "as they can't hear anything."

"But what if someone is home? Isn't that bad?" I ask.

"No. Not necessarily," he says. "Most people are too scared to confront you, especially if you wave a weapon in their face."

I can't fault his logic.

Cameron seems to be on a rant about Tom (bus driver paedophile in the next pod) who makes Cam's job as delegate harder than it needs to be. Tom, as I think I've described previously, is a fat fiftyish man with the worst hygiene in the wing. His clothing is perpetually stained with marks that look to be weeks old, and his hair is always a matted mess. He has rosy cheeks and a little Santa Claus nose sitting below his thick smudged glasses, but his personality is as disgusting as his smell. He'll always argue with the nurses and guards and apparently puts in the highest number of complaints out of everybody, which gives Cameron regular headaches. Tom is the poster boy for what a paedophile is, in my mind, and you would cross the street if you saw him coming your way – not because of any physical threat, but merely due to his entirely odious bearing.

Cameron rants uncharacteristically about Tom's incorrigible gossiping and rumour spreading, and he pins down two recent rumours that he sourced back to Tom's pod. Cam exudes such a mature patience with so many different people across the wing, as well as the various senior corrections staff and other civilians who interact with us here, that to see him privately share such harsh opinions about Tom is telling of the personal load he bears underneath. In two days' time, Cameron is heading back to court, although it's not for himself: he spends his free time helping other detainees prepare appeals or parole applications (now in concert with Arthur as our resident Professor of Law), and often heads along to court to support them. This most recent recipient of his assistance isn't even in our wing, and it shows just how prepared Cam is to help where he can and give his time and efforts to others who need it. He carries these burdens because he feels he can help people.

* * *

Canada has apparently just legalised marijuana, and Kenny, as our resident North America expert, has a wide range of opinions on this that ultimately result in a massive put down of his northern neighbour. He's convinced, he tells us all with his feet back hanging over the corner of the table, that Canada is full of left-leaning retards led by the virtue-signalling Justin Trudeau. We all nod politely as he speaks as if he is the spokesman for the entire United States and confidently proclaims how his country will never allow this to occur because there are too many people with common sense. I recall Colorado and perhaps California as states that have already legalised recreational marijuana, but he sets the record straight that I'm wrong and don't understand the country he left when he was four years old. I accept his position to avoid a pointless argument with someone who needs this strong piece of identity for his own sanity, and Kenny then, in keeping with our recent theme on drugs, explains how Canada's legalisation will crush the illicit American market, and it's hard to argue with his logic on this one. He and Jason discuss a proposed plan by the Australian Government to offer free heroin to addicts: a plan I don't think actually exists. I lift an eyebrow, as my own knowledge on such ventures only reaches safe injecting rooms, but I'm told that the offering of safe and readily accessible heroin would again crush the illicit market and, in turn, drive down drug-related crime. It's an interesting idea, but not one that I can see working – don't we have the methadone program? Here I'm informed by Jason that it's really no substitute for the real stuff and that addicts who want the high don't care about these alternatives, so why not make heroin available? It's a minefield, and I don't think they appreciate the heated debates that even surround safe injecting rooms and pill testing by the government, cocooned as they are inside the jail with only television and the odd newspaper as references (as indeed I now am). I do caution an opinion that I'll be the first to buy Jason his government-subsidised and supplied heroin should this farfetched scheme come to light. I expect Jason to dismiss this offer, as I can't imagine he would want to go back to that world of hard drugs, but he assures me that he'll be stocking up in such a circumstance to sell on for a profit. Somehow his own fervent support for the plan fails to notice this glaring inconsistency.

CHAPTER 13

"**M**uster recount! Muster recount!" crackle the loudspeakers in our rooms and common areas. It's a common enough occurrence in a prison of 400 detainees, who have to be accounted for five or six times daily lest one of us has escaped. Accounting for everyone and arriving at the magic number usually takes around fifteen or twenty minutes, and then the doors are unlocked again to permit detainee movement (except for the final muster of the day). The recounts are understandable, given the wide movement of detainees to various areas, and I would suppose that one in every thirty musters is a recount, which isn't really a bad strike rate when you consider it. Today, though, the entire jail is subjected to a recount when Jason arrives back in our pod from work and is somehow not counted. We know it's him when the officers return for the recount and realise that they have six, and not five, detainees in the pod, and the professional embarrassment registers on their faces quite clearly. Although Jason is, of course, innocent of any wrongdoing, Kenny and I give him a hard time for it anyway, as the recount threatens our Friday 'activities' hour at the gym, which also allows us to access a beard trimmer. With rogue hairs dangling down further over my mouth than they ever have before, getting access to the beard trimmer is the most important part of my day. Luckily, our small congregation of six assemble and we stroll through the jail under the carefree eye of Mr Barry, who is the corrections officer permanently assigned to the gymnasium. He's an officer with a good reputation, and I walk along with him and Arthur – whose beard looks equally ragged – and we catch up on the latest intra-wing gossip of the day.

Arthur, never one to shy away from sharing a controversial opinion or snippet of scandal, recounts how our detained priest, John Aitchison, made a fool of himself in front of the new deputy general manager when she visited the day before. A Canadian woman, she toured the prison to introduce herself, and John, in his harmless and soft plummy accent, commented that "this is a good jail, evidenced by the low recidivism rates". Arthur explains that in fact, this jail has one of the worst recidivism rates (perhaps owing to its wide holding of different category prisoners?) and that the comment is a little tactless. I confess to not finding John's remarks particularly scandalous and ask Arthur why he's in such a chipper mood, with Monday's impending apology for victims of institutionalised sexual abuse. Arthur leans in and dips his head into one of those confidential poses and I know I'm about to receive some new juicy nugget of information. Arthur confides that John's predatory past is one of the worst cases of Church interference and suppression: he was moved by the clergy from his British-based Anglican Parish after a bad scandal that involved sexual abuse of young boys in his charge, and he later was dispatched to Australia, where he was moved around at least two more times to bury his latest acts of paedophilia. I'm already put off by John's almost (sadly) clichéd background of predatory priesthood; this in no small part because certain persons in my sister's partner's family were subjected to clerical sexual abuse, causing ongoing damage and trauma. To hear now that John has a longer litany of unpunished offending just makes me shake my head and wonder how on earth this sort of thing was once okay to bury and forget about; that other senior members of those organisations thought it both morally and ethically appropriate to not inform the police. Arthur explains that John suffers frequent nightmares; he knows that John usually sits up late in the lounge room, dozing when he can, but not taking the risk of committing to a normal sleeping position.

I suspect that anyone reading this will feel very little sympathy for John Aitchison.

Often, when we're shooting a few basketballs at our standalone hoop, John will be walking by, and he'll throw his arms up and shout "Congratulations!" as a particularly difficult shot goes through the hoop. He's a pleasant and mild-mannered sort of person; he walks around with his hands clasped behind his back, either looking down or up, but never – it seems – where he's going. As we pass in the yard, his face will switch from one of complete absence of emotion to forced enthusiasm, though it then switches back too quickly to nothingness, giving you a very hollow sense of his real interest in you. When sentenced most recently (an additional five years on top of his already served two years) the judge accused him of being "arrogant" and said he "showed little remorse", which I think is an opinion of someone who doesn't know him beyond one dimension. His air of arrogance is actually an unavoidable aloofness that he carries himself with, and it's easy to mistake his wispy and fleeting attention as something more deliberate. John can be found sitting outside in the sun reading books written in classical Greek, and even Arthur seems suitably impressed at his linguistic ability, although I suspect there is a degree of academic jealousy since Arthur must consume his own ancient history in his native English. Arthur then tells me he can't picture John in his priest's regalia, but here I have to disagree, as I see it all too clearly. Not only can I see John wearing his white collar, but I can see him standing in front of a chapel entrance greeting his flock as they arrive for the Sunday service. Although I only know John as the grey and blue polo shirt-wearing detainee, to me he seems more out of place wearing this than his former professional attire that I only see in my imagination. What I can't imagine is the crimes he committed again and again across two countries and over a span of thirty or forty years. There is clearly a huge amount that John Aitchison, paedophile priest, has never answered for, and in some ways, I feel more angry at those who compromised their own morality to protect him time and again than I do at John himself. It's unforgivable.

So, come Monday, when the delivery of the National Apology to Victims and Survivors of Institutional Child Sexual Abuse (the National Apology) occurs, I suspect that John Aitchison will be keeping to himself and quietly reading a book, or merely leaning back against the wall he likes and enjoying the sun on his face. Many others convicted of sexual crimes against children are here too; some victims in their own right, such is the sad and depraved reality of sexually abused children growing up to perpetrate the same crimes on others. Ray (incorrigible racist; ponytail; friendly disposition) had a horrendous time in boarding schools as a child, suffering vicious physical and sexual abuse that clearly shaped and warped his mind so badly that he later subjected his own children to the same horrors. He'll listen as a perpetrator and a victim, an unfortunate cycle that is certainly not an isolated case here. It's something else to reflect on: how much can the sympathy for a victim erode away the hatred of the rapist or molester? Can both feelings exist neatly in parallel when you consider someone like Ray, or our now bailed former senior United Nation's officer Adam Carrington, himself a victim and later abuser of his own children? A victim, perpetrator, and a person: all of them.

Cases like Kenny, my snoring American neighbour, are equally sad but very different, in that it seems that the total repression of his self-identity and his troubled journey as a homosexual man built up and up and then culminated in him raping children (as a repeat offender). Then there are the South Asians we have, four or five of them (and badly over-represented as sex offenders here), who seem to have offended more as a sense of entitlement rather than from troubled childhoods. The four Indians and one Nepalese all come from affluent and educated backgrounds – without exception – and also cause trouble in day-to-day communal living through this ingrained sense of entitlement.

But those who are victims of the institutionalised sexual violence must, I can only humbly guess at, deal not only with the perverse acts themselves but also the disgusting failure of other trusted adults who could have helped. Helped to seek justice – not protect the villainous, that is. I wonder how much John Aitchison will reflect on his crimes and how he was protected by the clergy. Arthur tells me of the awkward silences that descend in their common area as the television brings up an issue relating to paedophile priests or the clergy who protect them. There seems to be a real consciousness of the awkwardness at least, but no one ever tries to console John or make light of the situation with an impromptu joke or comment. They only sit there silently.

* * *

Back in the pod, Cameron is sautéing onions, mustard seeds, salt and pepper as a base for a carbonara while we chat. Kenny is ranting at only half maximum fervour about people who adopt the New York Yankees baseball team as their favourites without knowing anything about them, or indeed the game of baseball. I happily tell him that I'm a Toronto Blue Jays fan, and then proudly admit I've never even seen a game of theirs on television. I used to have a ball cap as a kid, and that's enough for me.

"Yeah, but that's a shitty Canadian team. They shouldn't even be allowed to play with the Americans," he tells me. It looks like Cam and I are in for another lesson on how things really are. He goes on: "But so many people like the Yankees who haven't been to a game. Idiots, all of them."

"People can like whatever they want, Kenny," I say.

"Yeah, but they're not *true* fans. They just want to be American fans. Look how many Asian women wear Yankees hats."

There's no real point going further down the rabbit hole, but I do tell Kenny how much I dislike people telling me I'm not enough of a fan, or enough of a whatever. Gatekeepers, they're called; those annoying people in society who start their assertions with: "You're not a real [whatever] unless . . ." It's tiresome, and unfortunately, anything with a hint of Americano is right up Kenny's alley. His opinions on what real barbecue sauce is, or isn't, are about as fascinating an insight you can have from a man who takes such differentiations quite seriously. I suspect that as I go along I'll have to search harder for topics to bait him on and see how riled up I can get him.

We eat Cam's dinner on our small outdoor balcony and continue the chit-chat. Jason gorged himself earlier in the kitchen while working and so abstains from another meal, only emerging to belch and fart and make a nuisance of himself around the kitchen as we're trying to clean up. I decide to pull him up for smoking in his room again and he flies quite unexpectedly off the handle, even going so far as to throw a mean word or two at me. He's a zero to one hundred kind of person and he has never seemed more like the career criminal he really is then when his bad habits are being politely pointed out. The experience makes me realise how little patience I actually have for him once he reverts back to his bad-mannered self. Cam goes and tells him off fifteen minutes later.

The evening is quiet and a few decent movies are on, so it's nice to sit and watch them while checking some emails. My friend and his partner are off to Japan in March, and another friend brings me up to speed on her opinions of the men on the Bachelorette (they're all insanely and fascinatingly odd in ways that are fully described for me). With my window open, a cool breeze is falling through onto my bare feet and the few cars still passing on the nearby highway at this late hour let out a steady hum. The thing I miss the most (after women and whiskey) is being able to look up at a night sky. We have a few winter days where the planets come out before our five-thirty pm evening lock-in, but there's never enough time to sit and stare up (or out, as I prefer to think). Venus and often Jupiter don't disappoint, and Saturn can be caught if it's dark enough. Mars, impossibly red and beautiful, found its orbit right outside our main door window for a good week. We can stare out of this window between the five-thirty pm outer-door lock-in and the six pm inner door lock-in (when we lose access to our well-positioned window). Mercury, we never got to see, tricky and fleeting as she is and so close to the sun and horizon, but I hope one day we'll get her as she dips below the horizon. Being able to stare up and out into a black night sky is a luxury

I don't have right now, and I promise myself a decent telescope when I eventually get out of here. It's something I've wanted for years and I'm done making excuses for myself, and this prompts me to write up a formal bucket list for the first time in my life. I won't bore you with all the details, but family, travelling and experiencing lots of things I've put off in an already exciting life are there, and it was an incredibly cathartic experience to put it down on paper.

When I ask Kenny what his aspirations are when he gets out of jail, he just shrugs and tells me he'll work it out then.

"Sure, but what do you *want* to do in your life?" I ask. I tell him I want to hike in the Karakorum, go shark diving or – my ultimate goal (that I'm terrified I'll never get to do) – travel into space.

"Nothing. I'll find a job," he says.

"Nothing? You don't want to go to the Superbowl? Or even visit the United States again?"

Kenny stares at me like I've just arrived from the planet Mars and cannot understand the point of my question, and it becomes clear that he really is devoid of any grander ambition beyond getting out of jail, which I suspect is not even a pressing issue for him as an institutionalised detainee. When I tell him it's okay to dream and I explain how I hope to live long enough for space tourism to become a reality one day, but that I'm realistic about my chances, he doesn't even grasp at anything fantastical. I put the same question to Jason and get a similar initial response: get out of prison, find a job, get on with life, but when I push him for more he says he wants to visit his family around Australia. It's not overly ambitious, but it's something projected forward from the basic building blocks of a civic life. Perhaps I'm asking too much of Kenny and Jason; two people for whom self-actualisation is a higher hierarchy of needs that they've never had to consider. Freedom, income and homes is what they worry about, but I hope one day they both wake up outside of prison and cast an improbable but reachable goal for themselves.

CHAPTER 14

There is a tremendous thunderstorm outside, and the lightning flashes are crawling towards us, eventually striking close to the prison itself as the rain pelts down. All the fuses are thrown and anything electronic shuts off. After making a cup of tea, I notice our priest standing outside in the doorway alcove, just missing the worst of the rain, and I wander over to him to chat. He seems quite unfazed by the intermittent lightning that is close enough to be dangerous, and I even catch him looking up, although I can't tell if he's simply enjoying this intense storm, or possibly praying to be struck down by a deadly bolt.

As the rain lifts momentarily and the afternoon medication round is called, I interrupt his moment and mention it might be a little divine intervention, which receives a polite laugh. John curiously mentions to me he's not sure divine intervention would be appropriate for him these days, and I'm momentarily fooled into thinking it's some deeply introspective comment about what must be surely unease between himself, his crimes and the Almighty. I'm mistaken, it seems, since John goes on to aloofly tell me of a different and long-gone life when members of his flock once wished him to pray for a sunny day. They had a small fete planned and wished the Almighty to fit a little weather manipulation into his calendar. John thought it humorous that God would intervene on behalf of such an insignificant event, and informed his flock that God had heard them but had more pressing matters, which I find amusing in so far as I can't tell how serious he's being about his belief in some higher power. John is staring up into the growling storm almost like he's being admonished by an angry parent, but then merely comments that it would be far cheaper if we could simply pray for weather.

"How so?" I ask. It seems I have to bite.

"Well, we could abolish the Bureau of Meteorology, of course," he says with a Cheshire grin spreading right across his face; he's obviously using a well-worn joke from his priest's toolkit. He's wearing a garish and highly visible broad-brimmed orange hat above his cheap blue waterproof jacket, and he shuffles as you would expect from a sixty-something-year-old priest going to the guards' office for his afternoon medication.

Holding my steaming cup of tea, I also choose to walk slowly out in the rain, but with nowhere to really go I'm just enjoying the sensation of becoming wet in the thunderstorm, which has now returned to full gushing velocity. It's slightly chilly but just lovely, and I wander up to chat with one of the better guards who is monitoring the line of sodden detainees and the lovely (and dry) young nurse handing out their pills and potions. The guard is about my age, being mid-thirties, or perhaps even a touch older. Prior to becoming a correctional guard a few years ago, he spent fifteen years as a labourer. Now he wears a uniform with one stripe (indicating, I believe, three years' service) and when not working at the jail he trades currency from home, somewhat competently, he tells me. I'm able to chat quite easily with all of the guards because I'm still such a mystery to them, and I think they welcome these chats to try and peel back a layer of the onion and make their own assessments. I'm sure there is a betting pool on me somewhere, but I can't reveal anything, and I steer any topic away from myself or my professional background when it inevitably arrives. Although the guards aren't aware of why I'm here, they are aware that it's not for sexual crimes, so I'm very much in a different category to the other detainees, which amusingly enough, they seem to like to tell me. Rather, it's that I'm not able to be easily put into one of three detainee categories that the guards (or this one at least) have established. Firstly, there are the people who have had a bad day, similar to Michael Douglas's character in the movie *Falling Down*, and have gone off of the deep end as a result of some event or events that are very much out of the ordinary. Secondly, there are the 'scummy criminals', as they are described, who are destined for jail as a career choice. Then thirdly, there are the people in this wing. The guard explains that they're also normal people, except for the five per cent of their brain that is wired totally differently to the rest of us; it's that five per cent that enables them to commit heinous crimes against women and children. I agree with him and tell him that at least he doesn't have to sleep two doors down from Alwyn Baume and that I'm even thankful to have Kenneth Johnson as a buffer, despite the fact that he's a repeat paedophile in his own right. The guard nods at this and tells me he regrets reading Alwyn's statement of facts when he first started working in the jail. All the corrections staff can access these files on their computers, and he tells me that it is the one singular thing he wishes he could undo. It's quite a statement, given that he's probably read all of the other files, and he obviously still has powerful feelings about it. He goes on to tell me it wasn't so much the physical or sexual violence Alwyn visited upon his own family, but the psychology behind it all. He understands that Alwyn Baume is quite mentally unhealthy, but the crimes are so devastatingly evil he doesn't understand the reality of it actually occurring. Two other guards have previously commented on Alwyn Baume to me, sharing insights that have bordered on the unprofessional, but then they too are human and I think seek solace in acknowledging the horror of those crimes in particular. The psychology behind pointing accusingly to actions as grotesque as making your own daughters into sexual slaves for other family members, and allowing them to inflict torturous cutting and beating violence on your daughters, is apparently very important for these guards, and I feel the comfort in pointing to it myself. It's a solidarity with other members of our society that feels important. To acknowledge when people in our tribe have acted outside of the group's expectations.

The guard I'm with now admits to me his internal conflict: to know what crimes his prisoners have committed, versus his own desire to protect himself psychologically, and it's something I completely understand. To know or not to know. Either position brings its own problems. Having made the decision to turn my thoughts and somewhat odd experience into writing, I do feel a desire to capture more accurately the crimes of those detained here, and for completeness perhaps it would be appropriate for this to occur. But my perspective is not the criminality or legality of the situation relating to these detainees; it is more simply observing how they live as humans in their own little world, raising or not raising their crimes to me as a fellow detainee. I could ask certain guards or have people check online so I can find out about the acts, dates and victim profiles of their crimes, but I don't seek this gritty detail beyond what I'm incidentally exposed to, and I don't feel that a comprehensive coverage of their crimes is this document's purpose. I hope, therefore, should someone become intriguing enough to warrant additional probing, that the reader can do that on their own – and at their own peril.

I hope it suffices to write the generalities of what I hear, and that by identifying my neighbour as 'Jason the rapist' or 'Kenny the paedophile' I'm forgiven for trying to accurately portray the person I live with and am excused for not delivering titles for shock value alone, or for being lightly facetious about their crimes. I mean with utmost sincerity to enable you to append these labels to the people I live with, as I think their own humanity brings more fulsomeness to the evil characters we all read about in the news or watch on television. But I'm still not sure what to do with this perspective – to know that they *are* multi-dimensional, and human – except to acknowledge that it's *real*. And if I'm condemned for humanising the inhuman by exploring this experience and bringing colour to people who society wants to forget about and exile to another planet, I hope at least that the reader appreciates that I've never lost focus on the damage left behind by these offenders. I'm not pleading their case, but perhaps opening a back door that is usually locked.

* * *

Our phone calls last ten minutes and cost us around five dollars each, and we're lucky that each pod has a phone to use, so there is no horrible waiting in line and dealing with bruisers pushing in front of you, as I've read about and heard of elsewhere. All numbers (and email addresses) must be approved in advance, and are then called by us using a simple automated menu system. When calling, the recipient is subjected to a most awful recorded disclaimer delivered by a metallic female voice at the start of every call: "YOU ARE ABOUT TO RECEIVE A PHONE CALL FROM A PRISONER AT A CORRECTIONS FACILITY. THIS CALL WILL BE RECORDED. CALLS ARE LIMITED TO TEN MINUTES DURATION. PLEASE STAY ON THE LINE TO ACCEPT THIS CALL."

Pregnant pause.

"CALL HAS BEEN ACCEPTED."

At this stage, I like to annoy my sister by sticking to my favourite opening gambit: "Guess who?"

During one call to my sister, she tells me of some recent training she's done to be able to work with or around children, and it's fascinating to hear her recount some of the warning signs to watch for. In particular, she's told about the kinds of grooming tactics that paedophiles use to gain the trust of children, and that it rarely comes from total strangers, but rather someone known to the family (or indeed a part of it). Some of her fiancée's siblings fell for some of the exact tactics she's taught to look out for, and I can't help but think it's a little scary that these methods are so openly espoused as training. It seems logical that these methods are made known so they can be watched for, but it would also have to serve as a training manual for depraved predators looking to make some initial move on a target. My sister also expresses her amazement that the behaviour typically comes from quite young men and that it flies in the face of the notion of a scary and creepy old man who society more naturally sees as the stereotypical paedophile (the ignominious standing example being Dennis Ferguson, among other ghouls). Looking across the thirty-six sexual offenders and paedophiles here it's clear that many of them perpetrated their crimes as young men, but many have only been caught in older age as their 'historical crimes' are finally exposed. However, it's true that the worst of the offending (outside of Alwyn Baume's league of derangement) was done by young men (like Kenny and Burke) without the confidence or wherewithal to pursue adults for consensual sexual exploration. This assumes that many of the older men here started their offending quite late, which is an assertion that can't be made with any confidence given how sordid some of their tales are. Ray Layton (ponytail), for example, has been in and out of Thailand for his entire adult life (he's now in his sixties) and is only now serving time for molesting his own children. Some started once they became young fathers, being caught once their children came of age and could articulate the abuse. At least six men fall into that category here. They all seemed to abuse a position of familial or social trust, but then the wayward molester who approaches an unknown child in public is clearly something that also occurs.

My sister also tells me she's surprised by the victim statistics, and that more young girls are molested than young boys, despite the prolific news stories about predominately young boys being abused. Girls are less likely to report it, she's told, and in later life are less likely to abuse others as well, whereas something like eighty per cent of male paedophiles have been abused themselves as children. It's a desperate cycle that reinforces the compounding damage that institutionalised sexual violence has on its victims and overall community health.

* * *

Kenny cooks every Saturday evening and typically puts together a very edible stir-fry, often making a helluva mess in the process (but we never mind). Tonight, he's added an additional step of deep-frying crumbed beef strips that he's marinated all day, and I offer him my help as he seems at full capacity; his hands are dripping in batter as he works the shallow frying pan full of bubbling oil. He is quite the cook, our Kenny, and aside from his weekly stir-fry dishes, he also makes his own ice cream, barbecue sauce and a number of other treats like his pumpkin pie. December 2nd, Thanksgiving (held a week later on Kenny's insistence for a reason I don't fully understand), will be his biggest effort and we all wait anxiously to see what else he can produce.

The ice cream Kenny makes is worth further noting, given he has perfected it over the long years of his two periods of incarceration, and he's made something that would surely win an award if it was ever able to be presented at a competition. The first batch that I tried was phenomenal, being a creamy light peanut butter flavour that was amazing to try after months without any ice cream (which is one of my little pleasures in life). Kenny thought that batch too icy: he sat there with a big unmoving frown because the consistency wasn't quite right, and Cameron and I told him he shouldn't be so hard on himself. Kenny is suitably passionate about ice cream and has the right go-with-the-flow kind of personality (assuming he's not discussing something related to the United States) that would make him a good small retailer. With a little confidence boost to get him comfortable making some more eye contact, he could sell his ice cream and pumpkin pies and probably make a tidy profit doing so. I can see him, wearing an apron and a little paper hat, as he scoops his ice cream into a cone or boxes a slice of his pie, winking and telling his customer to come again. I mention it to him; Kenny smiles and takes the compliment well and says it's an idea that he might even think about. Cameron, writing an email out, audibly stops typing and cocks an eyebrow at me, no doubt wondering if I'm aware of where this is leading. Kids like ice cream. Kids and ice cream stores. It's not even that farfetched to imagine Kenny behind the wheel of an ice cream truck trundling down a quiet suburban street with that melody pouring out of a speaker up top. A gaggle of kids following him behind . . . and this is where the whole idea comes crashing down. There's a long enough pause for Kenny to pick up on the problem and start talking about NFL. He's in a safe comfort zone with the American football league and we fall easily into a conversation about what teams I should support, given I can only name a few, and we land on the Minnesota Vikings. As with the Toronto Blue Jays baseball team, I once had a Vikings cap I would wear fishing, and that's enough for me to give my allegiance over.

CHAPTER 15

The latest issue doing the rounds in the wing relates to Neil, our short Indian with the Sanskrit neck tattoo, and his making of odious omelettes early in the morning. Sipping my cup of tea, I listen patiently but without any real interest as the group of four or five older detainees from the pod next door natter on about it and complain that it's an outrage. Only fifteen minutes earlier, I had been sitting happily by myself on our park bench enjoying the sunshine and my book, but now have to smile and be polite while these latest non-issues are raised and hotly debated.

Sitting around and complaining about non-issues seems to be the national sport of our wing, and I suspect that it's a feature among all groups of closely detained people (whether prisoners, shipmates or whatever) the world over. Leading the charge on this occasion are Bill Scheeren and Brad Weir, who are also the two accomplished gardeners in the wing, with Brad, in particular, managing the large and well-producing central garden that is a real testament to his horticultural labours. Bill works equally tirelessly on growing herbs and spices, but where he delivers produce to enhance food, Brad produces the actual food – and lots of it. So substantial is Brad's garden that the prison kitchen accepts lettuces, cabbages, and all kinds of other vegetables as soon as they can be pulled out of the ground, washed and delivered, although of course, a few items find their way to us as well. He has around twenty squared metres of four-foot-tall mustard plants he is about to harvest, and a few surreptitious chilli plants that are either unknown to the guards or simply ignored as a naughty little luxury.

Brad has been here nearly as long as Kenny and Jason, and like Jason is in his mid-forties. He has a shaved head with dark squinting eyes, and weather-beaten skin that always seems to have a film of dirt from his work. He's often found in his black shorts and grey polo shirt, with sunglasses perched on his head (or sometimes deployed properly over his eyes) and is never seen in shoes. I think I might have seen him wear working boots once, perhaps twice, but he's quite comfortable in bare feet walking all over his garden, pulling up weeds, harvesting produce and tending to his crops. In the fifteen or so minutes before being locked back into our pods of an evening, Brad usually provides a good deal of entertainment as he chases away the boldest of the ducks that know it's nearly time for the garden to be left unguarded again, and it brings a smile to our faces watching Brad conduct short sprints across the adjacent yard, shooing the hungry birds away as they land like invading paratroopers around it. It's Operation Market Garden every day for poor Brad, and he does his very best in defending the ground. Sadly, these ducks are a fact of his life, and Brad watches his garden's nightly attrition from the barred outdoor area of his pod that provides a grandstand view but no way to shoo away the ducks.

I don't know why Brad is here; beyond the fact that he is a sexual predator, and it seems like he got a heavy whack of years given how long he's been here. Despite his serious nature, he's taken the time to show me around his garden with its various plots and its greenhouse, all the while chatting away about this and that and offering to get me involved if I want. (I politely decline – gardening has never been one of my interests.) He's a friendly guy, but you don't get very much emotion out of his crinkled dark eyes as he stands in line for medication or perches on the park bench near our pod. He seems to be contented with himself and his garden, and I think he enjoys seeing some of the other older detainees drag plastic chairs up near his garden to enjoy the serene days. Watching the ducks eat his garden all night must be a real hell for him, but he's at least beaten the rabbits by putting up a wire mesh fence that keeps them out.

The rabbits hop around eating whatever they can, and I personally love watching them every afternoon and evening as they bound and play with their white fluffy tails in the air. We're surrounded by so much wildlife that it takes some of the sterility out of the prison which everyone (except Brad) is very thankful for. The large mob of kangaroos perpetually beside our outer fence is a lovely constant presence and it's a shame that they can't find a way inside like the other animals; they would be spoiled silly by the guys.

Fortunately for Brad's garden, the nightly peckings are becoming rarer now as the summer rains turn everything green, giving the ducks plenty of other food options. The lush green garden no longer stands like an oasis among dried brown grass, and Brad can breathe a little easier from six pm to eight am, although we're deprived of our amusement every evening in watching him chase off the hungry birds.

Bill is a strange person when compared to Brad (and everyone else, frankly), and he seems a little more 'out there.' He's older, perhaps early sixties, and has closely cropped white frosted hair and an equally cropped beard, perhaps more like a goatee. He's gregarious and loud; someone who will walk past a group of other detainees and pretend to be the King of England, happily informing his subjects they don't need to stand in his presence. He's most certainly odd, and it has the effect of rubbing people either the right or wrong way, but no one who spends any time living around Bill is left undecided about their personal feelings and opinions of him. Like Brad, Bill is a sexual predator of an unspecified nature as far as I know, but it's not hard to see how his odd personality is suited to some kind of predacious behaviour. He has an overtly less guiding sensibility on how to act around people, but it's unclear if this is low emotional intelligence or just a brashness. When I first spoke to Bill, he offered to show me some of his wooden ice cream and matchstick constructions, which are impressive in both their practicality (lampshades and side tables) as they are in their ingenuity. Of particular pride is Bill's recreation of a lampshade that can be found in the movie *Shawshank Redemption*, and he had a screengrab emailed or mailed to him so he could recreate it, which he's done in fine detail. Bill's room is a marvel of hoarding with clothing, arts and craft materials and supplies, and other knick-knacks he's accumulated over years of detention. He also has blue ice cream containers full of ground coffee, acquired from the regular barista's courses, and he thrusts one into my hand after I smile at the smell of its contents, accompanied with a stern request that I return the container when I'm done. One week, Bill cuts dill leaves for me when I mention I'm pickling cucumbers, and another time he fills my hands with fresh coriander and spinach to add to a lamb curry. He'll hand it to you like he's handing over his first-born child, but he produces it nonetheless, and I think it gives him a real kick to be helping people via his modest herb garden. I like Bill, it must be said, but I can see how his loud personality can put people off. When I ask Jason over dinner one evening who in the wing he dislikes the most, he lands on Bill quickly enough to indicate there's a strong animosity there.

As we're locked back into our pod for a lovely warm summer evening, Kenny and I watch the rabbits bounding around and chat idly about nothing for a while. I tell Kenny about the afternoon sitting on the bench, trying to read and enjoy some solitude in the sunshine, when I recount being joined by the oldies and their conversation around Neil's stinking morning omelettes. I'm curious if this is how the rest of the jail is – worrying about small issues to fill the day, and I'm told that it's different in our wing because it has so many manipulative people.

"Manipulative?" I ask.

"Yeah, sure. It's their nature to be manipulative, and it doesn't get turned off because they're here." Kenny and I are standing, and he starts his flickering on-and-off eye contact, which means he's reaching for something close to his heart. I want to hear what he has to say and feel I have to draw him out a little more.

"I guess sexual offenders have to be manipulative. You see it here, do you?" It's as far as I'll go, and this is enough to start an insightful monologue. I'm trying to sound casually interested but I'm fascinated and want him to tell me more.

"I know the behaviour; you see it in nearly everyone here at some level. I see it in others because I recognise it in myself and my own offending. I've come to terms with it."

I nod and keep listening.

"Manipulating people to gain their trust is a part of it, and it's a skill some people have when they don't have other normal relationships. And it's not just manipulating people to like and trust you," Kenny tells me. "It's about isolating them as well so you become the only people they can trust."

At this stage, I'm surprised Kenny is talking about this so openly, and I ask him a question to probe deeper: "Of the people here, who would be the most manipulative?"

"Tom Johnstone. Straight away. I see it in him every day, and how he conducts his relationships here." Kenny isn't being spiteful but just giving me his cold analysis. We chat a little more about Tom, the fat, grubby bus driver who I learn was convicted of far worse offences than I had originally thought.

"And Glen," he tells me. I'm surprised he's named his severely overweight friend as one of the most manipulative people here, but he's also someone who knows Glen Vandavord well and can analyse his personality probably better than anyone else here. What he's *really* like.

"I don't call him the 300-pound octopus only because it's funny," Kenny says. "It's because he's got a tentacle around anything and everything. He's a textbook manipulative personality *without* strong adult connections. Glen will tell people whatever it takes to get people to like and trust him, and he's simply used that on kids."

All I can do is nod again.

"Glen won't admit it, but he's slowly coming around. I can accept it, my behaviour." Kenny shrugs as his eyes dart around anywhere but directly at me.

I thank Kenny for sharing his thoughts with me and tell him I'm interested in his insights and would welcome more. I think it's insightful for him to say as much as he does, especially about himself and his own behaviour. Kenny seems to be far further down the road of self-reflection and acceptance than anyone else in this wing, and I've already described his plans to live with another male detainee (who is currently detained elsewhere) as romantic partners once released. It's a degree of acceptance that I think is healthy and augurs well for his future, but also for the protection of future potential victims.

* * *

Late in the evening, Cameron and Dave Will come back from seeing their families at visits, and Cameron is in a particularly ropeable mood after a gronk from another wing called them "pests." A few members from another strict protection wing were already seated when the dozen or so members of the Women and Child Chasers came in, and one of the seated gronks loudly said: "Hey boys, we beat the pests!" which elicited a laugh from the group, and included a few family members. Cameron didn't hear the original comment, but on the way out of the room after an hour with his family, someone told him about it, and Cameron demanded to know who'd said it. The gronk had already left the room by that stage, but Cameron swore he would confront him the next time he saw him and ask the offender in question to repeat his remarks. That's the thing with Cameron: he's a big athletic guy who never has any problems in the prison because of his obvious physicality, and he's previously confronted everyone he could who threw those sorts of words at him. He's not a violent person and would never attack someone unprovoked, but he's also no shrinking violet; after four years of being imprisoned and called all kinds of names, he tends to prefer direct confrontation, and not once has anyone repeated themselves when he's tapped them on the shoulder a week or a month later and asked them to.

The term 'pest' is a consistent one heard here in the prison (and at other facilities according to Jason and Kenny), and it seems to accurately portray the kind of pathetic creature the generic sexual offender tends to be. The 1913 Webster Dictionary definition for 'pest' reads: "[a]nything which resembles a pest; one who, or that which, is troublesome, noxious, mischievous, or destructive; a nuisance. A pest and public enemy." Or, if you're a little more theologically minded, Psalm 41 also makes a reference: "[t]he pestilence that walketh in darkness." --Ps. Xci. This fits ninety per cent of the people in this wing of the jail; their crimes and personalities put up little defence to the contrary. No doubt there are other insults hurled at rapists and paedophiles, but I've only really heard that one word (with various appended adjectives) when I've been walking to the library, in the library or elsewhere around the jail with a group of other detainees from my wing. Without exception, there is normally a fence or some physical distance which protects the insulter from an immediate physical reaction, so to be told about the gronk who made his comment at visits is surprising.

Cameron is particularly pissed off: aside from the nerve of the gronk to insult their group, he's also violated the sanctity of visits, which is considered one of the few parts of the prison immune from trouble, feuds, violence and other general misbehaviour by all detainees. There's nothing altruistic or higher-minded about this inviolability; visits are the best conduit to exchange drugs, and when people cause problems that impact the visits schedule, they also risk disrupting the influx of drugs. Aside from incurring debts and lapsing on payments, disrupting or negatively affecting the availability of drugs is the easiest way to receive a brutal beating in the prison, and there have been more than a few younger detainees receive thrashings for unknowingly affecting drug swaps by fighting or causing some other disturbance. Such is the sanctity of visits, Jason explains, that members of rival motorcycle gangs will sit quietly next to each other when they're otherwise honour-bound to immediately initiate a fight with that person. Of course, the prison tries to prevent these various groups from coming into contact, but often newly arrived prisoners on remand will be mixed in and cause an incident before the corrections staff understand who is who and can take action to separate them. Keeping quiet about your affiliation until you can get the jump on a rival is a well-worn tactic here, and it's the reason the remand blocks are the worst place in the entire prison, with the possible exception of the volatile women's unit.

CHAPTER 16

Asolemn Prime Minister Scott Morrison delivers the national apology for victims of institutionalised sexual abuse. There's a lot of emotion from people in the crowd, and some are yelling out and demanding to know why these institutions in question still receive government funding. Former Prime Minister Julia Gillard, initiator of the Royal Commission, is given round after round of applause. The statistics from the Royal Commission make for grim reading: more than 250 survivors, some as young as seven, told commissioners in private sessions that they had been sexually abused in various contemporary (post-1990) institutions, with two-thirds abused by foster or kinship carers. An estimated 60,000 children were reportedly abused, and mostly by men (ninety-four per cent), while sixty per cent of the institutions were faith-based. During the speeches, a famous Churchill quote is offered which seems appropriate in gauging where abuse survivors are on their journey of healing.

"This isn't the end; this isn't even the beginning of the end. But it is, perhaps, the end of the beginning."

Melbourne man Robert House has commissioned Australian artist Peter Daverington to create a striking painting, *The Raft of the Clan*, (using the acronym of Care Leavers Australia Network). It's inspired by the 19th-century painting *Raft of the Medusa*, and Daverington used the idea of survival at sea as a neat metaphor.

In the crowd, people hold hands and stop to remember, or sing songs and comfort each other. Many people cry. I keep a curious eye on our priest John Aitchison throughout the day to see if anything registers in his behaviour or mannerisms: anything that betrays his awareness of what the day is. He's his usual aloof self, and I watch him standing around making small talk with others, with the same light mood that he has most other days. It's curious for me, and while I didn't expect to see him walking around self-flagellating and crying out in remorse, his too-light demeanour seems more unaware rather than defensive, and I suspect he's buried himself away from the media surrounding today's apology.

No one else in the Women and Child Chasers seems to pay much attention to the apology, and it passes quickly from the media within the twenty-four-hour news cycle. I had expected it would be a more prevalent issue for us here, but like anything else that relates to sexual crimes, shining the mirror back onto the offenders tends to result in them scuttling away back under their rocks. There is a tremendously low level of acceptance and self-reflection here (although exceptions do exist: Shaun the serial rapist, and Kenny the serial child molester), but for such a momentous occasion to pass so quietly through this inkspot of evil seems, somehow, unfair to victims.

A day or two later, a more significant event occurs in our sheltered lives. The status quo is upset by the arrival of a new detainee, but I quickly find out that this person is not new at all, and merely arriving back into the wing for the third or fourth time. We're told prior to being locked into our pod ahead of lunch that one of us will be going to another pod to make room for Brian Wilson. The name immediately elicits groans from Kenny, Jason and Cameron, who all know Wilson's reputation well, claiming he's a very difficult person to live with. Brian Wilson is seventy-eight and uses a walker to get around; he also wears a colostomy bag that makes him malodorous. His infirm bearing is the reason why he's coming to this wing, which Cameron now tells us is becoming a place to put older detainees who need assistance from others in their day-to-day living needs. Our pod, in particular, is where the corrections management staff are putting the problem (or in my case, mystery) detainees to keep them out of the way. Alwyn Baume and his mental health issues, Brian Wilson and his advanced age, and of course myself as a detainee with special circumstances. This leads Kenny and Jason to look at each other with a shared apprehension: they risk losing their highly desirable single occupancy cells through being evicted to another pod, and quite possibly even to a shared 'two-out' room.

One of the better (and older) corrections officers discusses the issue with us, and Cameron recommends that Jason be moved to the Transitional Release Centre, or TRC, which houses detainees with less than a year to go on their sentence, and who are allowed to depart during the day to attend work. The hour over lunch passes slowly and then the corrections officer returns with the news: Kenny is to be moved; then, strangely, Jason will move from his room to Kenny's, and then Brian Wilson will arrive and occupy Jason's old room. It's a kind of musical chairs that everyone assures me is par for course, but Kenny reacts badly to the news and starts to become more animated than I've ever seen him, arguing with the corrections officer. Kenny is the ultimate, malleable, easy-going prisoner who doesn't complain and accepts his lot in here, but he quite correctly points out that he's never been anything but compliant, and that it's accordingly unfair he's being told to move. I'm personally surprised too, as the corrections staff request Kenny's assistance nearly every other day to go and clean the disgusting and genuinely hazardous bodily waste spills that occur throughout the jail. Despite the fact he's paid for this job (seventy dollars a week), it's an unglamorous task that Kenny always does without complaint; responding instantly to the calls for him to attend this wing or that wing.

We all help Kenny to pack up and move into his new pod, which is only sixty or seventy yards away, and then await the arrival of Brian. Arrive he does: an entire hotel trolley of boxes and bags arrives along with a short, white-bearded man on a walker. He's quickly settled while Jason tells me a little more about his background, which still a week on doesn't fit with the person I'm observing. Brian, Jason starts, is notoriously difficult to live with, and owes his three earlier departures from this wing to disputes with neighbours over chores, food and his hygiene. He's a notorious local paedophile who abused his own children and grandchildren and has a large media footprint from his trial. He's a thirty-year veteran of the public service and has a deep personal interest in short wave radio, even going so far as to draft a book on the subject. His glasses sit over his hearing aids, and he also uses a device to assist his breathing at night, which he happily tells me stops him from waking with a sleep apnoea-induced headache. Overall, I can't help but feel that Brian is a pleasant-enough fellow, despite what I know about not only his crimes but his neighbourly manner in upsetting so many people. I suppose in some way my perception of this older genial man is a part of the deception he's been allowed to ferment with family victims. Sitting on our picnic table outside, I'm assured by others that Brian will show his true colours before too long and that his inability to get along with others will become more apparent. Given Brian is now located in the room directly opposite Alwyn Baume's, it will be interesting to see how those two get along.

* * *

On Saturday, I'm treated to my first 'ramping,' which is the lingo for a thorough and detailed targeted inspection. While I'm sitting in my room, the door is flung open and I'm presented with six or seven corrections staff and a dog and asked to leave while they go through everything. Of the six rooms in our pod, strangely only my room and David Will's room are searched (as are we), and then all the common areas are searched too. In some ways, the search is appreciably thorough, and in other ways, it's telling to see what they neglect to look at in detail. I'm subjected to a strip-search which I'm told later by Cameron was illegal, and I look over his shoulder as he opens the corrections policy and explains what justifies this measure, reading the detailed policy that seems completely neglected in this instance. It all comes down to 'reasonable suspicion' of a person hiding a 'sizeable item', and this suspicion must be formed by at least two corrections officers independently; arbitrary searching cannot take place. Now that I better understand their own policy, I plan to withhold my consent the next time it's asked and inform them that reasonable suspicion is needed, and that it will be administratively challenged if they proceed with a non-consensual search using force (which they'll have to employ). As someone with no interest in drugs or violence, I suspect that the searches are either random or of a spurious nature that falls below the threshold of 'reasonable'. I do accept that the corrections staff have a difficult job and that prisoners are loath to cooperate or assist them, but in my own case, I do not feel it warranted to undergo a strip-search if I'm following the rules, not providing positive drug tests and otherwise complying and being a trouble-free detainee. The search concludes with nothing found, which doesn't surprise me or them in the least. There is nothing in my room, of course, but I suspect one item in our food cupboard to be of interest, and despite the corrections staff pulling everything out they miss the suspect package that may have made their efforts worthwhile.

When I arrived in the pod, I was told never to use a particular box of unopened breadcrumbs, and while I never asked what was in it, I was told that I didn't need to know anything further. While I still don't know what's inside, I did let my curiosity get to me once, and asked why the breadcrumbs of all our ingredients were being used to hide contraband. Given how dry the contents are, it's easy to secrete objects inside without damaging them, I'm told, and also opening and then resealing (multiple times) the cardboard spout with a little white wood glue was a straightforward matter, given the corrections officers are unwilling to open food packages that seem to still be factory sealed. It also minimises the risk that a dog will identify the breadcrumbs as suspect, given the large volume of spices and ingredients that goes into the mix. I suppose it's logical and I wonder if the corrections staff will ever find their way into those breadcrumbs; however, I suspect I'll be disappointed at their processes. It's truly amazing how well done the resealing is, and I can barely tell that I'm looking at a box that's been tampered with.

* * *

In an interesting series of events, I soon find myself renewed friends with Crafty, one of our resident gronks (the other being his friend Thomo), after producing a chocolate cake for his birthday. With an excess of cake mix that we buy in our weekly food purchases, I decided that I could afford to use one to make a cake during the week, knowing that if it all went wrong there wouldn't be too much distress from my neighbours (wasting a cake mix and thus causing them to miss a dessert would cause some eyebrows to raise). The result is edible, and later that afternoon I found myself standing in the line for medication when someone mentioned Crafty would have a birthday the following day. As you might recall, Crafty and I have been on poor terms since I barked at him for his pushing-in line antics, and we've said not as much as a word to each other in the preceding three or four months.

"Your birthday, Crafty?" I ask.

"Yep, another one in here tomorrow." He speaks through a protruded lower lip that features a ring piercing, and he leaves it unconsciously thrust forward which gives him an undeniably ape-like look.

"Come on down tomorrow and I'll bake you a cake." The words fall out of my mouth before I mean them, and I now realise that I've committed myself to this course of action: baking a cake for this career criminal (though I stress career criminal in the pettiest of ways).

A few hours later word has spread of the great peacemaking cake and I'm told Crafty is excitedly telling everyone about it. The following day as I'm beginning to mix the ingredients (really quite simple with the pre-mix) I'm ambushed by another birthday, but this time it's for my fellow pod neighbour Jason. It's a good enough excuse for two cakes to go into the oven, and shortly we have a small gathering of happy prisoners wolfing down cake with custard and freshly whipped cream. The next few days and weeks see Crafty and I chatting idly as renewed friends, and I suppose it's a net positive to have reduced my adversarial list from two to just one (that one being the reclusive Alwyn Baume).

Our eighty-year-old prisoner Cyril (who is also the oldest, though only by a few years) finishes his six months of imprisonment and leaves us, returning to a presumably quiet life somewhere close by. For all the stress and worry of being imprisoned, seeing Cyril in here turning eighty and both arriving and leaving as an old man makes me thankful that I can finish this part of my own life and leave it buried neatly behind. There is a sad condemnation on a full life lived to spend time in jail so late (I believe), and I muse over how much of Cyril's behaviour was prosecuted, or allowed to pass without investigation and accountability. Many in the wing, including our law professor, believe Cyril would have been better receiving home detention, but he serves his time here in good-enough spirits and disappears like a vapour.

From elsewhere in the jail, a rather criminal-looking chap by the name of Jeffrey Lee arrives and settles into the bed freed by Cyril's departure. I introduce myself to Jeff, but he strikes me as someone for whom jail is a way of life, rather than an aberration to be tolerated once, and so we have no natural spark of commonality that connects us. He's perhaps in his early to mid-forties, with a shaved head of dark hair, and a curious roundness to him. He carries a few extra pounds, but his body shape is void of any angular definition, and his roundness and scruffiness is accentuated by a coating of drab tattooing which I suspect were received in ad hoc jail sittings. Topping off his appearance is a pair of glasses, which helps to give him the overall appearance of someone who spends a life sentence working in the prison library. Only later will I learn that his crimes are heinous enough to challenge Alwyn Baume's, and they include patricide, paedophilia and bestiality. Killing his own step-father would be bad enough, but when the police looked at his computer they found sexually explicit photos of children, and himself and a minor in compromising sexual positions with animals. He's also charged with unlawfully confining and causing actual and grievous bodily harm to a child. All in all, Jeffrey David Lee is a monster.

CHAPTER 17

As soon as I've convinced myself that Alwyn Baume has stopped focussing on me in his perpetual state of unhealthy paranoia, Cameron receives a three-page handwritten letter from him that accuses me of placing my drying laundry in areas deliberately designed to annoy him. The letter is intended for Cameron only, but he, of course, allows me to read it, and it's a new insight into Alwyn's mind in a way that is concerning, while simultaneously intriguing. The letter, oddly handwritten entirely in lower case (with the exception of Cameron's name which receives a full treatment of capitalisation) and full of rhetorical interrogatives, reads (I'll note that I am the occupant of room two, and Alwyn the occupant of room four: Alwyn decides not to name me for a reason I don't fully understand):

hello CAMERON,

a minor matter, have considered the possibilities, excuse any obtuseness.

this past week it has been noted room two has begun leaving clothes to be dried on a rack next to room four, not room three but room four.

some clothes eventually removed after a day or two, the remaining clothes, clearly dry, left on the rack for a further indeterminate period. why?

it was noted this morning (sunday 04/11/18) room two had again placed clothes to dry utside room four, not room five, not room three.

why? the area is not a designated drying area for all, you don't park your clothes outside room four, nor any purported convenience does room one, or room five, who at this point in time seemingly prefers to place clothes outside within the porch. until recently room two has recently placed clothes to be dried outside room two.

what has changed? surely it is no less convenient to park clothes to be dried outside one's own room. the plain fact is parking clothes to be dried outside room four is an imposition, unnecessary at that, there's ample space outside room two.

i removed the clothes rack and will continue to do so, to a position directly outside room two. eventually room two may resume placing clothes to be dried outside room two. but it cannot be assumed, given there may be a specific intent to impose. the anticipated refrain there being it's a common area, what's it to you?

presumably as intended, objections will there eventuate, threats will ensue. as had previously, you will recall, room two stated i would be tipped in "seven days", as has another recently been threatened. conceivably, this individual ~~conv~~ wilfully intends to intimidate.

room two's self-regarding arrogance and sense of self-entitlement quite apparent, as there known, one word from that quarter could most likely result in emphatic action, to the detriment of others so chosen.

at best, room two's action is utter thoughtlessness, though that possibility is doubted. at worst, and more plausibly, room two's intention is to egregiously impose, to provoke, to cause concern and unease.

i will not suffer oppressed inaction. it is acknowledged my perception may be substantially incorrect, however, an unnecessary imposition now pertains where previously there was none.

am not requesting you intervene, simply advising you of the potential for contention. as it is, the area there regularly becomes cluttered and more confined, consequently unnecessary impositions shall continue to be moved elsewhere, any eventual comment or objection from that quarter shall be ignored.

i have assiduously kept to myself, and do not speak with the individual, never will, and yet I am being unjustly confronted. the action may seem minor, the presumed intention and actual outcome is not.

Alwyn.

[sic]

Well, all that because I put a rack of laundry a little too close to his door! Needless to say, I was more than slightly bemused to read this letter and see how completing some simple laundry tasks so badly aggravated him. That evening I knocked on his door and as politely as possible offered him a chance to sit down and discuss any issues with me, indeed with a neutral third-party if required, but he merely stood in his doorway looking at his feet and refusing to even say a single word to me. I tried again a couple of hours later, this time even recommending someone who could act as the third person, but was similarly rebuffed. I asked Cameron for advice, and he explained that there was little to be gained trying to reason with Alwyn and that I was better off just continuing to do what I was doing and ignore him. So, I continued putting my laundry outside my own door, just as I had for seven months.

All was quiet on the washing front until three weeks later, when restricted space caused me to put the laundry on the other side, and again Alwyn started complaining to the other pod residents about me. On hearing this, I exited my room so he could speak to me directly, and each time he stormed back into his room. A few minutes would pass, and I would hear his door silently open and one of the others (typically Cameron, who had set himself up in the communal area) would receive a new tirade from Alwyn, and again I would exit and confront him. It's purely pitiful stuff, but I did want Alwyn to understand two simple things: that he should not touch my things in the common area (in this case my laundry), and that he should raise any issues with me or the guards. After a second day of Alwyn's behaviour, and with

Cameron's advice (and own frustrations having now dealt with Alwyn for four years) we brought a senior corrections officer in, which caused some amusement. Corrections Officer One McDonald (an older and mostly reasonable guard who was as tired of Alwyn as anyone else), and Corrections Officer Three Patterson (a senior, a no-nonsense and suitably direct guard) both took on the task. As McDonald (known to us rather informally and happily as 'Macca') arrived with Patterson during the afternoon muster roll call, the following unfolded:

McDonald: "Righto! I've brought Mr Patterson down here to sort this issue out. He's kindly given up some of his busy day."

Patterson: "Mr Baume, is there a problem?"

Alwyn Baume (mumbling after a short indecisive pause): "Well, I guess not chief."

Patterson: "Good!" And with that CO3 Patterson pivoted on his heels and left our pod, having stayed perhaps ten seconds. It's the kind of indelicate direct intervention the guards are good at, and it was nice to see Alwyn quickly disarmed.

After the problem has been resolved for another week or two, Alwyn then decides to raise his objections to the guards when my laundry, again due to the lack of enough room, finds itself too close to his door. After the guard has been brought up to speed on the earlier issue, he rolls his eyes and smiles at me and confides he wishes he didn't have to intervene. He asks what I want to do, and I tell him I'll just move my laundry and save us all the trouble. It's hilariously absurd how such a pithy issue can bring in so much entertainment (for me and the rest of the wing) and real concern (for Alwyn). As a pod (minus Alwyn) we decide to just keep the area clear of all laundry so he'll calm down, but Cameron wants to use this as an opportunity to make the case to have him moved out and wants me to raise it in one of the meetings I have with the senior management. I'm not convinced and feel Alwyn is best left alone in his own room, but he certainly seems to be focussing on me and has a problem with my special status. Laundry! Go figure.

* * *

After a lovely walk around the wing on a lazy sunny day, I find our gardener, Brad Weir, watering his impressive patch. We chat idly, as one does through most days, but I'm fascinated to learn of another little dispute boiling away in his own pod (my pod is the only one with six members in it; the other two pods are doubles, containing fifteen people each, and they sit in the middle and far side of the wing relative to our isolated spot). Brad is coarse and constantly finding issues with things, but we get along quite well as we only overlap in rare and polite chats like this one. Brad is at war with two others in his pod, the quiet and odd Juan Cruz, and the equally elusive John Gould, who together find issues to annoy Brad by using their manipulative qualities (he claims). At the mention of manipulation, I press Brad further and he tells me about Cruz and Gould, two people I have barely said a word to in the wing, saying that they are the textbook manipulative paedophiles who cannot simply exist harmoniously among a collection of people.

Gould spreads rumours to others about Brad, telling them that he's overheard Brad saying he doesn't like this or that person, and he even informs the guards about chilli plants being illicitly grown and camouflaged among denser produce. It's classic manipulative behaviour, Brad explains, as Gould is attempting to isolate Brad from others. However, in this case, it's not to befriend him, gain his trust and molest him, but to exacerbate the stress on Brad and those in his social circles. I have to think hard to remember John Gould, and when Brad reminds me that he's just had a hip replaced, it hits me. Gould is older, being in his sixties if not early-seventies, but curiously he has a rather hipster-like haircut that sees half his head shaved, with the top and other side combed over quite fashionably. He's otherwise nondescript: another old man in the wing with a sordid history of abusing children. While I appreciate Brad's opinions of Gould are heavily biased, it's still an interesting insight into someone with predatory behaviour who insidiously attacks another predator in the natural food chain of sexual offenders.

Brad stresses over his family on the outside; a teenage daughter has run away, and a younger son is facing difficulties in school, and his mood is channelled not inwards or at counselling help, but outwards into his day-to-day interactions with the wing. Like Bill, coincidentally our other gardener, people either love or hate Brad, and few people lack a strong opinion either way. Cameron, in his role as the wing's delegate and a natural leader among the thirty-odd sexual predators here, simply dismisses Brad lightly as an "idiot," but so said to convey that he's harmless and only channelling his frustrations externally. Cameron doesn't really *hate* anyone here (with the notable exception of Tom Johnstone [bus driver; odorous paedophile]); he is merely frustrated with certain people as a teacher might be. Even the problematic Alwyn Baume, someone Cameron has had to live near for four years, merely receives a rebuke of being too frustrating and tiresome, but there is no malice.

Brad then explains how John Gould decided to take an active interest in cleaning their patio just as Brad was drying some seeds across it. Gould clearly maliciously hosed away all the seeds, claiming later he was only cleaning and didn't realise they were there. If that was true, it was a fantastic coincidence, as he hadn't ever hosed the patio prior to that one occurrence, nor has he done so since. It's jail at its finest: pettiness exacerbated – and in this case by some of the most insidiously manipulative people society produces.

Just when I'm shaking my head at Gould's antics, Brad tells me about the time that Juan Cruz, the second-oddest person in here after Alwyn Baume, defecated in an empty soap dish and put it in the communal rubbish hopper, knowing that two or three members of the wing, including Brad, were required to sort through the rubbish for recycling purposes. It's a paid job in the jail, but one that leaves them open to that sort of disgusting stunt. Cruz is a little man, with an oddly – nearly pumpkin – shaped shaved head, and a little moustache. (The majority of people here are shorter than average – it's almost as if a lack of personal confidence in physical appearances has driven many towards molesting children.) He speaks fluent Spanish and has a heritage of South or Central America (I don't think he's from Spain proper) and a short, stocky boxer's build. He spends much of his time in our little gym pelting the punching bag and looks menacing enough, but he suffers from a crippling shyness that sharply contrasts with his physicality. However, the strangest thing about him is the pitch of his voice, which can only be compared to that of a nine-year-old girl. It's a terrible comparison to make, but an accurate description of the shrill, self-conscious piping that comes out of his mouth on the rare occasions he chooses to say something – which, for my ears, has been three or four times in seven months. He's often found wearing his minimalist sunglasses, punching and kicking the bag, lifting weights or quickly scurrying out of the way of other people as they move about the jail. He's a fascinatingly odd person; so, the story Brad tells of him defecating into the soap dish seems to fit his enigmatic personality. Nothing would surprise me with Juan Cruz, and despite how gravely shy and discreet he is, I see a real predation in him; as if he's a vicious meat-eating predator, but one close to the bottom of the food chain. Harmless to those above, and ruthless to those below. Most certainly someone who sends uncomfortable chills racing up my back.

* * *

I'm sitting in a room near the library in a prison book club meeting when I'm asked to return to the wing to meet with the prison's general manager. The book club is run by the indefatigable Belinda, and we're discussing Harper Lee's *To Kill a Mockingbird*, which I've only just read through a fortnight earlier. (Coincidentally, just after I'd finished it, Tony, the lanky former computer specialist, told me he owned a first edition of *Go Set a Watchman* and loaned it to me). Aside from being a welcomed intrusion of intellectual stimulation, these book clubs meets are our one-and-only chance to eat soft cheese, which Belinda brings in, so I'm not entirely pleased about the interruption.

Mr Ian Robb meets me back in the wing and we slowly walk around, catching everyone's eye as they try and decipher what's being said. Robb is, he informs me, departing from his current position. He confides that his boss, executive director Jon Peach, isn't allowing him as free a hand as he's used to, and so he's leaving to find something else, although he doesn't tell me what. He also makes a comment about Peach that makes both of us laugh, and it's clear that the two don't see eye to eye. He explains that his deputy is now aware of my situation and is my point of contact for anything I cannot discuss with the corrections staff. I nod and wish him well, and we chat for a quick five minutes before he leaves me with some advice, which rolls out of him in his thick Glaswegian accent:

"And just remember for your book, I'm six-foot-two."

I smile. He's referring to this collection of thoughts.

"It's funny you say that; I'm thinking about writing something." I have to admit to something, but I know he knows, and I want him to confirm it.

"Oh, I know you are, laddie. *I've read it.*" He smiles at me and offers a wink, then leaves me with a grin as he departs.

For the short twelve months that Ian Robb has been running this prison, he leaves with a good reputation among the detainees and my personal thanks for making my journey more bearable.

CHAPTER 18

The new week starts with some hilarity, which is always much needed. In this case, it's caused by the implementation of an anger management course run by the programs staff. I've never attended a program here at the prison and it's unlikely that I'll ever do so, given that no one knows what I'm here for. It's a lucky break; many others are subjected to programs run by hungover has-beens (or never-weres) whose pseudo-science instruction only seems to enrage the detainees and provide the sentence administration board ammunition to deny someone's parole. The most infamous of the programs is the ASOP: Adult Sex Offender Program, and the majority of the detainees in the Women and Child Chasers have horrible stories about never-ending courses, as a person only successfully *completes* ASOP when the course conveners decide they have completed it. It's precisely the kind of abstract and ill-defined structure that allows them to subject some inmates to an additional two or even three years imprisonment by improperly holding up parole. While I most certainly support programs that are targeted at helping paedophiles and rapists reduce recidivism, the first-hand stories I hear clearly show how much this program misses the mark. If anything, it is a dangerous indictment on a system that should be working harder to stop these criminals from re-offending and harming the most vulnerable in our community.

I didn't attend the anger management course that provided us such levity, but it was described to me in great detail how Ray (ponytail; incorrigible racist; molested his own children) and Glen (heavy and socially awkward; former primary school teacher; paedophile) set each other off before the course even started. On the morning of the first day, the convener had arranged ten or so chairs into a semi-circle and waited for the seats to fill. Ray arrived first, grouchy and frustrated at being made to attend the course (Ray, of anyone, badly needs to attend anger management therapy; hence the hilarity). Second in was Glen, who, for reasons only understandable by the socially inept, decided to prostrate himself on the floor and start stretching, providing commentary to Ray about what he was doing. Ray and Glen don't interact at all, and Ray clearly blew his short fuse and started yelling at Glen: "What are you doing, ya fuckwit?!" It went on and on; Glen just kept stretching and calmly tried to explain his movements, further angering Ray who stood up and started flailing his arms: "Why do I have to put up with this fuckwit behaviour?!" The course convener came into day one of anger management with one attendee shouting madly at another!

Everyone shakes their heads and smiles at the story that flows through the wing like a tidal wave, passing their own judgement about other times Ray has flown off the handle or Glen has demonstrated extreme social ineptness. Cameron and Dave Will (my tattooed neighbour – also Ray's closest friend in here) make a comparison to the retirement village in the *Seinfeld* series, Del Boca Vista. Given our wing is full of geriatrics and is similar to a retirement village, it's quite an apt comparison, and no issue can be too small to turn into an argument or major dispute; this of course was made clear to me through my own experience with Alwyn Baume and my laundry.

Despite my criticism of Ray, there is a very human side to him as well, as there is with all of the other paedophiles and rapists here. I personally get along well with Ray, and I often join him and Dave Will for a coffee and listen to the stories they swap. Both men have a very old-school view of the world and espouse the sense of respecting one's elders. They did it growing up and now they expect it in return.

Ray's volatile and abrasive personality limits how he shows affection to other adults, but one thing he does is to deliver food to people, including Dave Will. When Dave was in hospital for ten days with the worst untreated case of gout his receiving doctor had ever seen, Ray constantly came into our pod, asking after news from Dave and making large pots of soup in case he was coming back that day. (We ate a lot of soup in the week before Dave returned.) It was sweet, truly, to see Ray so concerned over Dave, and looking lost while his dear friend was unwell and in hospital. When Dave returned in a wheelchair, Ray, looking as nonchalant as he could, called him a "malingering fuck-wit," but I saw the relief in his eyes that his friend was okay. Three times this week, when Cameron has come back to the pod, he's found some cans of sardines left as a gift from Ray. It's how he says thank you and shows his approval. Cameron and I happily eat the sardines on toast and tell Ray about it, and then a few days later a can of sardines in tomato sauce appears on my bed without any explanation. It seems Ray approves of me as well.

The only other person who behaves in this way is Bill (herb gardener) who has similarly given me an ice cream container of coffee and containers of dried dates (yum) and is helping me attempt to nurse my chilli plant sapling into something fruit-producing (although it's not looking promising). Bill is as abrasive as Ray in his own unique way; as I've said, he often masquerades as the King of England to annoy others and shows his empathy by gifting. He's a real potlatcher and he gives far more than he receives, sometimes getting nothing at all in return. Jason (oafish neighbour; rapist), who hates Bill more than anyone in the wing, thinks his behaviour is only part of his manipulative bag of grooming tricks, and it does make me think twice about it. I'm still a little naive: I think everyone here acts out of goodness only, but I need to remember that I'm surrounded by people for whom manipulative behaviour has been the key to their grievous offending. But can't I still recognise a good act for what it is? Do I have to treat everything with suspicion and awareness?

It's this awful duality raising its head again as I live in this wing and among these predators, forcing me to re-examine the line of my own morality by acknowledging who these people are at every turn and every interaction: human beings worthy of empathy, dignity and even my respect. Why are other deplorable criminals worthy of respect; even that of society writ large? The *Underbelly* series of books and media parades some of the most vile thugs as celebrities, and even our own national folklore celebrates a brutal killer like Ned Kelly as a hero. Only a few weeks ago, the most notorious criminal in this jail, the widely feared Matt Massey, was released, and is spoken about in hushed respectful tones by others, and even the guards afford him (and his still-detained wife) a degree of caution that speaks to this aura. Matt Massey, a hulking giant with fierce fighting skills who brutalises people on a whim. His modus operandi is to identify drug dealers, inquire about making a large purchase, and then accompany the dealer to the source of drugs under the pretence of not trusting the dealer with his large sum of cash. Massey will then take all the drugs from the dealer or batter all and sundry into a pulp. It's outrageous predatory behaviour but has some sort of criminal honour about it that allows others to speak like he's a modern-day Robin Hood. Massey's behaviour does not then excuse or lessen the impact of those who have sexually assaulted the most vulnerable people of our community, but neither does it deserve your or my respect. The Matt Masseys and Alwyn Baumes are two sides of the same coin: predators on opposite ends of the food chain; but predators, nonetheless.

Ask yourself the following harrowing hypothetical: would you prefer a family member was raped or murdered? Faced with the lessor of two evils, the choice most rational people would make is obvious. But ask that same person if they'd rather dine with a rapist or a murderer, and I suspect most would choose the murderer. It's a curious reality that we deplore sexual offenders, and yet acknowledge their crimes in totality to be lessor than murderers, who in some perverse way still retain this odd acceptance. Ted Bundy, the Unabomber, Ivan Milat, Martin Bryant, Anders Brevik: horrible killers, all. But also celebrities, with books, movies, fame and immortality. Hundreds of victims destroyed, but it's not enough to turn us away and put these people in the same category we put sexual offenders. None of those I'm writing about here deserve fame or some twisted respect. Not a single one. But perhaps your curiosity brought you here (either that or I've personally guilted you into reading it), and now I'm engaging in the same hypocrisy by showing the prisoners here as something worth considering human. Perhaps you should reject all criminality as not worthy of your respect: throw away your *Underbelly* DVDs, your books on famous serial or mass killers, and don't give your criminal curiosity over to anything except to protect yourself and your family. It's certainly odd that we as a species are so curious about the limits and possibilities of human depravity, but it's nonetheless clear that this curiosity exists.

* * *

It was mainly Arthur's fault, but I'm the one who finished it off. We stood side by side looking at the wreckage, lying broken and shattered on the ground after a long history of abuse. The basketball ring had finally let go, and the myriad of repairs and careful usage came to a conclusion as a loping three-pointer broke the rim, angling it down at a forty-five-degree pitch. I took advantage of this by dunking the ball and ripping the rim the rest of the way down and off. We stood there, having known this moment was coming, and Arthur – the wily old professor he is – already had a scheme in place to replace the ring. The breakage has coincided with the prison maintenance team arriving and Arthur and I look at each other again as if it was a miracle. Surely this is too good to be true!

It was. The team are there to turn off the heated flooring in our pods, and what was always a comfortable (even luxurious) amenity is now gone until winter next year. It's amazing how chilly the floor is and I realise just how good we've had it since I arrived. If you're ever looking to find a convenient issue to complain about regarding how good prisoners have it in this jail, on top of large individual rooms with televisions, computers and showers, you can now also complain about our heated floors. Oh, how I miss that comfortable heat rising into the soles of my feet and toes! Cameron's nook in the common area is the one area of the pod the heated floors never extended to, and so he reminds us that cold floors are the reality for him and we should stop our complaining. Jason reminds him that the heated floors warm the entire pod to his benefit too, and he should join in our commiserations.

Tom (bus driver; odorous; paedophile), the only person Cameron thoroughly dislikes (even hates) comes rushing over to complain that the heated floors shouldn't have been turned off until next week and wants him to raise it as the wing's delegate. Cameron laughs and tells Tom he's "a lunatic," one of Cameron's favourite refrains for the nattering geriatrics here in Del Boca Vista, and then tells him to get lost in that super charismatically way that makes Tom leave without taking it personally.

Cam's dislike of him is based on long experience dealing with Tom's meddling and manipulative personality, and the fact that Tom is an incorrigible gossip to boot. Tom is constantly reporting others to the guards, spreading the latest rumours, and just generally making everyone's life harder than it ought to be. Tom lives with Arthur, Shaun Burke (serial rapist), MJ (good guy musician, fantasises about beheading his own family), David Cashin (former machinist, child pornographer and repeat storyteller), John Aitchison (paedophile priest) and others who are always reporting missing hot chocolate powder (last reports focus on the mysterious disappearance of one-fifth of the tub), or most recently a missing Mars bar from the fridge. It's comical and pathetic: stealing food as grown men. Our pod has none of the issues the others do, and we live in somewhat of a utopia when the haphazardness of our Del Boca Vista wing of eccentrics is summed and considered. Only Alwyn tries to drag out non-issues, but he's ignored and put back in his room.

Cam shaves, and it's the first time I've seen him without his salt and pepper beard, but he assures me the beard will be back in a few days. Four days later, Cam looks precisely the same – the same beard and haircut Sean Connery wears as Captain Markus Ramius in the movie *The Hunt for Red October*.

Dave Will's daughter gives birth to a baby boy (young William), and it's Dave's first grandson, so he's ecstatic about the news. He tells us about his six granddaughters, smiling and complaining that there are no boys, then catches himself and pauses; he looks up with an even bigger smile and proudly tells us that he loves his girls just as much. Dave Will really is a lovely guy, and someone, like me, who is in this part of the wing for different reasons. His vibrant tattoos, long white mohawk and handlebar moustache make him look menacing and, as he tells us, a few years ago he was a very different person, but now he's just a pleasant older man who cooks a wicked roast dinner every Sunday evening. We're all happy for him and pat him on the back, then go on to ask every morning how his daughter and the new bub are.

It's a piece of clean, pure, good news in the wing that makes me realise just how rare it is. Good news usually consists of someone getting paroled, successfully completing the adult sex offenders program or winning an appeal. It's all tainted in some way with sordid and grimy edges. But the healthy and safe arrival of the new bub is something pure. With six years to go before release, Dave absorbs every ounce of the news and sits back with the biggest smile I've yet seen on him. He looks content.

CHAPTER 19

The lunatics of the Del Boca Vista Women and Child Chasers were at it again this morning, with Ray (ponytail) and John Gould (old man, hipster haircut) arguing about how best to fill in their anger management booklets over a cup of tea. The arguing wasn't serious; Ray and John know each other well enough to joke about anger management through becoming angry themselves, but the boiling emotion is only a convenient and light social façade.

It's one of the first times I talk to John Gould, who as you'd recall spends his time with the odd Juan Cruz planning pranks that involve faecal matter, but he seems a more interesting man that I had given him initial credit for. Of course, everyone in here has their own unique and multi-faceted story, but after hearing about Gould and Cruz's disgusting antics I thought that would erase any further curiosity. It hasn't.

John Gould's anger management booklet is out because he's illiterate, and he is receiving help in filling out different sections, despite Ray urging him to scrawl in the few horridly coarse swear words he knows. John's hipster haircut is also interestingly complemented by a smile that has half of the usual number of teeth, however, like his hair, the missing teeth are all neatly arranged to one side (the left when looking at him) so that it almost has a deliberate cosmetic look about it. Gould's life has been mainly spent living on his small sailing boat, which he has taken around Australia and no doubt further beyond. He shares a story to the table about a fierce storm he was caught in, and one that he thought might be the end of him. He buttoned-down all the hatches and crawled into his bed below while the boat was thrown around so violently, he was eventually knocked unconscious. It's a scary tale, and one that he tells without much obvious embellishment. He finishes scratching a few entries into his anger management booklet and then gets up and leaves.

Ray and Dave Will sit and chat and share mainly the same old stories, though as always I catch a new one here or there. Dave is recounting a day spent rushing from pet store to pet store with a uniquely coloured and very dead parakeet trying to find a replacement. The poor bird, owned by a lady whose house was being cleaned by Dave, had been killed by the liberal application of the potent cleaning chemicals that were being splashed about, and the yellow, green and red combination couldn't be found anywhere. Aside from having a rare colour scheme, the bird also said a word or two, and Dave knew the old lady got it to talk regularly enough to add another layer of complexity to his plan. He ended up stuffing a blue parakeet into the cage, and the old lady was none the wiser (or was polite enough not to bring it up to Dave when she realised later). Dave, with his mohawk and tattoos, would have been quite the sight holding the dead parakeet up by its feet when he was asking for a replacement in these pet stores.

Back in the library, I run into Taylor Schmidt (murdered someone for fun; learning a new language; studying for a business degree) and we sit side by side, run through some vocabulary and chat idly. He's a great source of prison gossip but the stories tend to follow the same banal theme of drugs and debt and violence that blurs into one continual theatrical production without much variance (probably much like these pages). It's clear he's a smart guy; he simply went way off the rails at an early age; however, his curious insights are sometimes so far off course that I can only stare at him like he's four years old or suffering from a severe head trauma. His perception of how the real world functions exposes him quickly, and when he tells me that he's planning to "beat the system" by travelling to the Cocos (Keeling) Islands (which, he tells me, as Australian territory would be eligible inside his likely parole conditions – I very much doubt this) and get plastic surgery before heading into Asia, I'm momentarily and genuinely stunned. He actually tells me this and asks my opinion on it; an earnest face staring back at me waiting for feedback. I can only smile and nod and perhaps caution that Cocos Islander cranial facial surgeons might not have the best reputation in the world (and most certainly don't exist at all) and suggest indirectly that he should finish his parole period within continental Australian boundaries, for everyone's sake. Taylor is the logical opposite to the educated idiot: the uneducated smart person, and this is clear in his cerebral fluidity: quickly grasping language concepts, putting together credible papers for his bachelors, and discussing certain current events. I hope he lands on his feet once he's released in another seven years, but I would suggest fifty-fifty odds on the chance that he falls back into strife, possibly being absorbed into some illicit activity in south-east Asia that sees him stuck in a less-forgiving legal system. I honestly hope he makes it, and I would not be surprised in the least if I opened up a newspaper in the year 2040 and read about him as a multi-millionaire entrepreneur having made some ridiculous idea work and prosper. Likewise, I wouldn't lift an eyebrow if he found himself back in the same prison. I do hope it's the former.

During the same library session, Kenny (African-American serial paedophile – my former neighbour before he was turfed out to make room for the old and decrepit Brian Wilson) cracks open a newspaper and discusses the ongoing David Eastman trial. Eastman, who I've never met but is well known to many of the people in my wing, was infamously jailed for the 1980s murder of Colin Winchester, who was the second-most senior Australian Federal Police officer at the time. Eastman spent nearly thirty years locked away before being acquitted and released in 2014. The Crown decided to prosecute him again, and the case has been a newspaper favourite with a climax nearing as the jury retires this week. Kenny assures me that Eastman, should he be found guilty (again), will be put into my pod as another one of the 'untouchables,' which Kenny has also begun calling us to his own great amusement. Eastman has never stopped professing his innocence and for his entire incarcerated time was a serial litigator, dragging the prison and other inmates through the courts over petty matters because he could. When one of the lawyers representing the prison protested that Eastman was a vexatious litigator, the presiding judge pointed out that many of his complaints were substantiated, therefore, he was not a vexatious litigator and the prison needed to start adhering more strictly to the law and its own policies. Kenny's rigid adherence to his opinion that Eastman will be placed in our pod all comes to nought when the jury returns and finds him not guilty. After his lengthy incarceration, I can only imagine the damages he's going to seek.

It's always nice touching base again with Kenny, and he returns to our pod often enough to play the board game *Catan* with Tony and Jason. Kenny asks me to play but I can't muster the interest to learn the rules or sit down like they do, although I do respect the commitment to this same game that has made an almost daily appearance in the seven months I have now been in jail. Kenny instead gets me into *Transport Tycoon Deluxe*, which is one of the forty-odd games we can play on the prison computer system. Having a computer in my room makes this game more accessible, and before too long I find myself fully engaged in building complicated railway and logistical networks in a game that eats the hours away. The game has a fascinating and welcomed depth to it, and I learn that Kenny is behind its installation onto the system a few years earlier. Kenny is somewhat of a savant, having applied his appreciable smarts to the game since early childhood, and is such a wealth of knowledge that I feel he should almost aim any post-incarcerated career into transport and logistics. Aside from all things American, Kenny will also talk about track density, signalling, efficiency gains, lines and nodes as credibly as most qualified and experienced logistical officers I came across in the military. I tell Jason, who is hunched over the same table he was playing *Catan* on but is now studying from some textbook for his own business degree program, that his time would be better spent throwing the textbook away and playing *Transport Tycoon Deluxe*. I get a wry smile in return but tell him I'm somewhat serious. It's all for nothing, however: Jason is more of a *Warzone 2100* player.

Belinda the librarian tells me Shaun Burke (serial rapist and burglar serving a thirty-six year sentence) asked after a sci-fi book that I currently have, so later in the afternoon I swing around to his pod (next to ours) and drop it off. I haven't read it yet, and I explain I'll be happily stuck with Kim Stanley Robinson's Mars trilogy (*Red Mars* and *Green Mars* were great; *Blue Mars* is dragging so far) for the next week or two, and leave it with him. An hour later, Shaun appears at my doorway with seven well-thumbed classical sci-fi books and asks if I would like to read them. The books are Heinlein, Asimov, Clarke and another and I quite happily tell him I'd like to look through a few, putting the stack on my shelf. You can no longer buy books, but enough people who have been around long enough (like Shaun, Tony and Cameron) own private collections that the guards cannot confiscate, so I'm surprised when Shaun goes on to open this part of his life to me. He's been in jail for twelve years now and has another eight or nine to go before he can apply for parole, so I feel a weight in his stack of sci-fi books that far outstrips the mere quantifiable metric: this is his own private universe of escapism. Over the next couple of days, I finish my trilogy and go on to read Shaun's two favourite books: Heinlein's *Stranger in a Strange Land* and *Time Enough for Love*. Shaun smiles widely at me as I tell him of my interest and progress (Shaun's smile is framed on the absence of his four top teeth) and I can tell these books have brought him a great deal of joy and escape.

The guards decide to ramp (conduct a detailed search) of Shaun and pull apart his huge number of belongings identifying contraband along the way. He doesn't collect things for illicit purposes; Arthur, who lives in the room next to his, tells me he is more of a bower bird who collects things that might be useful or need repairing for their own sake. He's a good source of rubber bands, string, knick-knacks and odds and ends, and people from other pods often stop by to see if he can provide something. No doubt the corrections staff will claim the identification of the contraband (I don't learn what it is or care enough to ask) as a great success, and for Shaun, this represents another indistinct blip in the middle of his crushing sentence; something to be forgotten next year, or in five years. Or nine, when he can apply for parole.

"I've earned every year," Shaun will say about his sentence, and it certainly sounds like it when I hear about his crimes (the link to my own sister's friend still chills me). His pacing of the yard takes on a fortnightly menace as he clearly stirs internally about some terrifyingly unknown psychological ailment that returns to him like a yo-yo. A birthday, some news from the outside, or goodness knows what flips him into fifty tight speed-walking laps, head down, in the corner of the wing. He's left alone and watched silently by the others, or with low murmurs of speculation, during these periods.

Kenny watches and shrugs his shoulders. People "do jail differently," he tells me, without concerning himself any further. This is Kenny's home: incarcerated. It doesn't matter which jail; he's a citizen of detention and considers life outside of locked doors as a foreign universe that he doesn't try to understand any more. The last time he was released and he visited a bank, he couldn't understand why the young lady at the window was being so nice; so helpful. What was her angle? What did she want? In Kenny's universe, people befriend to obtain something or an advantage. Contemplation of charity or even pleasantness for its own sake is a part of the universe Kenny hasn't lived in, and it's frankly scary hearing that from a recidivist serial paedophile who has clearly used kindness as a vile sexual weapon. As Shaun Burke races past in his psychological funk, Kenny couldn't seem more different; but they have both been moulded by the same long periods of detention, and it's an interesting contrast into how people with lengthy sentences cope with their realities.

CHAPTER 20

Taylor, my erstwhile language student, is beaming in the library as the civilian head of education in the jail explains that his latest business course essay garnered a distinction grade. It's not his first – and not likely to be his last – and is further proof of Taylor's mental faculties and ability to apply himself to something other than crime. Nearby, Jason is standing around, nervously waiting for his grade on a quiz he took recently, and all of our congratulations to Taylor seem to be making him more and more uncomfortable. I jokingly tell Taylor he should open a bottle of champagne and celebrate, and in return, I'm treated to Taylor reminiscing over once enjoying a glass of whisky that one of the corrupt guards had smuggled into his wing (the glass tumbler was a nice touch). This guard, Taylor tells me with great gusto, is the primary supplier of illicit mobile phones, often making as much as a thousand dollars per device brought it, and he also regularly supplies drugs and other knick-knacks. I'm told his name and given a description, but I won't record it here. I'm simply amazed that this is allowed to happen and wonder how much the senior management knows about and accepts these things, as any serious effort to have these corrupt guards fired surely cannot take much work from an intelligent and focussed person with the right access. It's a system I don't understand, and I frankly can't wait to get away from; I've spent too much of my life surrounded by good and honest people to feel comfortable in a place where devious and mendacious people thrive on both sides of the fence. This must surely be the most frustrating job for the honest men and women who work as corrections officers.

While in the library, someone points out Alwyn's son Kane. He's not what I expect, if I'm being honest, and the thirty or forty-something man sitting on the couch looks muscular, confident and even slightly menacing with his strap beard and jutting jaw. I discretely but intently stare to see any familiarity and barely make the genetic link. Alwyn's ethnicity is itself a curious and not at all obvious blend, but Kane looks like the product of two Caucasian parents. On the couch next to Kane is the far more juvenile-looking Taylor Schmidt, language materials in his lap, who has told me of previously beating up Kane and "jumping on his head." This was presumably one of those three-on-one gang beatings, as Kane looks like he would dispatch Taylor without too much trouble, but I'm later told Kane's fitness focus is a very recent and defensive posture to prevent future occurrences of violence. Despite that fact that Kane himself was sentenced to a heavy stretch of jail for the rape and torture of his female siblings, I cannot help seeing him as some horrible victim. That the sick and depraved Alwyn Baume raised the man sitting in front of me makes me genuinely and simultaneously fearful and sorrowful, and I see a pitiful victim and a deadly predator in one. Kane is the detainee delegate for whichever wing he resides in, and Cameron tells us often of Kane arriving at the meetings clearly high from drugs. I've not yet met the Baume wife/mother (and most certainly never will) but I cannot help imagining what kind of person she is, and the family as a loving unit seems nearly as preposterous as the horrendous crimes they've perpetrated against the younger daughters.

As we start the process of leaving the library (which involves us going through a series of airlock-like doors) a member from a different wing tells us through the slightest gap in the door: "you cunts should burn," and then promptly disappears into his own crowd. There are a few sniggers from our group; a smiling Navin takes the gronk's verb as transitive and wonders where the missing object is, but I can't help but smile at how unconfrontational the gronk was. We are hardly an intimidating group; mostly made of old grey men and awkward heavy juveniles (juveniles in the thirtyish to fortyish age range: Glen, Kenny, etc) but the verbal abuser disappears so quickly and meekly that it somehow stands out as odd; even pathetic. In some way, I expected stronger and louder abuse, but so far it's been from people speaking though closed door and across fence lines. Not being one of the despised rapist or paedophiles allows me to ignore any abuse (even if I'm an intended victim in the group) and I smile and try to analyse the interesting way groups interact happily but then have these little moments. When I'm casually chatting with Cameron about it that night, he tells me of often returning to the library or kitchen and tapping the person on the shoulder to remind them what they said. It's amazing how many people back down when actually confronted with their behaviour, to say nothing of the implied retaliatory threat of violence. In some way, all the criminals are cowards and deal with confrontation badly, but then we don't mix with the dreaded 'mains' who live in the blocks. The amount of violence there speaks to their nature being very different, and it's interesting to consider that the other groups we mix with in the library (or anywhere else) are also where they are for their own protection. Anthropologically dissecting the prison would be a fascinating project.

* * *

Alwyn's continued nagging presence in my world returns in all its regularity, and this week he decides to seek out Cameron to discuss his concerns regarding the long-forgotten (at least by me) laundry saga. Uncharacteristically, Cameron loses his patience and tells Alwyn he doesn't want to hear about it, that he's been dealing with the same issues for four years, and if he has a problem with me, he had better sit down and work it out, or consider moving into a new pod. Cam tells me of this encounter and I'm somewhat thankful that he's finally put his foot down and closed one of many doors Alwyn has to complain or raise these non-issues. We know he's not mentally well, but it seems unfair that we should always be so accommodating of the fact and absorb what conflict he generates rather than allow the guards to acknowledge it and put him somewhere more suitable. There is now momentum to have Alwyn moved along, and I would be surprised if he finishes the month in his current room.

* * *

Cameron's shorter-than-usual temper seems to revolve around some dental pain he's suffering since having a tooth removed last week, and when it gets too much for him to bear, he sees the dentist again who is surprised to tell him that his jaw is broken. It can't be too bad, as his treatment plan involves some over-the-counter pain killers and friendly advice to chew on his non-broken side as much as he can until the jaw heals itself. A tough guy, our Cameron. He also seems to be in an uncharacteristically flat mood and I'm not sure what else is on his mind. He's previously told me the following month is a hard one for him; with birthdays, his wedding anniversary and Christmas coming close together.

My special status in the jail and wing draws the ire of those around me when a hand-held Sangean brand digital radio I ordered arrives promptly. I'm bemused at Cameron, Jason and Brian's amazement and frustration that the detainee finance request I put in a week earlier has resulted in me receiving and signing for this radio today, and Cameron tells me of one that he's had in the system for eight weeks, which is possibly even lost. I shrug my shoulders and tell them none of this is my doing, and I shouldn't be blamed for the way things are, even offering a wry smile in my defence. Jason immediately begins to start listing the things he wants to buy through me until I put a stop to any notions and explain that there is probably some other logical explanation to this. The coincidences have neatly stacked up enough to make the pleading of any case of coincidence a fruitless exercise, but I try anyway. I'm disappointed in the radio itself which requires AA batteries (rather than a rechargeable lithium ion battery like most portable electronic devices these days) as I have no desire to buy batteries every other week to occasionally listen to music or news on the small white device. Before even five minutes has passed, the elderly Brian Wilson, who incidentally is such a fan of short wave radios that he's writing a book on them, offers to buy it off of me. Having paid $116 for it I tell him it's his for an even hundred, and we're shaking hands before I realise I could have easily recouped all of my money or even made a profit. Cameron walks back into the room and also jumps into action, telling me he'll buy the radio off me if I don't like it, and I can only point to Brian hunched over the instruction manual with an earpiece in and explain that he's the new owner. Cam laughs at missing out by mere seconds on the deal, but the whole experience has motivated him enough to go and complain to the finance section about his own stalled purchase request.

* * *

On a lazy summer Friday, Corrections Officer One Ross, by far one of the better guards, informs our pod that come Monday we will need to make room for a new and older detainee who will be joining the untouchables (as Kenny has been describing our pod). Yesterday Gary, one of the quiet, older sexual offenders in the next pod over, was released on bail and has left an empty bed. The new person coming in is older and cannot climb onto a top bunk, and so they plan to put them into a single room much like they did Brian Wilson a month ago. Cameron is frustrated that the corrections staff asked our pod to identify a person to leave, but I try and tell him that it's a good way to involve us in decisions that help achieve their outcomes without upsetting people unnecessarily. I explain to both Corrections Officer Ross and Cameron that Alwyn Baume gets my vote to leave, but it looks like Jason is on borrowed time, having only narrowly missed out when Kenny was turfed out for Brian Wilson (indeed Jason had to move to a different single room in the same pod), and having none of the 'untouchables' aura around him. Alwyn is mentally unwell, Brian is old and wears a colostomy bag, and Dave and I are non-sexual offenders with special circumstances. That leaves Cameron, the delegate and leader of the wing who manages the untouchables for the corrections staff, and the ordinary vanilla rapist Jason. Jason doesn't need to be in this pod and is lucky that he's here at all, so I suspect that come Monday he will be departing for this new older paedophile or rapist (though all older detainees seem to be here for paedophilia – the obvious exception is the sixty-eight-year-old Arthur, who is a convicted rapist but no paedophile).

Arthur visits our pod regularly and seems to be wearing down Cameron's patience (and indeed mine) with his incessant and never-ending discussion about his own case. He claims innocence and legal injustice but fails to see that none of us really care enough either way for him to have to convince us. I would love to give Arthur the benefit of the doubt on his innocence, but curiously he often cites a number of brain specialists who claim he has trauma resulting in diminished responsibility and a poor understanding of appropriate behaviour. I don't know if Arthur is claiming his innocence, or if he's claiming he wasn't sound of mind when he supposedly perpetrated the rapes. You cannot argue *uno flatu*, or in one breath, that both are correct, and yet he does. Either way, the long arguments in his own favour are tiresome enough to make Cameron roll his eyes and others to politely peel away. Poor Arthur is also trying desperately to get approval for transitional work release, which would see him depart the jail during Monday to Friday working hours. A young lawyer friend of his named Tom has recently started his own firm with a partner, and Arthur has jumped at the possibility of attending his practice and working as a legal assistant under the jail's transitional release program. Unfortunately for Arthur, the Law Society has frowned on employing a convicted rapist in any legal role, and he doesn't seem to interpret Tom's slow to non-existent communication on the matter as a polite brush off. Tom may not be eager to fight the Law Society head-on in the early and formative period of his new business. Cam and I seem to see this but don't have the heart to tell Arthur, noting he's sure to come to his own conclusions soon enough.

* * *

In the line for medication, Thomo (gronk, friend of Crafty) has a baby magpie perched on an improvised glove, and it's undeniably sweet to hear the story of him and Crafty rescuing the abandoned baby chick, and commit to looking after it. Crafty and Thomo are two dubious criminal stereotypes but seeing them in this role of adoptive parents is a nice contrast to their weekly scheming and old stories of boosting cars. The little grey-feathered bird sits happily on Thomo's arm as he wiggles a finger under its beak. There are smiles everywhere, and I even contribute a fat white grub I found earlier when relocating my dying chilli plant to the garden. Standing in line too, Shaun Burke is also smiling at the bird, and then takes the opportunity to ask me how I'm enjoying his favourite book, Heinlein's *Stranger in a Strange Land*. I tell him truthfully that I really enjoyed it, finishing just last night. I don't tell him of the curious passage I stumble across on page 281:

"Nine times out of ten, when a woman gets raped, it's partly her fault."

It would be unfair for me to draw too much inference from this single passage in an otherwise lengthy story, but it's eyebrow-raising nonetheless to read this in a book a serial rapist claims is his favourite of all time.

PART III

"I learned how to comport myself
among trolls, elves, hobbits or goblins.
I learned that a friend can be lost to
greed and avarice. I learned that solving
riddles may be as important a survival
skill as bowmanship. I know how to
talk to a dragon, and that it's best not to."

Karen Joy Fowler

CHAPTER 21

The corrections staff in the jail are a professional cadre who for the most part do their job well and treat us fairly. We're addressed as 'Mr Surname', and answer back with a similar formality. The guards are Mr or Miss, and in the cases of the more informal and easy-going guards, colloquial 'ockerisms' are allowed. Thus, CO1 McDonald allows us to call him 'Macca' and will, in turn, call me by an informal name; as he does with others he has a comfortable informality with. Some of the others call the guards 'chief', though it's a throwback to calling teachers 'Sir' or 'Miss' that I've never really liked, and so I avoid it as a rule. The guards have four levels of formal rank, ascending from Corrections Officer One through Four, with a blank rank slide, one star, two stars and a crown denoting the corresponding levels. For all Correction Officer One (CO1) ranked officers, they are also allowed to append a chevron (or stripe) to their slides that correspond with years of service, so while a new officer might have no stripes, the majority of officers comfortable with holding a base-level of rank will have three stripes showing seniority and experience.

Most officers with three stripes seem comfortable in the job and don't have the chip on the shoulder than many younger officers seem to carry. I assume this sternness comes from both training and the inexperienced exuberance that all prison guards under thirty-five seem to have on their faces. The younger ones, with one outstanding exception, are all compensating by trying to be meaner and sterner than the prisoners, and while that tactic must work well in the blocks and rougher parts of the jail, in the Women and Child Chasers' wing they just come across as inexperienced. I find it an annoying kind of attitude when anyone asks anything of these younger guards and they act like they're granting you an early release through their personal intervention; whereas, the older salts can engage you at the human level without adopting a sense of superiority. There is also a third group, and you'll have to forgive me as I'm going to group this cadre by race alone. The over-representation of solidly built Polynesians and slimly built South Asians is too true to ignore, and this group tends not to (thankfully) have any chips on their shoulders like the younger Caucasian guards do. They're the most pleasant and easy-going group, as a general rule, but lack some of the problem-solving skills that the older three-stripe officers have, although I am constantly amazed that some long-serving officers don't understand the most basic of prisoner processes that presumably haven't changed in years.

We don't have any truly bad guards in our wing, although there are certainly a few who no one bothers if they have a detainee request or a problem that needs fixing, and this tends to result in the better guards receiving an avalanche of attention when they start a shift. CO1 Wilson and Campbell are solid and sought-after guards, as is CO1 Ross (female). Miss Ross executes the most effective shift, if I had to choose, but the two others bring a much-appreciated humanity into their roles. Others like Browne, Alford, Tuvulu and Barry are all good as well, and then there are always ring-ins from elsewhere in the prison. Of all the regular officers that come down, probably Alford and Sidlow have the more controversial and wider-ranging opinions along the spectrum, but both are good in their own respective ways, and as many opinions exist as there are people to make them. Mark Alford spent fifteen years as a concreter (and some say still moonlights on his days off) and has a youthful energy about him that can put others off. He wears his heart on his sleeve and speaks with detainees from a well-meaning but somewhat acerbic wit that is either 'got' or 'not got' by detainees, and it's something I have had to warm to over time. You can tell he's repulsed by the paedophiles in the wing (indeed, he's confided in me that he is), and while he's professional, he sneers at the worst of them from his muster roll call book or up in the wing's office when answering some question or query. Some really don't get him: Arthur thinks he's a mindless goon, and the former priest John Aitchison simply doesn't detect the sarcasm.

"Excuse me officer, but I didn't receive my newspaper today," John will ask in his earnest tone, hands firmly grasped behind his back. He seems to pronounce each of the three syllables in officer like they are individual words: *off-i-cer*.

"Not my problem," Mark will reply curtly and not at all seriously, but before John catches the pause and asks again, or bats away the jibe like others do, he's pivoted on his heels and is walking back to his pod, defeated. It's not the outcome Mark wants, but this is how those who don't understand his wit deal with him. Cameron often wishes he would recognise this and regulate his behaviour with detainees like John, but I suspect that Mark doesn't lose any sleep over it. Of all the guards, it's Mark Alford who I sense wants and craves intellectual acceptance from some in our wing the most, and will wander into discussions about international relations or politics while idly watching the medication line, or comes over to a few of us sitting down and starts chatting quite normally, confidently offering an opinion or questioning something. Beneath the fifteen years of concreting and all the roughness you would expect in a prison guard, I feel that there is a good and honest heart there. There is not a chance Mark Alford would bring drugs in, or sell phones or other contraband, and I think that has more to do with his character than anything else. He's a gravelly character with a few facial scars from puberty, and I can somehow see him in high school with long greasy hair and a gold chain around his neck. I hope he sticks it out in this job and even rises to the next rank – and tempers his hard-edged personality with something these poor old men aren't so put off by.

Kylie Sidlow is as different to Mark Alford as can be, and she is also probably the most controversial corrections officer in the wing. The same age as Mark (perhaps thirty-five), she's a fierce personality and someone whose shrill tone of voice is unforgettable (and unmistakable), and the seriousness in which she takes her job is infamous; she is the corrections personification of a strict martinet. I suspect that being a corrections officer is both a very important part of her life and a big part of how she defines herself. It's welcomed, frankly, to have someone who so assiduously follows the rules and works to get things done for the detainees, but there is also at times a lack of self-awareness that sees her cross far beyond the authority of a simple level-one officer, and this has previously drawn the ire of both detainees and other corrections staff. One of my first interactions with her was a disappointing one, as I was seeking her advice (with another detainee) on how to put a complaint in about an incident that occurred with a more senior guard in visits. When speaking with Kylie about this, she implied that we receive a number of privileges in the wing that only exist because of officers like her, and that, should we pursue this complaint, those privileges might disappear. I was frankly appalled that she inferred this to me (and in front of another detainee), and without one second's hesitation included what she had said in the complaint that went up. Both she and the other officer involved in the complaint (the much-loathed Corrections Officer Two Boyce) were counselled and sent to work in other parts of the jail for a number of months. Tom (grubby paedophile; former bus driver – Cam hates his manipulative behaviour above all others) admonished me for raising the issue with Sidlow, based on the fact she "got things done when others don't". I told him to piss off, and that unacceptable behaviour is just that, and that has formed the crux of our relationship since then, although recently it has warmed slightly. It was unfortunate that Kylie Sidlow allowed herself to be absorbed into that issue, but she has a number of stories following her whereby her judgement has shown to be lacking just enough for a more senior corrections officer to intervene. When she was still regularly working in the pod, she would come in and yell "Muster!" and then laugh as

Jason would emerge from his room, topless, with his stomach and bad prison tattoos protruding out grotesquely (he would often offer a slap across his own stomach). They shared a moment that was only appropriate for them in that context, and Kylie would even make a self-disparaging remark about her own unfortunately wide build (her hips having a pronounced girth), or her trendy purple haircut. That worked for her and Jason, but I was always a riddle for her – some mystery she didn't understand – and so I was treated as badly as possible within her professional bounds. I tried to speak to her as politely as I could, in one case asking her to follow up an issue with a watch coming into the jail, explaining that my friend had tried to drop it off and had been rebuffed three times, despite the approval that existed. I asked if she could make sure a copy of the approval was sent to admissions and was told angrily by her that "I know how to do my job thank you!" She's hard work for certain people like me, like Mark Alford is hard work for others like John Aitchison.

We don't have much interaction with the next three levels of corrections staff, but they do make their appearances. Of the one-star Corrections Officer Two level (CO2), probably Miss Dwyer is the most frequently seen, and she is a friendly but still very stern officer. With shoulder-length auburn hair and pretty features, she is the best of friends or the worst of enemies, and most hold her at the respectable distance she has earned in her time as a guard. I suspect she has a particular dislike of fellow female CO2 Boyce (the one I had an issue with), as Dwyer shared a discrete word with me the very next week when she had replaced Boyce at visits, and even offered me a smile. I like her, as many others do, and her frequent appearances for our final pod lock-ins around six or six-thirty pm are met with comments over our dinner (typically being served or eaten then), and I never fail to offer her something to eat, despite the strict rule prohibiting guards from accepting any food from us, less we try to incapacitate them in some way.

The next level, the two-star level threes, are the area problem solvers, who typically make an appearance when there is an issue significant enough to warrant their attendance, or when they're curious enough to follow a level-one officer around for their musters. I'm aware of three substantive CO3 officers: Frame, Kent and Martens, and two that often act in that rank: Patterson and Morey. You'll recall Patterson from his attendance at our pod over the Alwyn laundry issue, but otherwise, I've only seen him in passing, never making conversation. Morey is another controversial figure, and he is a younger officer who is always wearing his sunglasses and happily chatting with prisoners like Cameron. He over-promises and under-delivers, Cam tells me, and is not an officer that has earned a very good reputation among the prisoners, many of whom caution interactions with him as something likely to be used against a detainee later. It's a curious reputation, but one he has earned across a wide number of detainees. Frame and Martens, I've never dealt with, and my one interaction with Kent, where he made a disparaging comment to me when we were once handcuffed together, left me thoroughly unimpressed.

Of the final level of corrections officer, the level fours who wear a crown on their rank slides, there are five substantive officers, and one, Terry Gibson, who often acts at that level. I've had the most to do with Gibson, who has attended to me when the general manager has been busy, and occasionally Collins will come down to our wing given he is in charge of the operations branch. I've never met Anthony Johnson, who runs the accommodation branch; Rust who runs the security branch; or Mark Bartlett who runs the services branch. CO4 Jack Russell is acting deputy general manager under Ian Robb's deputy, Corinne Justason, who is handling the top role of the jail since Robb's departure. She reports to Jon Peach, executive director of corrections in the state, who in turn reports to the chief justice.

Some of the lower-level corrections staff we routinely see talk about the incipient politics that run through the entire uniformed staff, and the various cliques that exist to serve different interests. It's hard to see how a small and long-serving organisation like corrections won't develop problems similar to the Federal Police or even Defence Force, in that it's hard to bring fresh people into roles with responsibility, noting the normal ascension of rank is required to reach the uniformed jobs of responsibility. You encounter a paradigm where 'dead man's boots' rules the roost, and people can only be promoted up with a significant impetus on those next in line. It stifles fresh thinking and restricts competent people from being employed at a level appropriate to their skills, and they often go on to seek employment elsewhere, leaving a shallower talent pool. It's difficult: fighting ships need career naval officers to lead them, and so corrections branches need career officers too. But I'm not convinced – the Australian Federal Police is perhaps a better model of bringing in qualified and competent unsworn skills, although the politics of uniform-wearing sworn officers and civilian unsworn officers will always presumably exist.

Across the entire jail, there is one guard who stands out to me as a favourite, and that is the single-star-wearing Corrections Officer Two Gary Frew. Of modest physical proportions, Frew is a short bald man with square black glasses who speaks with a slightly high-pitched voice and exudes a welcomed positivity in every interaction he has with the prisoners, which typically comes when he works as the supervising officer at visits. He jokes and cajoles detainees and even other staff, but his barbs and jabs are always good-natured, fun, and contribute to an overall feeling of harmony, which cannot be underrated in the volatile atmosphere of an incarceration facility. He also applies healthy doses of common sense to situations that make one feel that there are thinking and compassionate corrections staff; during my one and only extended visit of two hours, and after drinking far too much coffee, he allowed me to quickly slip into a nearby bathroom that is typically prohibited; the risk of detainees handling drugs in that environment is ever-present. However, on that occasion, Frew made a judgement call assessing that I was *not* up to no good (he was most correct in that assumption) and allowed me a quick two minutes alone to relieve myself and enjoy the second hour chatting with a dear friend who had visited me from interstate. By giving you a degree of trust – his trust – you feel compelled to ensure that it isn't broken or compromised, and it makes you want to be a better detainee by letting you show good behaviour. While there are some prisoners who will no doubt abuse anyone's trust without thinking twice, there are certainly other middle-of-the-road prisoners who would respond well to an approach like Frew's; they take on an increased degree of personal responsibility and want to show they are worth that trust. Conversely, detainees who are treated perpetually like liars and thieves (of which many detainees are not) will take advantage of the very few opportunities provided to take something or do something they know to be wrong, as it's seen as a rare chance to 'get one back' over the corrections staff. Perhaps it's a chicken and egg scenario: give wider trust to make detainees respond positively, but firstly identify good detainees worth this increased trust. With drugs and violence already rampant inside the jail, I would suggest that an increase in attitudes like that of CO2 Frew could only help at this stage. At the very least, treating those in a cottage environment with more trust would improve detainee morale and thus behaviour, noting that any lapses in good behaviour will see them removed back to the far more unforgiving blocks. (And if you believe that detainee morale is something irrelevant and should be ignored, look at the genesis of every single prison riot since the inception of holding people against their will.)

CHAPTER 22

Believe me, I know how much you're hanging on for another update on the Alwyn Baume saga, and I'm pleased to bring you the latest (and, one hopes, final) development in what is a tiresome adventure for everyone concerned. With yesterday's announcement from the guards that we are expecting a new person into the pod on Monday, Alwyn took it upon himself to volunteer to depart, and by early afternoon had shifted to the pod next door. When I saw him packing his things, I thought he was merely moving into a different room in our pod, noting his room is alone in having bunk beds, and that perhaps he wanted to avoid having a new person put in with him. Imagine my pleasant and unexpected surprise when Alwyn started to roll his belongings out the front door and into his new pod, in this case sharing a 'two-out' room with Ali, our Lebanese Papa Smurf lookalike. It's a victory for everyone, and I tell Cam and Arthur how surprised I am at Alwyn's rather humble departure from a desirable single room to sharing a room in one of the busier pods next door. From Cam, I get a raised eyebrow, and he explains that Alwyn's decision was one of pure survival, noting he was advancing towards a situation where the guards would 'tip' him from the wing into a far more violent cottage or even the much-dreaded blocks. In the previous few days, I had had to resort to providing Alwyn a letter of my concerns regarding his behaviour and arranged for MJ (Hemingway lookalike; mental health issues) to act as a neutral third person and provide the letter to Alwyn. His previous behaviour of finding another detainee to focus on and demonise has usually resulted in that person threatening or indeed physically assaulting Alwyn, and they ultimately end up being removed from the wing, giving Alwyn *precisely* what he wants. Cam lists the six others since 2014 Alwyn has done this to, and with only one exception, he has always been rewarded after having antagonised someone else and persuaded others he was the victim. It's insidious and manipulative behaviour of the worst kind.

Unfortunately for him, after reason and adult methods of mediation had failed to calm and dissuade him, I merely made my case in writing and handed over a letter expressing my own concerns about his manipulative behaviour. I failed to give Alwyn Baume what he wanted: a confrontation that made him look like the victim, and he took my letter to Cameron explaining that he didn't understand it and didn't know what to do. Cameron merely told him it was all in there and he should reply in kind, speak with me, or address the behavioural concerns I raised. Or he could move – which is what he ultimately decided to do.

On paper, Alwyn's pattern of manipulation was so starkly obvious that it left him very few alternatives. The guards and other detainees saw it too, and Alwyn realised that his tried and tested modus operandi had failed, and he risked being booted from the entire wing now as I was firmly anchored through my special protective status. It was a smart and logical play by Alwyn to move into the pod next door; it makes me think his manipulative behaviour is more to blame than other obvious mental health issues, which everyone seems too quick to excuse his behaviour with. Cameron thanked me for stubbornly holding Alwyn to account and giving him some respite from being constantly annoyed, although he believes it will go on once Alwyn finds the next person to fixate on and complain about. Arthur and some of the others predict that Alwyn will quickly come into conflict with Ray Layton (ponytail; incorrigible racist) and Ian King.

King is a quiet long-timer around the wing and he is a tall Aboriginal man who could easily pass as the African-American musician Ray Charles (the similarities go far beyond just race). Indeed, King's nickname is Ray, leading to confusion with the comparatively short and Caucasian Ray Layton who lives in the same pod as him. To make matters worse, a few years ago in a different part of the jail, someone assaulted King seriously enough to destroy one of his eyes (this lends weight to the Ray Charles comparison: he is half blind and wears similar boxy sunglasses that are offered cheaply by the prison), so both King and Ray have one bad eye, which makes describing either one of them a confusing experience, despite their obvious other physical and racial differences. While King is a quiet and discreet detainee, in my own experience, many are wary of him, and tell stories about constant conflict and a grating personality that has driven a fair share of past issues; those in the know swear he and Alwyn will clash. We'll have to wait and see, and while I don't wish any others to have conflict with Alwyn, Cameron and Arthur seem to think it's a certainty that will go some way to further vindicating my own wearisome troubles since arriving.

That's the thing about manipulative people like Alwyn: you start to question your own sanity and perception and wonder if you're doing something wrong, when the creeping and twisting methods the other person use are precisely designed to sow the sort of discord that draws in sympathy from others. Looking back at the past seven months I even feel a flash of anger that this shark-eyed monster tried to twist the reality around me, and I can't help but think that his and other's claims of mental illness are overdone. Living among some of these horrendous rapists and paedophiles has at times been vile enough, but to personally feel the encroaching vines of a predator – caught in the middle of a web I didn't realise was being spun around me every day and every week – feels very real, and I'm thankful I managed to cut through it before I became Alwyn's seventh victim in prison. I could easily have swung a punch at him or grabbed him by his collar; shaken him into a satisfying crumpled mess on the floor in front of me. I can nearly see his hidden crooked smile as the guards would have intervened, nabbed me as the perpetrator, and dragged me to a new pod. (Or, would they? My status here makes this an uncertain outcome.) I didn't give Alwyn what he wanted, and he was rational enough to leave one of six of the most desirable rooms in the entire prison to save himself from a worse fate: leaving the wing altogether. He swapped his spacious room for a cramped box without a computer, television, shower, toilet or sink, and instead is now sharing a bunk bed with someone else. Faced with a letter that called out his behaviour and neatly packaged his previous pattern of harassment, he fled to save his own skin, and it's precisely the cowardly response you would expect of someone who spent years raping and torturing his own children along with his wife. The severity of his crimes beggar belief and I can assure you that Alwyn Baume does not deserve your sympathy or concern. Those black shark-like eyes of his. It sends a chill up my spine.

* * *

With the room vacated, our new neighbour is not long in arriving, and in the afternoon, I'm shaking hands with Robert Sirl, who asks me to call him 'Chappo'. Sirl is forty-seven and has a nearly black beard and ponytail, and is covered in a number of faded tattoos across his arms and legs. Unlike Dave (neighbour; mohawk; tattoos) who is covered in richly coloured and well-finished tattoos on his legs, arms and head, Sirl seems to have had his work undertaken a few decades earlier but by a professional, unlike Jason (other neighbour; ogrish convicted rapist), who's had all of his tattoos done inside jail. Jason, Sirl and Dave are thus perfect canvas examples for bad, good and excellent tattooing, respectively. Sirl has been in the jail for six weeks and has had previous periods of detention. He seems completely bewildered by the sunny gardens and open cottage environment he's landed in, and his amazement continues when we show him our provisions, and explain that he can help himself to anything he wants (there is no labelling or theft like in the other pods – or indeed in modern workplaces). Saturdays are one of my two regular nights to make dinner, and when I put the crispy fried chicken, mashed potatoes, salad and gravy in front of him I can tell he's nearly dumbstruck with his luck in landing here.

"What's in the gravy?" Jason asks me halfway through the meal. Some of the savoury condiment has found its way onto his white undershirt.

"Standard Gravox; but I fried off some onions, then added a little dijon mustard, thyme, cream and pepper," I answer, "and a little cornflower to bring the consistency up." Sirl is looking on, mystified.

"Oh, don't worry, these cunts are right into it," Dave Will says to Sirl seriously, waving a right index finger (that stops shorts at the second knuckle – errant shotgun apparently) towards Cam and I; we both smile in return. Please don't roll your eyes. Instant gravy *can* be fancy, thank you very much.

Look, I don't mean to over-represent our reality: it is jail, but we are undeniably the best pod, in the best wing, in the best jail you could ever hope to be held in against your will, and that's a view shared by anyone and everyone. I'm personally surprised to see that this is the first time six of us have eaten together, noting the reclusive Alwyn kept fastidiously to himself in his room.

After dinner, Sirl surprises us all by delivering an impromptu poem about his detention, and we all laugh at the clever and passionately delivered limerick he recalls by memory alone. Later, asks me to write it up for him so he can enter it into a writing competition that our librarian, Belinda, is running.

What have I done for such bad karma,
I want to get out, I miss my mamma.

I'm sitting in Goulburn with no TV,
every prick in here is picking on me.

Writing letters 'till I run out of ink,
every cunt in here tells me I stink.

Got no money, my account is broke,
been rolling up bible and tea-leaf to smoke.

Every night I can't get to sleep,
my cellie tells me: "Don't make a fucking peep".

I miss my lady I love her so much,
but she's going to leave me, she won't stay in touch.

My feet were covered, I had a pair of Nikes,
first day an option: "Shoes or the spike".

I had no choice, now I've got one thong,
please tell me Lord: Where the fuck did I go wrong?

I told the screw I need welfare,
he give me the bird, he didn't fucken' care.

Been here a month too scared to shower,
got a mad fucking rash from runs and scours.

What can I do? I can't find a rope,
I can't make a noose, I'm a fucken' dope.

I won't use a razor I need 'em to shave,
don't tell any cunt, I'm not really that brave.

Not long now, only a year to go,
will I make it through? You never fucken' know.

Well, that's all for now, the screw just hollered,
doing it fucking hard; doing it fucking solid.

Dave explains that he knows Sirl from the outside (as does Ray) and that he's a good guy. At this stage, we all assume that, like Dave, Sirl's life has been threatened seriously enough in the jail to warrant his arrival in the Women and Child Chasers (making the current count of non-sexual offenders five: Dave, Crafty, Thomo, Sirl and myself), although I'm sure we'll learn of the exactness of his offences soon enough. He doesn't seem to be a paedophile or rapist, but then I no longer have any idea what typical means in this context. In the evening of his first night, he's already chatting to Cameron about his case, but I can tell that his no-nonsense attitude and Dave Will's immediate acceptance bodes well for our new neighbour. Lately, I've surreptitiously asked Dave about his opinion of different people in the wing, and he has strong and immediate opinions that derive from his own background of dealing with people in the criminal underworld; he evaluates people quickly and has yet to miss the mark in my estimation. Interestingly, he despises the elderly Brian Wilson who arrived in our pod a month ago, claiming his hygiene (his colostomy bag is only part of the problem – he's a grubby hoarder too) and offences against his own children and grandchildren make him someone barely worth a hello (though Dave is never failing in his politeness). I've personally yet to have any issues with Brian Wilson, though I find his offences repulsive, and aside from a little laziness one might expect from someone in their late seventies, he comes and goes as he needs to. His hearing aids make any conversation an impossibility, and his natural warmth and smiling, slow-strolling stature around the wing don't imbue any of the grandfatherly qualities one would expect, but instead seems to somehow exacerbate his predatory nature, in so much as you know it's a convenient camouflage. For some reason, Dave Will just sees this hidden character.

Arthur, studious professor that he is, finds time to have our basketball hoop fixed, and before long we've returned to our enjoyable sessions in the warm summer afternoons. Arthur recounts dinner in their pod the night before, and how he had to tell off poor Father John Aitchison for taking a second helping without permission. I smile and look at Arthur as he tells me about how out of line John was, given they were planning on packaging up the leftovers for the next day. It's a non-issue: an Arthur speciality, and reinforces Cameron's discreet desire that

Arthur never land in our pod and bring these issues with him (not that Cameron or the rest of us would put up with this). I hear Arthur tell his story about John again, and still cannot grasp or understand what he did wrong in helping himself to seconds. Arthur, for all his company in the wing, seems a tad neurotic and controlling, wanting to have an iron grip on how people ought to live around him. It's no different to many of these older men who have never had to live and compromise with others until their period of incarceration.

* * *

Arthur, Dave Cashin (bald head; missing teeth; machinist) and Bill Scheeren (herb gardener; grating 'King of England' personality) and I sit idly on their pod's patio and chat among ourselves. I'm interested to find out that Bill was formerly a leader of some kind in the Scouts, and this starts to illuminate the circumstances surrounding his sexual offending. Like John, our priest, Glen Vandavord (awkwardly heavy; socially inept; friend of American Kenny) our teacher, Arthur, our professor, and now Bill, our Scoutmaster, we seem to have every clichéd paedophile occupation you can think of, except this is no cliché – it's people formerly in positions of extreme trust who have violated that trust in the most unimaginable way. Bill is the son of a Dutch diplomat and lived for a time in Amsterdam as a child, and then later in Ottawa, Canada. He has no hint of a Dutch accent, and clearly spent a significant amount of time in Australia, so it's an interesting revelation for me. I tell him that I was in the Sea Scouts as a youngster, and proudly earned my silver boomerang and a handful of other merit badges. I'm not sure if he was in the Scouts when I was – being in his late-sixties he would have been forty-something – but it's a concerning thing to contemplate as I do with others who are convicted of historical sexual offences (which I assume Bill is – I should ask someone who knows). His reticence to talk about the Scouts beyond casually mentioning it makes me feel it is intimately linked to his own offending.

CHAPTER 23

A feeling of being 'the new guy' followed me around for at least three or four weeks after I arrived in not only the prison, but this wing. It was only after I saw someone else arrive and be taken around, introducing themselves to forty new people within an hour or two, that I had a feeling of being settled.

That first person in after my own arrival was a tall (taller than Cameron or Tony; perhaps six-five) Swedish-Australian by the name of Dan Burman. He fits the profile of the wing by being well into his sixties, if not seventies, and he has a close-cropped head of blond-grey hair combed straight back and a mouth full of gnarled teeth. Quiet and pleasant, Dan is also deeply religious, and so he formed a natural friendship with Father John Aitchison that has endured over the past six months. They pace the wing together and will sit side by side in two plastic chairs next to our small greenhouse, with a commanding view over Brad's garden and down into the open end of the yard, which is a lovely wide-open grass space perhaps the size of a soccer field (we are most definitely blessed with space). I've previously said a few words to Dan; polite greetings in passing mostly, but we had our first conversation today as we were eating a Thanksgiving afternoon meal that the industrious American Kenny had put together.

Indeed, Kenny's effort to provide the Thanksgiving meal was a long time in the planning (and the promising!) and before Kenny was evicted from the room next to mine we would often be subjected to wonderful 'test' meals or sauces, so he would be sure to get it just right on the day. Naturally, a few of us helped with some preparation, but no one deserves to take the credit away from Kenny, who had spent a whole week politely asking for and receiving refrigerator space in the different pods or permission to borrow additional utensils and ingredients to pull the day off.

As the three-thirty pm deadline arrived and passed, Kenny asked the assembled wing (of which perhaps three-quarters or around thirty people had attended) to show some patience as two of the much-loved prison chaplains were shortly on their way. These two ladies arrived and marvelled at the tables of food, and quickly started around the room with smiles. It must be an experience for these chaplains to visit with and speak to some of the most violent and unhinged members of society; smiling and placing a motherly arm on them and showing an affection and patience that just doesn't come from anywhere else inside of prison. Both of them are said to be so loved across the jail that they could walk unharmed across any yard in the middle of a full-paced riot, and perhaps even receive an apologetic and protective escort to one of the barricaded doors. Only our librarian, Belinda, would also receive such passage.

Cameron as our delegate and anointed leader opened proceedings and explained the effort that Kenny had put into preparing the Thanksgiving meal, and quickly handed over to him to say something more substantive. Kenny hadn't wanted to speak, and I would understand how addressing any sort of crowd was not really his style, but he spoke most credibly and explained what the holiday meant to him, and that, despite the fact we were all prisoners and perhaps at a low point in our lives, it didn't mean we couldn't gather and share a meal and give thanks for whatever good there was in our lives. He received a well-deserved round of applause, and I noted how throughout the next forty minutes people came up to him and shook his hand, thanking him for bringing a little normal civility into a day of incarceration. With a quick prayer from the chaplains, we stood and moved to the tables to collect our plates. As we were setting it up, Cameron and Glen had separated the savoury and sweet items and strategically positioned the cutlery so people would be forced to canalise into a certain direction. Cameron wanted to quickly explain the rules to everyone before we began eating, but I scoffed at him and told him to leave it alone: with a life full of pesky rules and constraints the last thing we needed was any more. Let anarchy reign and get out of their way! Cameron smiled at me and agreed, and people moved along as they pleased.

After collecting my food (and, I'll note for the record, undertaking a respectable catch of some falling meatloaf Kenny had tried to spoon onto my plate) I sat down with Dan Burman and John Aitchison. We exchanged a few niceties before John remarked that the tables of food reminded him of a gathering of soldiers in a barracks. I looked up, thinking it was said for my benefit, and heard Dan nod his agreement. I asked Dan if he had served in the military, and he looked at me and said he had served in Vietnam under national service. I'll admit I was pleasantly surprised and asked him about his experiences. He recounted how he had emigrated from Sweden with his family only a couple of years before, and as a newly minted Australian citizen had been called up, and completed his training in Singleton, Puckapunyal and Canungra and then spent all of 1969 in South Vietnam as a machine gunner. I then happily told him I'd been a military officer and had served in Afghanistan. We shared a knowing smile and spoke about our time overseas at war, recounting the complexity of not knowing who the enemy was, and not wanting to die in a politicians' war (both our wars qualifying as one of those). We promised to meet again and perhaps even share a photo or two. I told Dan of my own family link to Vietnam, and that I had in fact been to Nui Dat, Long Tan and Vung Tau – all areas where Australians had a presence in the war – on my first of three trips since 2013, and I felt a real sense of history for those who had been there in uniform. There is something to be said about the link of Vietnam veterans and us contemporary veterans. When they came back to an unwelcoming and hostile country in the sixties and seventies, they then suffered the further indignity of being told by many Second World War and Korean War veterans that Vietnam wasn't a real war. I cannot imagine how much more piercing that would have been, but it is a credit to the Vietnam cadre that they treated us marvellously on our own returns from East Timor, Iraq and Afghanistan. I remember my own return to Australia after a bitter tour in Afghanistan: I told my family not to visit me at the airport but to wait for me at home as I didn't want to make a fuss. As I cleared customs and walked out into the arrivals, a large crowd of well-wishers welcomed me home with applause, and I quickly turned right, embarrassed, to make it to the taxi rank. There, waiting discretely but in significant numbers, was a group of Vietnam veterans from the Returned Services League, who mobbed me with slaps on the back, cheers and a job well done. It was all too much for me, weary upright junior officer that I was, and I got misty in the eyes as these old men, denied their own honourable return, slapped me on the back and told me they were proud of me. It's a memory that still makes me emotional.

And so, hearing that Dan was a Vietnam veteran, no matter what his other sins might be, drew me to him in a way that is inexplicable but very real. Both Arthur Hoyle and Dave Cashin speak about missing national service by days, and it's nothing I've ever judged them on, despite their somewhat occasional awkwardness that arises when they ask me about Afghanistan (though I don't tend to bring it up or talk about it much). I feel they're self-conscious about missing out, but I don't ever judge them on how fate or even their own desires shaped that part of their life. In some ways, Dan and I are very different veterans. I had been a professional officer with a career; I served in East Timor and elsewhere in the Middle East before I went to Afghanistan in my mid-twenties. I wanted to go, and it was the professional highlight of my military career – the best and worst of my life up until that experience. I had graduated from the Royal Military College, Duntroon, before I turned twenty, but I had another half-dozen years to prepare for *my* generation's war. Being sent into the jungles of Vietnam as an eighteen-year-old machine gunner must have been harrowing. I had picked Dan as a religious oddball, which now hardly seems fair, and I also can't claim to know what he's in jail for and will have to make discreet inquiries, though I dread hearing he is here for crimes of the worst kind. He is a sexual offender.

Stuffed full of food, we all retire to our own pods and wallow in our happiness. The afternoon put on by Kenny is nearly too well done, and I find myself slipping back down from the high point of near-normality, similar to the feeling I have after returning from visits with friends and family. Only Arthur seems able to find the negative among all the positivity, and he shuffles over to me accusing Crafty of leaving early with a plate of sixteen desserts, and saying that Neil Sirowi was a glut focussing on a particular bean dish. I don't know how he manages to stay so firmly anchored in the nitpickery nothingness of every banal situation, and I expect a little more from him as an academic. I've already recounted Arthur's recriminations of John Aitchison for taking a second helping of dinner a few days earlier, and it's a pattern that I wish he would cool off from. Being in jail *is* horrible; of that, there is no doubt, but we are surrounded by enough beauty and happiness and soaking summer rays to enjoy ourselves somewhat; it takes a concerted effort to go around making everyone feel just a little bit worse. It's something we could do without, and I'm happy that the mischievous lout Crafty made off with sixteen desserts and that Neil stuffed himself on that bean dish he clearly found so delicious.

* * *

Chappo, our new pod neighbour, continues his starry-eyed appraisal of his new wing, and I nudge him and tell him he's lucky to have arrived when he did and not a few days later, or he would have missed the Thanksgiving feast. He seems incredibly content and happy with himself, and Dave Will has taken him under his wing and is still introducing him around, helping him learn the lay of the land. It's lovely to see the two long-haired, bearded and tattoo-covered men chat and help each other out, and seeing Chappo respectfully listen to Dave is somehow tender in a way I would never try and explain to them. They are both undeniably dangerous people who have wrought harm through lifetimes of criminality (although Dave has lived a life of honest hard work in parallel – proudly never missing a day of work in a cleaning business he ran), and so seeing them delicately stirring a mug of steaming tea and making sure they put the right amount of sweetener in (you'll recall sugar is contraband – one can make alcohol with it), or the correct splash of milk, is for me an insightful glimpse into their humanity. These two also have an odd criminal honour about them that the sexual offenders can never have, and they swap stories of violent debt collections or shootings and laugh or shake their heads at vignettes where they both know the people involved. In some ways, these men have a straightforward sense of righteousness about them that I saw in people in the military and even the developing world, and you know that good and honest interactions with them are likely to be treated with similar behaviour in return. It's a version of *pashtunwali*: the Pashtun tribal honour code, and itself a system that has self-regulated Afghan tribal behaviour for thousands of years in lawless territories filled with feuding warlords. Concepts like *nyaw aw badal* (justice and revenge), *turah* (bravery), *khegara* (righteousness), *pat, wyaar aw meraana* (respect, pride and courage), *nang* (honour) and *naamus* (protection of women) are all compatible with this unwritten Australian criminal code, although two critical components of *pashtunwali*: *melmastia* (hospitality) and *nanawatai* (forgiveness or asylum) are seemingly given little weight in the Australian version. Perhaps Dave and Chappo will be more receptive to my comparison of *pashtunwali* to their worlds, rather than gushing sentimentally, which is likely to only earn me two confused stares in return.

CHAPTER 24

During the Monday morning rollcall at eight am, barely conscious and with my hair sticking up in all directions, I patiently wait while CO1s Scott Campbell and Mark Alford tick us off of their muster sheet. It's the first time they've both been on since Alwyn Baume left our pod on Saturday morning, and both officers are aware of not only the ongoing issues between us, but also Alwyn's earlier antics in the wing and wider prison environment. Both officers ask me jokingly what I did to cause the nearly unheard-of self-eviction, and I merely raise my hands in capitulation, before pointing a thumb at Dave on my right and jokingly telling them he's next. Coincidentally, Dave has three laundry racks set up, including one that comes right up to my door so I swiftly push it fifteen centimetres to the right, which garners a quick laugh from everyone.

It was always such a non-issue, and we can all laugh at it, but I hear later in the day that Alwyn still thinks I'm trying to make his life uncomfortable and doesn't trust that his moving away has resolved it. I'm done engaging with him now that he's left, but it will be somewhat of a curiosity to see what odd conspiracies he spins when he can't even misinterpret my daily physical existence around him into something it isn't. Hearing this latest piece of news makes me even more convinced that this isn't the last time Alwyn Baume's antics and crooked perception of reality will affect me.

* * *

After lunch, I'm standing in the medication line listening to Shaun Burke talk to Jason about methadone, and how he's addicted to it despite never having had a heroin habit. This catches my attention.

"What do you mean you didn't have a heroin habit? Then how did you get onto methadone?" I interrupt and ask.

"The jail doesn't give a fuck," Shaun starts off. "As soon as you have a pain problem, they'll try and put you on methadone."

"Methadone? But it's here to replace serious opioid addictions, isn't it? Heroin, that sort of thing."

"Yeah, well, you just try and get pain relief stronger than over-the-counter crap."

"The doctors don't prescribe it here?" This seems ridiculous.

"They're too scared. It's panadol or methadone – no one *ever* gets anything else in the middle."

I'm genuinely surprised (something happening less and less as I learn more about incarcerated life) as Shaun Burke explains in detail about how three bulging disks in his spine had crippled him to the point of accepting methadone from the prison doctors when he probably needed an X-ray and a far-less-potent pain killer. As a result, Shaun lines up each morning as one of the addicted 'methadonians' and receives his small plastic cup of opioid drugs in drinkable form. My sister, whose housemate was brutally bashed and raped by Shaun Burke during his violent crime spree more than twelve years ago, probably doesn't care much about Burke being in crippling pain, but I'm astounded that a health system that seems to put so much effort into avoiding patient addiction would slap someone onto methadone for pain relief. Shaun then had to be operated on so his bulging disks are no longer tormenting him; he now has a functioning back *and* an addiction to methadone. (Incidentally, Cameron had a similar problem and operation while detained – however, his single bulging disk wasn't bad enough for him to ask for or accept an offer of methadone.)

Shaun Burke is angry about it: he feels compromised in a way that he never wanted, but here he is each morning lining up with the start of the shakes to get his magic potion. He tells me it takes about twenty minutes once he drinks it for him to feel the effects, but sometimes this is only around a ten-minute period, which he blames on his fast metabolism. His protruding stomach seems to disagree with this last assertion, but I don't point out the obvious contradiction.

"Can't you ask to come off it? Don't they help people do that?"

"I don't care what they say, you can't come off it unless they deny it to you, which they can't," Burke says.

"And besides," he goes on, "people will just to turn to smack, which you can get if you have the cash."

"But if there's a shortage of heroin, smack, whatever, surely people would eventually overcome their addictions?"

"Drugs come in – it doesn't matter. And besides, what else do addicts get up to when they're bored? Once you know you can get the high, people just think about the next hit."

"Sounds like it causes a lot of problems." This seems like an understatement to me.

"They just don't care. Fuck it – put people into liquid handcuffs." (This is Shaun's tidy euphemism for methadone.) "Just keep giving it to people, and say you're helping heroin addicts recover," he tells me.

"When people aren't on heroin to begin with?"

"Yep. Wonderful system isn't it?" At this point, I get one of Shaun's toothless grins that makes him look like a homeless man who has never owned a toothbrush, and I leave the line and wander back to my pod, where Cameron, Dave and Chappo are sitting outside on our park bench. I quickly relay the conversation that I've had, hoping for corroboration or additional insight.

Interestingly, Chappo, who tells me he was formerly a prisoner in Goulburn Jail, explains that methadone is the biggest contributor to recently paroled or released detainees turning to heroin, perhaps even for the first time in their lives. He explains that finding somewhere appropriate to get methadone, since the addiction is just as strong as when they were in prison, and coping with all the regulations and paperwork can be near on impossible; this then drives people to shoot up heroin instead. It's perhaps the cruellest irony of all: prisons that put detainees onto methadone, sometimes for years, and then release them into the clutches of heroin, which then dominates and destroys any chance they may have had of re-entering society and staying on the right side of the law.

Now, if you're like me, you'll shake your head and wonder why these people don't take more control of their lives and avoid the obviously well-known traps of hard drugs, but it seems somehow unfair that a system designed to (or at least pretending to) help drug addicts is not just failing in that, but is even *making new addicts* by seeing methadone as an appropriate non-heroin-related medicative option. Sure, roll your eyes, but then find the person whose house has just been burgled by one of these state-produced heroin addicts and ask if they find it ludicrous.

Well, no matter what your thoughts are, the idea of a race of zombie-like prisoner addicts known as the 'methadonians' makes me smile (believe me I know it shouldn't), and I wish that just one morning I could watch the long docile lines of super-compliant drones slowly wander towards the nurse's station like the living dead. Unfortunately, with only three methadonians (Shaun, Crafty and Thomo) I'm told the effect won't be the same (twenty is a good number, Jason assures me), plus the early-morning activity would require me to be up and out of bed at eight am, which falls decidedly short of being a good enough reason for this night owl. With my levels of "morning drunkenness", as Kenny used to describe me at the morning musters when I'd stand next to him in my doorway, I'd be probably be competing with the methadonians for the most zombie-like impersonation anyway.

* * *

Outside our pod on the floodlit grass and garden, dozens of rabbits are bounding about and coming closer to our patio than ever before. They're so close, in fact, that we joke about snaring a few to make into rabbit stew, but Jason advises against it: an Asian detainee he knew once captured a pair of ducks and ate them and was charged for animal cruelty in the process. Jason described the pillowcase of feathers the poor detainee tried to explain away when the police arrived in the jail to interview him, and his claims for a cultural exemption fell on deaf ears. So, our rabbits remain unmolested and enjoy the wide-open wing, which between six-thirty pm and eight am remains lightly patrolled and mostly ignored by two bored guards.

I've heard of other detainees being charged again for some other offence, and of course, this usually relates to violence, which is an inevitable reality among incarcerated groups. My first night in the prison, when I was shown my temporary room in the solitary confinement 'management unit', saw me placed in the cell next to Tara Costigan's killer, who was being further punished for a recent assault on a Comanchero bikie gang member (months later the local paper had an article about his conviction for this). Not many assaults – Cam and Jason agree perhaps one in ten – will receive any attention from outside authorities, and those that do are usually a result of injuries that are so grievous as to make hiding them an impossibility. Sending someone to hospital tends to draw this kind of unwanted intervention, so the act of severely beating someone without inflicting attention-drawing injuries is quite the terrifying art. You would think this might make violent antagonists focus on finding ways to minimise facial injuries, but Jason swears that the repeated stomping of someone's head is a sound way of inflicting a memorable and uncomfortable non-injurious beating, and despite split lips, black eyes and other facial bruising, this can always be explained away from a boxing incident, sporting incident or something else, and even broken noses can be set by the attending nurse. Jason also explains that when a significant and advantageous size differential exists between the antagoniser and victim, volleys of large repetitious open-handed slaps can be a terrifying way to brutalise someone without breakage. Thus, it's the broken arms, legs and ribs that send prisoners to hospital, and then police to prisons to investigate and charge the aggressors. It fits with the kind of simple unwritten rules one finds all over prison. It's also gosh darn terrifying: battering people's faces to deliberately avoid breaking something, but then that's how a place like this functions. If you ever meet someone who claims to have 'stomped on someone's head' while in prison (and I truly hope you don't), just remember you are in fact talking with an artisan schooled in prison violence tradecraft.

It goes without saying that many of the paedophiles and rapists in this wing have received their fair share of prison beatings, which explains why they're all housed together in the Women and Child Chasers' wing. Dave Cashin recounts a particularly vicious beating he took in the blocks: a large bruiser twice his size attacked him without any warning, smashing his only pair of glasses and badly bruising his face. Dave explains how horrified his wife was when he arrived for a visit covered in bruises and without his glasses; she made a scene demanding one of the guards explain to her what had happened. They shrugged in response, and Dave told her that no one cared enough to follow it up. The same guard told him he was lucky it wasn't a worse beating.

Another time, Glen Vandavord was held down in a common area while two gronks took turns swinging a broken kettle by the cord into him until he started crying, begging them to stop. When they did, they explained that if he told the guards they would repeat the treatment, but this time use the heating element of a working kettle on him. Glen never told the guards and soon moved out of the blocks.

Jason Dodd, in and out of jail for the past fifteen years, has received a large number of beatings, but oddly enough none since he was most recently incarcerated for rape a few years ago (his other crimes have been drug and alcohol-related). His first-ever prison beating came when he innocently enough asked a guard (or in his language: a "screw") about something, and afterwards, he was invited by a few detainees to go up and see someone who wanted to see him. When he arrived, the senior detainee explained the rules to Jason: he was not to speak or converse with the guards for anything, and he risked being labelled a 'rat' if he did so again (a rat being ranked only slightly higher than a sexual offender, or 'pest'). At the end of the lesson, he was told he was going to be beaten up, and three other detainees got to work on him. He considers this a lucky experience; many others were beaten without having their misdemeanour explained to them, and so Jason is relatively circumspect over this formative education. Jason admits to hurling verbal abuse at sexual offenders before he himself became one, but he never participated in any violence against such a person. In a previous incarcerated life, Chappo has both hurled verbal abuse and physical violence at sexual offenders, and now finds himself on the other side of the fence, similar to Jason.

* * *

Chappo's third night with us sees him treated to a delicious mango lamb curry, with a simple accompanying daal and some homemade naan. I miss the chilli (desperately) but Chappo doesn't, so he enjoys dinner and comments about his ongoing disbelief at his recent change of scenery. Earlier in the day, he expressed some regret in forgetting to purchase some sunglasses on the monthly 'buy-ups' form, and so I dug out my own pair, which were doing nothing but collecting dust under my bed, and gave them to him. I had a pair of prescription sunglasses come in shortly after I arrived, so I didn't mind parting with the gawky Ray Charles-esque wrap-around design, which seem to both fit and complement Chappo's busy bearded face nicely. Initially, he didn't seem to believe I didn't want anything in return for them. If anything, I was actually quietly happy to part with something superfluous; but of course, I take a little selfish joy in doing something nice like this.

I think I get a kick out of the reaction by not wanting anything in return, and I had the same feeling a few months back when I gifted Craig Stevens (hand-sanitiser drinking; Ford Anglia back tattoo) a pair of new shoes I received that were slightly too small for me, and when I later baked the cake for Crafty's birthday. Cameron does it too, and a few others around the wing, but usually you don't give away something of value without getting something in return. Not in prison. But it feels good to buck the trend and do something nice for its own sake.

CHAPTER 25

Inever thought I would be so happy to see a frozen bag of spinach arrive, but with a few new food items on the weekly shopping list a little variety is always welcomed. Among the standard items we expect to see, a kilogram of green curry paste also arrives, as well as some hotdogs and buns. We should have received some olive oil, but the crew that go out and buy the goods on our behalf (wouldn't it be lovely if they let us do it?) bought the olive oil in glass bottles, which is a tremendous no-no for detainees, lest we shatter the bottles and use the shards to attack the guards, each other, or indeed ourselves. It makes sense; the more violent cottages around the jail would surely take advantage of it, but the rule's not necessary here in the Women and Child Chasers. Being denied glass bottles of olive oil seems preposterous when we have a large butcher's knife bolted to a one-metre chain on our kitchen bench, noting it wouldn't take much to pry it loose.

Meanwhile, our frozen hockey-puck-sized spinach servings go into the freezer, and we all agree to hotdogs for lunch tomorrow, which is effectively this night owl's time for breakfast. If you ever watch your life melt away in front of a group of arriving police waving an arrest warrant, I recommend you grit your teeth and hold on desperately to two ideas: firstly (and critically) keep your mouth shut, and secondly, remember that if you do end up in jail, you can have hotdogs for breakfast.

Controversy around the food orders is at fever pitch in the other two pods (really four pods joined in pairs) as the Christmas period requires the ordering and delivery of three weeks' worth of produce, which is predicted to play havoc with all the warring old men and insanely incompatible occupants. Our pod will be fine, but it should be interesting to see how much additional tension arises when people either run out of food, fight for freezer or refrigerator space, or simply clash to have something to do. Arthur, in particular, seems to have an illogical stranglehold on what people ought to eat, how much of it and when, and the strict conditions under which a person may take a helping of seconds, or indeed draw leftovers from the fridge the following day.

* * *

The early afternoon period sees a foreign movie shown on SBS (made somewhere in the Balkans, but I can't get a hold on the accent) titled *Innocence*, which is about a highly esteemed doctor named Tomas Kotya (Croatian?) who finds himself accused of molesting a fourteen-year-old patient. We follow Kotya, who we find out early on is innocent, and see his entire life crumble around him as Olinka, the girl, walks the police through a credible statement that makes everyone believe he's guilty. During a commercial break, I mention it to Cameron, and he tells me the movie has been on before, but he couldn't bring himself to watch it as it's too close to home for him. Cameron doesn't talk a lot about his convictions, except to say it was a misconstrued piggyback he gave his female friend back in 1991, and that a good deal of maliciousness went into the accusation and trial. I'm simply not positioned well enough to form any critical judgement of Cam's guilt or innocence but suffice to say the case was robust enough for the jury to convict him, and for the judge to sentence him to a not-insubstantial fourteen years of prison. He's deeply bitter about it and speaks about the Crown prosecutor Trent Hickey with a venom that is out of character for the happily married father of five. Of the many sad faces adorning the identity cards next to our cell doors, Cameron's pronounced frown is marked in its deep sorrow, being taken after the lengthy three years of accusation, investigation, prosecution, conviction and sentencing had concluded, with Cameron photographed on day one of his 5,110 days of detention leaving behind his family. I can't imagine, even with my own circumstances, what he must have been feeling, but it is a credit to him that he has served as much of his sentence as he has with a focus to help others, and remaining an involved and loving father to his four boys and one daughter through phone calls, emails and bi-weekly visits. His wife, Kathleen, and his children are as much victims in this affair, and their own perseverance through a tough journey is commendable. American Kenny was correct when he told me early on that families serve time as much as the prisoner.

In better news, Doctor Kotya is found to be innocent and the victim of an elaborate conspiracy, but I find it interesting to reflect on a movie that in the age of #MeToo and 'Time's up', is still socially acceptable enough to be portraying men as the horrible victims of false accusations. I don't deny that it happens: it's a terrifying reality and one that chills any person to the bone, including myself, but as the United States supreme court nomination process for Brett Cavanaugh showed us, it's an area fraught with overzealous emotion rather than cool-headed fact. I do believe in the presumption of innocence, and that the burden of proof is on the system, and while it must make it a horrible process for a victim to engage with, I don't think the alternative is a worthwhile world to contemplate living in. The golden thread of justice is so critically important to a well-functioning modern society that I'm glad there has been a re-balancing of sorts in the past twelve months, and that hurled accusations are no longer enough to condemn someone. Don't get me wrong, there needs to be more work done on drawing victims out and supporting them through the process, but this nonsense about believing victims without question is incompatible with the presumption of innocence; perhaps believing victims to secure a proper investigation is more appropriate. People who automatically believe either the victim or the alleged perpetrator immediately and with near-religious zeal are unhelpful in the best case, and dangerous idiots in the worst. Both parties need to believe religiously in the *process*, and trust it to find out the truth.

You might think someone sitting in jail and espousing the merits of the justice system is a bit rich, but you don't have to look too far into history, or even across countless international borders today, to see what happens to a society *without* the presumption of innocence as a cornerstone. The illusion of due process is not justice. So, did Cameron Tully sexually assault his female friend, or Arthur Hoyle rape his students? They both profess their innocence. I don't know the answer, truly, but all my faith and trust in our justice process, imperfect as it is, makes me feel the system got it right on both accounts.

After the movie finishes, we spend the remaining Tuesday afternoon locked into our pod of six, and Jason and Chappo start chatting about their own crimes. As I've mentioned, I'm yet to hear what Chappo's charges are, and whether he is with our wing because he's a sexual offender or, like Dave Will, simply here for his own physical protection. It turns out that Chappo was charged with statutory rape (in Australian legalise: sexual assault of a consenting minor) and was caught in bed with a fifteen-year-old girl when the police arrived to arrest him for something unrelated. Chappo swears he didn't know her age, and pleads respect for women, saying additionally that he would be the last person on earth who would hurt someone in this manner. He seems genuine in this and comes across as a kind of loveable Australian larrikin; someone who is known around town for going to bars with his red parakeet on his shoulder and has a larger than life personality. When I stay quiet and slowly nod, he feels a need to go into a physical description of the girl, ensuring me that the "great tits, tight arse, black tank top and little skirt" had him fooled, but I just don't understand how you can end up in bed with a fifteen-year-old child as a late forty-something-year-old man. Sure, I've seen underage girls who could pass for eighteen, but something about it doesn't add up in a way that I can see myself falling victim to a similar situation. Only fifteen . . .

Jason decides to pipe up and tells Chappo about his own charge of raping a sixteen-year-old girl. If you, the reader, aren't familiar with Australian law, then you might be surprised to learn that the consenting age for sex here is sixteen, and that Chappo's crime would have been a legal act in a matter of months. Thus Chappo is technically a paedophile and Jason is technically a rapist; Chappo will go onto a national register and have restrictions placed on his travel, possible residences (no proximity to schools), types of occupation (none with children; no door-to-door work) and other similar constraints that will last his full natural life. Jason won't. It's a curious opportunity to see the law split down the boundary fence, and while I don't intend to moralise on what's worse: consensual sex with a fifteen-year-old girl, or the non-consensual rape of a sixteen-year-old girl, it seems like something is missing in Jason's sentence. Both charges utterly repel me, and I have a strong sense that both men failed in their own responsibilities to better control their circumstances and see the vulnerability in their victims. Admittedly, I don't see the far more insidious predation on very young children that many of the bad paedophiles in the wing are guilty of. It's almost as if the kaleidoscope of criminality, which clearly features so heavily in Chappo and Jason's lives, muddied their judgement into making horrendously bad decisions. But it's still a world apart from those men who, from stable and successful positions of trust and community prominence, prey on younger children in a far more methodical and serpentine way. I'm not excusing Chappo and Jason for what they did, but the slope of depravity quickly falls away into dark places here.

Having previously told us how he used to wear a parakeet on his shoulder for amusement in bars, Chappo also advises us that he eats eggshells for their calcium and protein. When Chappo was still a prisoner in Goulburn Jail, a muscled friend confided to him that eggshells were the secret to his bulk, and so now we have a little plastic food container on the bench full of shells for his consumption. He's certainly an animated character, our Chappo, who has an odd resemblance to Rodney Rude crossed with King Neptune (that beard and build). His claims of keeping a tennis ball in the air with seventy-six consecutive kicks receive polite nods all around from Arthur, MJ, Dave Cashin, Cameron and myself, as we sit together in the last hour of the afternoon before we're locked back inside. The weather is threatening rain, and a few rainbows are appearing pleasantly in the distance.

MJ decides to walk out onto the large flat grass area between our bench and the bushes where the rabbits congregate and lie down flat on his stomach. He looks marvellously relaxed and uncaring about people's opinions of this, and I hush down Arthur and Dave who start shouting at him and disturbing his quiet and obviously blissful moment. He's back before too long and sitting with us, and I'm interested to learn that the Hemingway-esque friend of mine, who incidentally suffers horrible dreams of murdering his own family, spent the first forty-some years of his life known as Kevin James Austin, which is the name his adoptive family gave him as an infant. Only after all that time did he decide to find his birth mother, and he quickly adopted the name Michael-John, which is what she knew him as before he was given away for reasons he doesn't mention. It's a touching story and I ask him if he ever responds to Kevin (he doesn't look like a Kevin – he's strictly an 'MJ' or an 'Ernest' in my estimation) but he doesn't; it's not who he is any more, he tells me.

I wish I knew more about him, as his life seems more a series of uncontrolled major events, rather than that of a simple well-functioning man who woke up one morning and became a sexual offender. He's a pleasant if plain conversationalist, and never has a bad word to say about anyone or anything, always smiling happily and being content with whatever or whoever is around him. I know he's a former musician, and he has a tattoo on his forearm that looks somehow military but I know is not. It's two crossed feathers or wings (a bird?) on an emblem that might be a band. I'll have to ask him next time. He seems genuinely out of place in here, despite fitting the profile in age and gender, and he exhibits none of the common manipulative and insidious little traits that slowly draw the others together into something discernibly homogeneous; different species for sure, but from the same branch of predatory lineage or animal. I don't see it in him, but I don't doubt he did whatever he was convicted of doing. Even the bemused and befuddled Dave Cashin, someone who seems to have been caught up in a net of other sexual offenders without really knowing what he was doing (he claims), shows the little signs of being the predator that might still lead a child away from a distracted playground, share child pornography online (what he's convicted of) or do something equally horrendous.

But not MJ; his faults seem much more opaque and driven by his mental health challenges. If his physicality can be best compared with Ernest Hemingway, then his manner would be approximated as someone who would make an ideal shopping centre Santa Claus: jovial, easy-going, patient, simple – an entertainer at heart. He would probably do fantastically in the job, and I can see him in the red and white outfit, bouncing a child on his knee and promising toys, while a line of excited kids and bored parents wait behind his snowy throne. But it's a fantasy. MJ is here, serving five or so years in prison because he is a sexual predator too. The undeniable besmirching mark written across the head of all these men now and forever. It has had the effect on me that I can never again look at a strange man, and not wonder seriously if this perfectly ordinary person is part of the same category of offender. In this zoo of evil predation – the Women and Child Chasers – too much superficial normality exists; too much easy trust; too many smiles and warm personalities. You must be tired of my judgemental and accusatory words, but it's for my own sanity that I need to capture these thoughts and try to unpick them along this journey; one that feels like I'm navigating in a storm, not knowing where I am, but understanding that I have to get somewhere or follow some cardinal direction, or else be lost forever. I wish I had the flashy one-dimensional monsters to hiss at and then forget, but I don't. I simply don't. Their humanity is too apparent, and their normalcy too chilling, and I don't know if pointing to them and labelling them as monsters is justified or arrogant, just as equally as I don't know if sitting down and accepting them as fallible and caring human beings makes me somehow complicit or enabling. *Can* I be friends with a paedophile or a rapist?

Could you?

CHAPTER 26

Being the night owl that I am, I tend to find myself in a sprightly mood around midnight when only Cameron is still poking about in the common area where he sleeps. Dave Will also stays up late but chooses to sit and watch television in his room until around two or three am, and then impossibly wakes up at seven am for the morning muster. How he manages to survive on such little sleep is a mystery to me, and I feel sorry that the days must feel like a never-ending eternity for him.

It was one of these late nights when Cameron and I got talking in the kitchen, and he decided to pull the stove front off of its hinges to give it a good scrubbing. After we puzzled over the latch mechanism for five minutes, the front door and all the internal racks came out, and we were happily scrubbing and chatting as the clock turned to midnight. We were going about this task as quietly as we could but inevitably woke up Jason, who popped his head out of his room to investigate the commotion.

"You two are going to get piss tested tomorrow morning," he tells us. Both Cameron and I looked back at him with cocked eyebrows waiting for his explanation, which he seemed to take pleasure at delaying behind his grin.

"If the guards see you scrubbing and cleaning this late, they'll assume you're both amped up on amphetamines or ice."

Sure enough, fifteen minutes later, we spied the night shift guard staring curiously through our pod windows at us, but he then quickly departed, apparently not thinking much of it, as both Cameron and I make for unlikely addicts. It's always interesting for me to have Jason (or anyone else used to incarcerated life) translate the foreign world that I live in, and I can see how similar behaviour could be a clear cue to guards that there were people hyped up on drugs and in need of testing. Indeed Thomo (non-sexual offender; user of the illicit tattoo gun, blond ponytail), who lives with his best friend and fellow gronk, Crafty (non-sexual offender; oafish; pierced lip), is both a methadonian and an obsessive-compulsive who spends most of his free time constantly cleaning his pod, to the chagrin of others. When Cameron once lived with Thomo, he had to tell him to *stop* vacuuming more than once a day because the incessant noise of the vacuum cleaner was annoying him. Having Thomo happily cleaning the entire environment ensured an otherwise pristine area, but it was quite the balancing act on how much was *too much*. I have no doubt that if the same guard who peered through at Cameron and I went and saw Thomo and Crafty undertaking the same chore, at the same time, they would be spot-checked for drugs the following morning. And yet there we were, chatting idly as we degreased, scoured and re-assembled our own oven like two jacked addicts trying to burn off a high.

The following day in the library, I see a newspaper article that catches my eye, and one that concerns a member of our wing, Gary Leslie Marsch. Gary, a seventy-three-year-old former primary school teacher who was jailed for molesting a thirteen-year-old student back in 1978, has just been released on bail ahead of a retrial, and his original convictions of indecent assault and buggery, which seem as outdated as Gary is, have been set aside. I've sat across from him over a few hands of poker and chatted when our paths crossed in the wing, and ultimately have found him somewhat unremarkable. Gary is an unassuming older man with a full head of grey hair, and he has the pleasantly symmetrical features of someone who was probably quite handsome in his youth. He wears tinted glasses on frames that seem better placed in the 1970s, but still seem to work on him as an older former teacher. His quietness seems to derive from his shame of being a convicted paedophile, and he has a reserved way of speaking to others around him. I suspect this quietness is him weighing the benefits of providing an intelligent opinion about something, or simply staying quiet and allowing the conversation to flow on unimpressed upon. Gary would have been thirty-three or thirty-four years old at the time of his offending – close to the same age I am now – and I find it interesting how my perception of the average paedophile is changing from the clichéd old man to these much younger predators. Gary, like Glen Vandavord, was a primary school teacher in his mid-thirties when he molested his pupils, but I can't see the genial old man in front of me as a predator. Gary seems like an ordinary person; someone who has formed functional adult relationships for social and romantic ends, and I wonder how he brought himself to do what he did all those years ago. I'm not aware if Gary himself was sexually abused (which seems to be a far more prevalent condition in the paedophiles and rapists in this wing then I thought), or if he has something wrong with his mental wiring like some of the others. Glen, in comparison, is lumbering in both his physicality and emotional intelligence, and I can see how he turned into the predator that he is; but Gary seems like one of these ordinary people, who, for reasons I don't understand at all, are able to perpetrate incredible evil on other people. Gary is the paedophile you walk past in the street and never notice, or the teacher you might hand your children over to without that 'Alwyn Baume' warning ringing, and that, in this observer's humble opinion, makes him the deadliest kind. It will be interesting to see if he returns to our wing as his retrial plays out.

After reading about Gary and his retrial in the library, I return to the wing with a few new books and set myself up outside our pod in a chair just short of the sun. With a ginger beer (one of my guilty weekly purchases) and Viet Thanh Nguyen's novel *The Sympathizer*, I have approximately five minutes of blissful privacy until Bill Scheeren (herb gardener) comes walking over and sits next to me. After the thirty seconds of continued reading fails to send the message that I'm closed for business, I put down my book and listen as Bill inexplicably unfolds his life story to me. It's almost as if he knows I'm writing about my experiences and is making a deliberate confession to me. I've written a little about the eccentric Dutch-Australian and former scoutmaster that Bill is, but he unfolds for me a rich and confronting description of how he started his offending in his early twenties and concluded in his mid-twenties. Interestingly he refers to his "victim" as simply that: there is no gender, name, age or other descriptive information, though Bill stresses to me that his under-aged victim was "consensual," and yet seems to acknowledge that what he did was wrong, and that consent couldn't be given. He explains that he felt he was empowering his victim and wasn't taking advantage of them, and that he too went through a similar experience with an older man at the same age (this is the only clue that his own victim was perhaps a boy, rather than a girl). He even told his mother about the older man and was told (horrifyingly) in return: "It's fine – boys are just curious at your age." She did not consider that her son was confiding in her that he had been abused. I'm merely listening to Bill as he unfolds all of this to me, and I don't have to ask any questions or make any responses for his monologue to continue.

Bill stresses to me that he was "fondling", and not "molesting" his victim and that it took a psychiatrist to sit him down and tell him that he was indeed a paedophile: a word that Bill initially rejected outright as not applying to him. The psychiatrist offered to treat him and conduct electro-therapy by attaching wires to his testicles and shocking him when shown child pornography; Bill understandably refused to subject himself to this torture but continued with his psychiatric sessions. His treatment left him at peace with his shame, but he felt that one last cathartic action remained: his confession to his victim. The victim listened to his apologies but withheld their forgiveness, explaining that a confession to the authorities was what they wanted. Bill refused and went on with his life for over a decade, mistakenly believing he had closed that chapter of his life.

Still racked with guilt over his crimes, he confessed to the police in the mid-nineties (and chronologically twenty years after Bill's offending), who told him that the twelve-month statute of limitations had long expired, and while they were appreciative of his honesty, they wouldn't be pursuing the matter any further. It was another decade later when Bill heard over the radio that the implementation of new grandfathered laws (i.e. applied retrospectively, regardless of no law existing at the time of the offence) meant he could be prosecuted. A phone call came shortly advising him that precisely that would be occurring. Before he was arrested, he flew to Canada – not to flee – but to say farewell to his brother, knowing what a child-sex-related conviction meant to his chances of leaving the country again, and then returned to Australia to face his long-overdue trial. He was initially sentenced to twelve years in prison, then had it reduced to eight years, then again finally to four years, all on account of his forthrightness and cooperation during the process. His victim was shocked, as Bill tells me, thinking that it was a "light sentence" and not worthy of what Bill perpetrated on them. At this, Bill offers an accepting shrug and thinks he should have to spend more time locked away but can only do what the judge orders. He then laments the "awful grey zone" he felt he sexually matured in, and that his experiences of both being molested, and then doing the molesting, never gave him a clear idea of what was right and wrong.

Bill's monologue is the most forthright explanation of a person's offending I've yet heard since joining this wing, and even Kenny, always willing to dive into his own manipulative behaviour and discuss it openly with me, never descends into this amount of detail. I ask my first question of Bill, who is sitting next to me in slumped comfort having delivered his confession, about what he thinks of others in the wing: who does *he* feel is the most manipulative person here? Like Kenny before him, he tells me the awkward Glen Vandavord is high on his list, which surprises me as much as when Kenny told me. Surely, I ask, there just has to be others more manipulative than

Glen? "No," Bill tells me simply, "Glen Vandavord is one to watch." Bill also names Ian King (tall Aboriginal man; Ray Charles lookalike) as a very manipulative person and shudders when he recalls how King, who volunteered as cricket coach, deliberately isolated and molested young boys that he targeted for their psychological vulnerability. It's behaviour Bill heard King describe in the adult sex offenders program during group discussions. It's also behaviour King uses on other detainees for non-sexual reasons, and Bill tells me he's a chameleon in disguise playing the role of a hapless old man who has already been in prison for ten years and isn't a threat to anybody. "Don't be fooled," is Bill's concluding advice.

* * *

The conclusion of an interesting week in the Women and Child Chasers sees the return of Kylie Sidlow: a notorious but ultimately well-intentioned guard. Sidlow is a squat woman of perhaps approaching forty years, and she has a close-cropped head of purple (or fading purple) hair and glasses. She assiduously sticks to the rules no matter how banal, and to Chappo's surprised displeasure, he is sent back from the nurse's office to replace his singlet for a proper shirt. It's a thirty-five-degree day, but rules are rules, and Chappo reappears without much fuss two minutes later. During the final evening lock-in, Sidlow says hello to Brian Wilson (old; hearing aids; molested his own children and grandchildren) with whom she has a very vitriolic relationship. Before I arrived in the prison, Sidlow's personal dislike of Brian saw him 'tipped' out of the wing into a more uncomfortable part of the jail, and it took him a good seven months to return (if you'll recall, displacing Kenny from his room). As she marks our six names off her muster sheet (the guards move from pod to pod for these quad-hourly rollcalls), Brian oddly makes a disparaging comment about Sidlow's shrill voice (and shrill it most certainly is), which he thinks is funny but just comes across as rude. Both Cameron and I apologise on his behalf, and she shakes her head and shares our amazement that Brian would seek to push his luck. Sidlow is given a very hard time by many detainees here, but she works diligently and (mostly) incorruptibly in a thankless role, and frankly deserves more respect than she gets. During the same muster rollcall, she informs me that she is my new case manager (all detainees are assigned to a corrections officer for routine internal administrative matters; a civilian case manager handles all external matters) and asks how I've been. Bless her, she thinks I might be bored, given that I'm not a sex offender, I don't have a chance to do any of the mandatory courses that the others routinely throw tantrums over. I assure her that I'm kept suitably occupied and am happy but take the opportunity to raise a minor matter over a weekend newspaper delivery, which she promptly fixes on my behalf.

* * *

Cameron and I finish the evening arguing lightly over the negative impact that homeschooling has on a person's sociability; I point to the awkward Glen Vandavord as my example, and Cameron points to himself as his. We conclude, and agree to disagree, when poor Cameron's ongoing toothache gets the better of him, and he seeks out and uses a pair of tongs to break off a protrusion that has been aggravating him since his tooth removal the fortnight before. He does this only an hour after discretely cutting up Dave Will's steak dinner for him, as the old bugger's own teeth wobble loosely and give him problems. I'm glad for the first time in my life that the military simultaneously yanked out all four of my wisdom teeth when I was a freshly minted officer. I merely presented myself all those years ago and said I had some minor discomfort: forty-eight hours later I was under a general anaesthetic wondering why I had opened my mouth at all, but now I couldn't imagine having to get the prison dentist to provide such prompt service.

CHAPTER 27

Well, it's finally happened. I've been personally called out for verbal abuse, and in this case from a gronk in the library. I was sitting there reading the newspaper when the gronk sitting next to me got up to leave and barely mumbled "fucken pest" as he skirted out of the room. It was the same one who a few weeks earlier waited until the door was safely closed before saying something through the window. I was more amused, to be honest – after eight months in the prison living with sex offenders, this was the first time someone felt me worthy of a verbal barb, and it also came the day after I shaved my facial hair into a Van Dyke or Musketeer-styled look (a moustache with an arrowed soul patch – oh yeah). It was the most offensive facial hair style I could craft, short of donning a National Socialist-inspired squared moustache, so I don't blame this gronk for thinking I was a sex offender. After he said it, I found Taylor (language student; murderer) and we went to a quiet classroom nearby to do an hour of language tuition. I used this gronk as an example in our lesson, and I was surprised that Taylor felt angry that I had been abused, and his emotion ran high enough to last the entire lesson. When we left, I pointed to the gronk in question, who happened to be in a corner of a camera-less hallway between the library and a small courtyard, and got quite the reaction from my student.

"That's him!" I smiled and pointed, not intending anything other than to acknowledge that he was there.

Taylor immediately went into attack-dog mode and grabbed the gronk by his shirt, pinning him up against the wall. The gronk was a forties-something prisoner with more sinew than muscle and had some semblance of Aboriginal heritage.

"Oi! Listen here, ya fucken cunt!" Taylor began in earnest. "*He's* not a pest, alright! First and last warning or I'll fucken stomp you, cunt!"

In response, the petrified gronk muttered a "Yeah, alright," and Taylor released him with a push.

Look, if I had known Taylor was going to respond like that, I wouldn't have so flippantly pointed the offending gronk out, but it was in some way fascinating to see a little hard-man prison justice handed out.

Our lesson had concluded because Taylor's wing was being taken back, so after he'd left I was happily recounting the experience to Arthur and some of the others and I pointed out the gronk still cowering in the hallway.

As the group of us laughed and smiled at him, he became animated again and walked up to Arthur to confront him. Before anyone could intervene on behalf of our erstwhile professor, Arthur decided to stomp on his foot and sent him running to safety in the library. This became the funniest thing anyone in the wing had seen in a while, and so did the rounds like wildfire, with people telling the story of how our own professor Arthur Hoyle had put this antagonistic abuser in his place. The next day in the library (we go on Wednesdays and Thursdays) the aforementioned gronk was conspicuously absent from his wing's representation.

* * *

Come Friday, a few of us go along to 'activities', which simply means access to a full gymnasium, indoor basketball court and hairdressing facilities (that detainees use themselves) a short walk from our wing. In our wing, we do have a small gym, basketball hoop and hair clippers (we are one of the few wings to do so) but getting access to these more substantive facilities each Friday is welcomed. Unfortunately, being scheduled for late afternoon Friday means that this weekly activity is cancelled probably three times out of four, so as we arrive with an overcast sky threatening a large thunderstorm, it's a welcome chance to spend an hour somewhere other than our wing or the library. The gymnasium has a corrections officer appointed; one of the better ones who always helps the detainees with finding and printing things off or sourcing sporting equipment, and generally treating them like humans (understandably, not all guards afford the paedophiles and rapists here much respect). Corrections Officer One Barry doesn't wear the normal blue uniform but wears a hybrid-physical activities version, much like physical training instructors in the military do.

I'm asked to relay a request to CO1 Barry from Thomo, who you might recall is jointly parenting a young magpie with his friend Crafty, and he wants a photograph taken with the bird on his shoulder to send his son for Christmas. Barry has a digital camera in his "fortress of solitude" (as Kenny describes the big, empty gymnasium and adjacent office which Barry alone occupies) and takes photographs for detainees on request. Taking a social photograph of a prisoner is an improbably complex process that requires release forms and signatures and is organised by Barry as one of his responsibilities. Photos must be taken in or around the gym, so Thomo, who cannot bring his feathered child to activities, needs Barry to make an exception and come to him. I explain all of this to CO1 Barry and grit my teeth, half-expecting him to flatly tell me "no" and roll his eyes, but he couldn't be more helpful and makes arrangements for the following week. I happily pass the news back to an appreciative Thomo.

Returning from the gymnasium, we see the skies unleash the start of what becomes a vicious two-day thunderstorm, and thunder and lightning crack and flash around the prison in a tremendous display. As I'm reading in my room, there's a knock on the door and a care package from the Salvation Army materialises with candy, cards and other knick-knacks, which is appreciated. I'm not religious in the slightest, but it's nice to see the kinds of people and organisations that remember those of us at the bottom end of our luck, and the smallest gestures can and do make a world of difference. My bag of candy lasts three days; Jason's lasts three minutes.

Another foreign movie makes an impression on me as the thunderstorm outside continues its rampage: *Presumed Guilty*, a French film and harrowing true story of Alain Marecaux, a respected lawyer, husband and father whose life is shattered by false allegations of child abuse. Similar to the Croatian film *Innocence* mentioned earlier, I find it interesting that another foreign film has a premise that is a man fighting a false accusation of paedophilia. I suppose, being in the wing that I am, I've become acutely aware of references and portrayals of sexual offending, right down to odd humorous snippets like in the movie *Vacation*, when the dad is faced with describing it to his son.

"Hey, Dad, what's a paedophile?"

"Well, son, when a man and a boy love each other—"

The wife cuts him off.

I've yet to see many movies about men who *are* guilty, although I know that they exist; for example, Kevin Bacon's portrayal of a paedophile in *The Woodsman*, and the horrific British film *The War Zone*, which I had to turn off and couldn't finish viewing years ago.

Aside from movies featuring sexual offenders, I seem to also catch every snippet of news with a story of some predator being arrested or sentenced. This includes the news that a young army officer and helicopter pilot named Rhiley Boyson was sentenced to three months in Holsworthy military prison for sticking a beer bottle up a prostrated colleague's backside, or that eighty-four-year-old former priest Thomas Fulcher was sentenced to four years in a Tasmanian prison for abusing young boys. We seem to be awash with these predators in every facet of our lives, and it's making me hypersensitive about it. A friend of mine who visits most Thursdays, and incidentally works in the passports office at Foreign Affairs, tells me that there are approximately 18,000 people on the 100-year 'banned-from-obtaining-a-passport' list, based on their sexual convictions and under-age victims.

* * *

With our two weeks' worth of food and a continuing thunderstorm outside, eating seems to be a good way to pass the time, and Chappo decides he's going to go onto "double rations". He's not putting on weight as fast as he would like, he tells me, which surprises him, considering he was on "two to three grams of ice a day" before he was jailed. I slowly nod at him and am somewhat amazed at his confession of having such a substantial drug habit. He seems like the kind of person for whom drugs is a part of his normal lifestyle, but two to three grams a day seems excessive. I guess people find their own vices, but I can't imagine how he functioned as a person with a habit like that. This all assumes of course that that is a substantial amount of the narcotic; I am the first to admit that my knowledge of such things is poor. Could two or three grams of ice per day be nothing? I'll ask Jason who is sure to set me straight on it.

Chappo has settled in well and loves being in this wing of the jail. While Cameron, Arthur and I mope around, conscious of being without our liberty, Chappo almost acts like he's won the lottery. Every meal makes his eyes happily glaze over, and he conducts himself through the days with a nearly too-bright-to-bear optimism, but when his son turns twenty-one Chappo falls into a flat mood, and we sit on the patio and chat while he tells me he wishes he could be there for him as a better father. Chappo and I are very different people with very different lives, but he undoubtedly exudes a sense of tough luck optimism; the battler on ice, perhaps, and like a few others in here seems to be far more a product of his circumstances than someone who turned a functioning life to predation. Chappo clearly considers the law as a set of recommendations rather than absolutes, and I don't feel I can ignore his most recent charges: the disgusting statutory rape of a minor. However, I do believe he has a good heart, and suspect the vortex of a non-civic lifestyle contributed to his recent charges, as I don't see the hungry predation in his eyes that others carry all too easily. Perhaps Chappo is the playful orca that doesn't understand its own physicality, but certainly not a prowling shark in the depths. I do see a difference.

Another for whom I don't see a great deal of natural predation leaves our wing and the jail for good. Nilander 'Neal' Sirowi, the short, happy and punch-drunk former boxer wins his parole and is notified he'll leave us in a few days to start the deportation proceedings to India. Neal is a friend, and because of our similar ages and ability to get along we chat often, and I enjoy his effervescence and windy laugh. Cameron jokes with him that he's got to receive his departure beating, and incidentally, I learn this is a real and very serious thing that happens in other parts of the jail. For us, it consists of Cameron playfully rolling with Neal in the grass until he puts him into a number of submission positions, but it's done so gently that the greatest risk to Neal is him nearly choking on his own laughter. Cameron, who helped Neal apply for his successful parole and was sitting next to him when the sentence administration board made its decision, now moves onto Owen Crockett and David Cashin's applications. Neal was given such a hard time in Arthur's pod and seemed to be the xenophobic focus of a bunch of old cranky white men who took exception to anything Neal said or did. Arthur, much loved as our cantankerous professor, would whine to Cam and I about Neal's latest odorous curry, or that he had the gall to use too much flour when making naan, or other silly and quite unnecessary issues we both dismissed with a roll of the eyes. As Neal leaves a few days later, I give him a big unapologetic hug and wish him well in getting on with this life back home. The place feels a little less happy without him, and when Arthur tells me later "good-riddance", in regards to Neal's departure, I walk away and leave him to his own thoughts.

We don't know who is coming into replace Neal, but Alwyn Baume has sufficiently upset his roommate, Ali (Lebanese Papa Smurf), that he has moved himself into Neal's old room, and told Alwyn he can deal with the new person as he's quite fed up with him. In the saga of Alwyn Baume, it's surprising that it only took two-and-a-half weeks from moving into his new pod to upset them all, and it seems more than ever he risks being 'tipped' from the wing altogether. He's also put a formal complaint into the guards that Peter Middleton (very old former author; paedophile) was urinating on the floor of their communal toilet, not having the confidence or wherewithal to just go and speak to him about the matter directly. I barely see Alwyn now given he's in the pod next door but did catch him recently sitting outside as I walked past. I lifted a hand in a very friendly and non-confrontational wave (can a wave *be* confrontational?) and he merely stood up and walked inside, ignoring me. Alwyn has been to see Cameron about his stress with Ali leaving his room; he is worried about who might come into the wing and become his new roommate. Cameron sits him down as he always does and listens like a patient father, despite Alwyn being twenty years older; old enough for the implied roles to be reversed. They're the same listening skills he's honed as a father to a young autistic son (his equal-youngest of five [and fraternal twin to a sister]); in some ways Cam has become the father of all the lost and wandering souls in this wing, dispensing his fraternal care and protection not to five of his own children at home, but to those here who are lost around him. Alwyn Baume, like Glen Vandavord, Kenny Johnson, Jason Dodd, David Cashin, Owen Crockett, Neil Sirowi and many others, relies on Cameron for a sustenance that society has deemed them unworthy of receiving: respect, patience and even hope. I envy *his* patience, simply because I don't have it.

I expect more from the people around me and have no time for behaviour that pitches short of what ought to be expected from full-grown men. It's not purely about their crimes, though that is an undeniable part of many of them, but rather their inability to get through a mundane incarcerated life without creating unwanted trouble, or losing the excess weight they want to lose, or finishing court-mandated courses on time, or doing what needs to be done. Functioning; being a person who produces goodwill, or finishes their chores, or does whatever the thing is that's expected of them, rather than standing there expecting the world to come and apologise to them for their situation and give them something for nothing. I'm tired of being around hopeless people – some who know it, and some who don't – and it's psychologically draining to socialise with them when they are happily existing in prison without a life to return to, or plans to restart one. And that's why Cameron helps me too: lifting this burden of frustration which he also shares and discussing unapologetically our grand plans and lofty aspirations for the future; acknowledging all the potential in front of us. I feel Cameron does this for himself as much as for my benefit, and he unwinds about his seven-year journey – three years at trial and four already served in prison – and how he dreads but accepts the remaining two-and-a-half years he has to go before being released back to a family that's lost him for so long.

When I share these thoughts with him and point to his patience as something remarkable, he explains that it came slowly, and wraps it into a neat nautical metaphor.

"You're swimming against the rip-tide," he tells me, "and you need to realise no amount of effort will take you directly back to shore – if you try, you'll drown. You can let it take you further and further away from dry land, or you can swim sideways to slowly escape the current." I see his logic, but it seems more aptly applied to his pitched battles against legal injustice, or securing someone's parole, and leaves me wondering if I'm any better equipped to build more patience into the social relationships here when I feel overwhelmed by hapless mediocrity and often disgust for the other person. An arrogant position, no? I don't deliberately fight against every developing relationship here with a paedophile or a rapist, but I am conscious of not being easily swept out into the ocean where my sense of morality can weep away from entropy. I think I'm genuinely scared of what others will think of me. "What do you mean you *liked* them? Are *they* your friends?" Even mentioning the human side of Shaun Burke to my sister (Burke, as you would recall, brutally raped and attacked my sister's friend as they both slept in a share house one evening) made her flash with understandable anger. But I don't want to do something and say another: I need to try and find that piece of ground where I can plant a flag and cry loudly: "*Here!* This is where I stand." Maybe my answer lies in expanding Cam's metaphor; swimming between flags, or around a distant and dangerous buoy knowingly, rather than a single static moral position that cannot reconcile all of these feelings at the same time.

CHAPTER 28

Arthur and I are shooting a few hoops when Shaun Burke (serial rapist) lets out a god-almighty yell. He's standing around ten metres away and pointing at a brown snake that's sliding away from him, heading under a fence where the hot water system for the pod next door is located. The snake is well over a metre long, and it slid over Shaun's right foot as he was poking around in the small garden located in front of their pod, leaving Shaun ashen-faced and full of adrenalin. As a few others show up and start poking around to flush the serpent out, Shaun recounts the interaction when I notice he's finally received his new orthodontic teeth. He's also clean-shaven, and with his new teeth, he looks remarkably different to the goatee-wearing toothless vagrant of only a few days ago. He still has an unfortunate paunchy stomach and is rapidly going bald, but he's managed to transform himself into someone who doesn't look like he sleeps under a bridge and eats out of a garbage can. As he describes the size of the snake, a few people shake their heads in disbelief, and I'm forced to speak up and verify that it was indeed of the proportions described. A minute later the snake emerges from under the hot-water tank and slides under the building itself, giving some of the assembled onlookers the evidence they need. For some curious reason, Tom Johnstone (grubby and odious paedophile) rushes up to the guards' office and grabs Corrections Officer One Browne, who shows up and shrugs his shoulders at the problem in front of him. Why this group of Crafty, Thomo and Chappo decide to poke sticks and carry on like they've never seen a snake before seems odd. Their behaviour seems to feed some juvenile curiosity but only ends up portraying poor judgement to the bored onlookers.

Shortly, the small group dissipates to carry on with their day, and I'm left sitting at our wooden picnic table as Tom Johnstone starts discussing his legal case with a few others. As you'll recall, Tom is the former bus driver and public servant who I now learn molested a number of kids on his bus and was sentenced to ten years prison. He spent two years and $200,000 fighting his charges but knew he was going to be found guilty, and he nearly fainted when his lawyer told him at his sentencing hearing it could be fifteen years. After the verdict of ten years came down, he asked his lawyer about appealing the decision and was told he should accept his sentence and not risk getting hit harder. Tom recounts how the judge told his lawyer in a private sidebar that he wanted to "hammer his client", and thought he was a "disgusting man", which leaves me in silent agreement as Tom supposedly assumes we'll take his side in the matter. Tom clearly feels a real and genuine anger with how he was treated, but there is no self-reflection or admission of his own guilt that demonstrates an acknowledgement of the damage he's done. Even Shaun Burke will admit he deserved every single one of the thirty-six years he was sentenced to, but not so Tom. To make sure I understand his position I ask him if he pleaded guilty, and what he expected the verdict to be.

"Oh, I'm guilty," he says without a nano-second of reflection, "and I knew I would be found guilty too."

"So, you feel you received a crushing sentence?" I say.

"Yeah, of course; bloody Burns [the presiding judge] had it in for me from the start!"

"But you *were* guilty? . . ."

Tom makes his case passionately that the sentence (which could have also been heftier at fifteen years) was a personal attack on him, and I find it odd that he can't seem to reconcile in his mind that this is precisely what *any* sentence is. I'm not sure what he expects: the sentencing of a criminal *is* a personal statement on an individual's actions, and Tom seems to have some mistaken opinion that there is an impersonal formula for sentencing paedophiles like him. Enter the number of children, their ages, the type of molestation and frequency and hey presto – you get ten years jail! It's nothing like that, and the judge will look at these rapists and paedophiles and consider a range of mitigating or influencing factors: cooperation with authorities, contrition, recidivism, any personal history of being abused, but also specific and general deterrence, community safety and to meet community expectations. Perhaps Tom doesn't want to admit to this reality; that his sentence is a reflection of him, and not of a biased or broken judiciary. There is nowhere to hide when a judge is staring over their glasses and looking down on a criminal in the process of being sentenced. Tom's lack of contrition makes his already repugnant personality stink that little bit more, and I feel particularly sorry for his victims.

* * *

A new guard arrives down in our wing and I immediately sense a familiarity that I can't put my finger on. I ask another guard as offhandedly as I can muster what this other guard's name is, and have it confirmed that he's a former school friend of mine. I am sure he hasn't recognised me, and so decide to retreat to my room for the rest of the afternoon in case he suspects who I am and comes for a second look. I'm a special detainee – you'll recall, for reasons outside of my control – and having someone recognise me could cause a number of issues.

Shortly after, when I've convinced myself that this guard doesn't know who I am and that I've done a fantastic job of avoiding his scrutiny, I get a knock on my door and he appears. I invite him to come inside and quickly ask him if he knows who I am and what my background is. He tells me he does recognise me from school all of those years ago, and that he first recognised me here when I arrived in the prison eight months earlier. He also knows not to ask any questions about my circumstances, and that he's been told by the general manager to leave me well alone and not tell any other guards that he knows me. In some ways, I'm comforted when he explains all this; I don't need to scramble and make certain arrangements as a result. Do believe me – I want to tell you more so you can better understand, but it's just not within my power.

So little does my school friend know, that he takes the opportunity to lean in and ask me what the story is, and I can only stare back at him innocently and put my hands in the air. I can see through his eyes the whirring away of his own various conspiracy theories, and I diffuse the situation by promising that once I leave the prison, we will go for a beer and discuss everything. This will never happen, but it pricks the remaining tension between us, and he starts to ask how I'm going in here and if I need anything. I don't take his offer as anything improper: it seems more like a genuine question from a professional officer, and I thank him and tell him I'm fine. He's wearing a star on his shoulder (making him a level two officer, or simply 'CO2') and I tell him it suits him. He waves my compliment away with a smile and explains that he's only acting up for the day, and then busies himself looking at a photo on my wall. We chat for another couple of minutes and he explains that he and his partner have a baby (six months old) but asks that I don't mention it to anyone else in the wing, which I don't. As the conversation shifts onto my fellow detainees in the Women and Child Chasers, he asks how I'm tolerating living with "these people", and he hisses the words through his teeth, clearly wanting to use more vibrant language. I share a few concerns, some very real, but there's an impossible gap between us to try and explain these multi-dimensional predators to someone who only sees one dimension; someone who has closed himself off – both as a guard and newly minted father – to the criminals in this wing. We part with a firm handshake and a shared smile, and I'm left feeling oddly exposed in a world where I have layers of protection and purpose on top of who I really am, and I wonder how close I've come to being outed in a very detrimental way. But it's a bullet dodged, or not fired at all; only sliding noisily into the chamber and being pointed at me but nothing more. An uncomfortably held breath released, perhaps.

* * *

Pope Francis has issued an edict to the world that clergy members guilty of sexually abusing children should confess their crimes, which I assume means to law enforcement agencies and not simply to each other. The edict comes the same day that I watch a two-part historical documentary on the papacy that is pleasantly narrated by the actor Liam Neeson, and I have a chance to tell our resident priest, John Aitchison, that I have a 'selfie' with the Pope in the Vatican City. Now, truth be told, my photo is me in the foreground and the Pope standing by a window high above during his weekly Sunday sermon, but John seems impressed nonetheless as I describe it. When he asks me which Pope it was, my memory goes, and I can only crudely reply "that Nazi one", to which John frowns and tells me I'm referring to Josef Ratzinger, otherwise known as Pope Benedict XVI. I asked John if he'd heard about the incumbent Pope's edict, and he tells me has, throwing his arms in the air and saying in his slight British accent: "Oh well!" For the first time, I don't feel like letting him off the hook and I ask him if people will respond by confessing. He can only shrug and tell me that people are motivated by self-interest, and won't self-incriminate without a good reason, quoting Cardinal George Pell's health concerns and recent forthrightness with authorities.

"Ha! But he's escaped to the Vatican himself!" I say, shocked that he would hold Pell up as an example. John doesn't seem interested in chatting further (this is clearly cutting too close to the bone), and he shrugs again and smiles his genial priest's smile at me. Liam Neeson's soothing Irish voice tells me Pope Francis is the 166th person to be appointed in the role, and I can only wonder how many millions of innocent young children have surely been sexually abused and denied justice because of all that this powerful lineage represents. The judiciary stripped John Aitchison of his religious titles by convicting him, and he now sits in this prison, a shattered apostate without any remaining vestige of honour, his piety and efforts amounting to another signpost for the corruption of the church. But for every Father Aitchison, I suspect that ten or even twenty guilty members of the clergy remain at large, to say nothing of the hundreds of thousands (millions?) who throughout history perpetrated similar crimes against the youngest in their flocks. I'm not a religious person, and while I can appreciate the historical and even contemporary significance of religion to the world, that it still holds itself up as any bastion of morality leaves me puzzled and scratching my head. This is clearly not just a contemporary opinion: even in Dante's pre-renaissance *Inferno* (Canto XIX) is the papacy corrupted, with the Pilgrim and Virgil finding the tortured Pope Nicholas III waiting for his successors, Popes Boniface VIII and Clement V, to push him further down into lower Hell. Eternal torment for freely distributing ecclesiastical offices to family and confidants; mere simony! Surely Dante would have condemned the papacy to the bottom of Hell had he known about the extent of child sexual abuse. Or perhaps not? The protection of children from sexual predation is a far more contemporary obligation and one that had to break down Church doors to be heard, with all the major monotheistic religions still unapologetically anchored in antiquated bronze-age social values. Sure, *autres temps, autres moeurs*, but scripture and precedent are no longer an excuse for behaving contrary to the moral norms and values of today's enlightened age. I hope a few of the guilty priests out there take Pope Francis's advice and turn themselves in.

* * *

Back in the comfort of my pod of six, two weeks' worth of food arrives to cover us over the Christmas and New Year period, and we all store it away as best we can. I pack the three dozen or so meat portions into our freezer, playing a game of Tetris and squeezing it in with little room to spare. Bags of lamb, chicken thighs, sausages, beef and pork all fit in neatly, but the five or six frozen chickens are awkward in their rounded bulk and sit on top of everything else alongside some frozen vegetables. The other pods are fighting and arguing over fridge and freezer space, and are being forced to throw away produce that they can't agree should stay in. It's a debacle; one that we completely avoid given how well we all get along, and it sounds like the other pods will be facing additional tension when certain food items invariably run out before the next resupply in a fortnight. Brian Wilson seems to avoid most of the hard work, and when I leave the pod for a half hour he decides to go into my room and help himself to my television remote. He has some issue with his and is trying to problem-solve whatever the trouble is, but when he hands me back my remote (which is when I realise he's gone into my room) I tell him with obvious annoyance to ask my permission next time. His immediate response is to tell me that I wasn't in my room to be asked, and therefore implies it couldn't be helped.

"Then you wait," I say.

He shuffles out after his scolding and Dave Will, who vehemently hates Brian (I don't hate him – his poor hygiene and bad hearing simply annoy me) pops his head in and unleashes a tirade against him – not because Brian molested his own children and grandchildren, but because he is a grub, and there is something in Dave's background of running a cleaning company, and the spartan way he lives (we both joke together that we live like Japanese priests – neat and minimalistic) that simply and decisively irritates him. Brian's room is a complete shambles; it's almost as if the guards have gone through and conducted a detailed search, scattering things here and there, and his requirement to wear adult nappies causes his room to emit foul odours that are pungently unmaskable. This same smell wafts off his clothing and person at mealtimes and around the pod.

Look, he's an old man, and while I don't blame him for this fact, his ability to make a mess even brings the slovenly Jason Dodd to tell him to pick up after himself, or wipe down the kitchen benches – Brian

Wilson is the geriatric slob no one wants to live with. But he tries, and this makes me want to be more patient and give him a chance. He's currently experimenting with baking biscuits and making a French onion dip for Christmas lunch next week, and the mess he's been making recently is a result of this process. Dave dismisses these efforts unceremoniously: "I won't eat anything that fucking *grot* touches," is too hard a line for me, and so I sample Brian's baking efforts and comment on them when he asks me how they are. I feel sorry for Brian because he's so widely despised, and it's a feeling I wish I could eradicate in some way so I could just brush him aside like the others do, and not worry about him, in the way that I don't worry about many others. But there's something about how vulnerable Brian is that makes me feel oddly protective of him, and while I have my limits with him when he does something silly like go into my room without permission, to me he's just the lonely old man without a single friend here. But then he's also the shitty old paedophile too, so I just don't know how I should feel. It's this same tired old issue of contradicting feelings that has no easy answer, except to bury my head in these pages and pour out the mess of words you see. Being an empathetic, moralistic and judgemental arsehole is hard work.

CHAPTER 29

Jason Dodd (neighbour; oafish rapist) cannot find suitable accommodation that would allow the sentence administration board to grant him parole, and it's an issue that's now plagued him for six months. Indeed, his civilian-appointed case manager, a pleasant enough fellow named Phil Hawkins, had already secured a place for him to live at a caravan park, but his parole application was denied as the new address was located too close to a pub. This wouldn't be an issue for most people, but as Jason was heavily intoxicated when he raped his victim, the board quite reasonably thought the proximity to a pub made the caravan park unsuitable.

Everybody is outraged at this and tries to console Jason about it, telling him that the system is corrupt and he'd received an unfair ruling. As I'm listening to this, I have an odd sense of walking against a large crowd of people while second-guessing if I'm heading in the right direction after all. There is a very real sense in the wing that a prisoner who has completed the lower end of their sentence (i.e. the non-parole period) has the right to be immediately released, and that serving the parole period of their sentence in jail is some violation of their human rights. (It isn't.)

Some here have resigned themselves to serving the full period of their sentence, not wanting to complete courses like the adult sex offenders program or to live under restrictive parole conditions. This includes Tony Wyatt, MJ Stratford and Alwyn Baume, who have all accepted this fate, but the majority want to leave as soon as they're able to. Many of these people do the right thing and complete the courses, stay out of trouble, and secure work and accommodation for their release, but Jason doesn't seem to want to take any responsibility for his situation. This, then, I find perplexing; Jason admits to raping this poor girl and often jokes about how many other things he got away with, and no one else around me like Cameron, Arthur or others seem to think that the system has done anything but miscarried in their decision on his parole. Cameron thinks that the government housing department is leaving Jason to linger in jail instead of finding a subsidised house for him, and Jason has taken on the aura of a persecuted human rights advocate, which is making him insufferable to be around. When I mention that no one owes him anything – particularly a home and a job – he unwinds on an odd rant that includes his perceptions of government corruption, nepotism and how he's being screwed as the ultimate victim. Once he finishes, I'm shocked at how far away he's removed himself from his circumstances.

"Jason, you raped a sixteen-year-old girl!" I tell him. I'm a little surprised that the words come out so easily – raising people's sexual offences in front of them is taboo in the Women and Child Chasers.

"Yeah but I've served my time already for those fuckwits!" he fires back.

"You haven't; you've still got a parole period on your sentence."

"Well, *they* won't find me somewhere to live!"

"It's up to *you* to find a place to live."

"Well, how am I supposed to do it from in here?" He seems exasperated but is still missing the point of my own outrage.

"Phil's doing his best for you. No one owes you anything here – it's all on you; don't you understand that?" I say.

At this stage, Jason swears at me and walks out of the pod for a cigarette, and I feel he's heard nothing of what I was trying to convey. He seems to have genuinely removed his act of depravity – his raping of this innocent young girl – from his current circumstances and doesn't seem able to process it intelligibly. It's perhaps a combination of denial and shame, coupled with a lack of honest self-evaluation. For me, this makes his crimes worse; he has learned *nothing* from his punishment it seems, and he's prepared to blame anything and anyone else but doesn't seem able to look in the mirror and admit he's his own worst enemy. The reality is that the dominoes started falling when he pushed the first one, and no matter how scary or overwhelming he finds the resulting tsunami of consequences, *he* is to blame. *He* chose to rape the girl; to rip away her innocence without thinking about the consequences to her. In some ways, Jason doesn't deserve his parole, as he has apparently learned nothing, and I only wish he would honestly admit to the sentence administration board what he's said to me today. Jason Dodd: the remorseless and callous rapist who is also my oafish and lazy neighbour. I cannot hide my disgust at knowing how little he's atoned.

Coincidentally, Phil Hawkins, Jason's caseworker, is assigned to me when mine is moved onto a policy role elsewhere in the jail. Karly Yates has seen me a half-dozen times or so since I arrived, and we always chat and have an enjoyable five or ten minutes before she departs to the next person. The caseworkers help the detainees to complete external administration or help manage other aspects of their lives they understandably cannot manage from inside the prison, and I never really had any work for Karly; instead, we would often joke about her workload of managing fifty (fifty!) other detainees across the prison. Our interactions with civilian staff are limited to these caseworkers, the medical staff, the education staff and our librarian, Belinda. They all wear a special belt with a red panic button, and they're required to press it in acknowledgement as it buzzes every five or ten minutes; the idea being that instead of making a conscious act to press it during an emergency (presumably eliciting a violent response from an already aggravated prisoner), one simply has to leave it alone long enough to activate it. Of course, there is also a way to activate it by holding down the button (if circumstances permit), but the constant buzzing and acknowledgement is a regular and odd occurrence when discussing anything with the civilian employees here.

I had an embarrassingly 'gronky' moment with one of these civilian staff, and feel it was one of my more poorly behaved moments in jail. I was taken to see one of the prison doctors for a minor foot issue and was sitting in his office as he came in and looked up my file. He suddenly stood up and left to speak with the nurses, asking loudly enough for me to hear, "Who is he?" and "Why was he sent to me?" In the room with me was another man, perhaps in his fifties or sixties, and wearing the blue polo shirt of a remandee. I turned to him and cursed the doctor, saying something along the lines of: "This idiot doesn't even know who I am! This place is a joke," when the doctor returned to the office. He apologised for the confusion and then asked if I wouldn't mind if the new doctor listened in, as he was doing his induction, and motioned to the blue polo shirt I'd spoken to a moment earlier. The blue polo shirt revealed itself to be tucked in, and he was wearing a panic alarm belt and staring at me oddly. I felt embarrassed that I'd cursed to this doctor about his colleague, and, coupled with my Van Dyke facial hair, realised I had come across as precisely the kind of disrespectful low-level gronk I personally despised. To make matters worse, the doctor was perfectly efficient and helped me with my issue, leaving me with a smile as I stood and walked out.

* * *

Alwyn Baume, who less than four weeks into his new accommodation has already driven his roommate Ali (Lebanese Papa Smurf) out of his room, is now complaining to Ray Layton (ponytail) that the common area fans are too loud. He's turning them off constantly, despite the temperature being thirty-five degrees, and Ray has finally confronted him, telling him that he's "going to cave his head in" if he keeps causing issues and that people in the pod are already sick of him. It's a remarkable effort by Alwyn to so quickly alienate the people around him, but he's used his manipulative tactics to secure a single room again, albeit with a spare bunk that risks new conflict with whomever they bring into the wing to occupy it. Dave Will (tattoos; mohawk; neighbour) sits at our table for dinner giggling to himself about the confrontation he witnessed, and how Alwyn looked shocked at receiving the verbal spray from Ray that he did. Alwyn again goes to see Cameron and spends long periods talking with him about the current issues, returning four or five times the next day. Cameron relays that Alwyn wants to be moved to a single room up in 'management', which is the solitary confinement cells usually reserved for punitive stays of twenty-eight days or longer. With at least ten years left on his sentence, this would be an unlikely solution for any normal detainee to seek out, but then Alwyn Baume is the isolated oddball who would make it work. However, the corrections staff don't want to reward his bad behaviour and give him what he wants, and so Alwyn is forced to reconcile the fact that he must live nicely with others in this prison.

The following day, we hear that Bill Scheeren (Dutch herb gardener; former scoutmaster) has been moved into a new pod to escape Ray Layton, and now occupies the room with John Aitchison (paedophile priest) that Neil Sirowi left vacant when he was deported a week earlier. This leaves Alwyn Baume free to occupy Bill's old room, which – with a single bed only – means a new arrival in the wing won't have to share a room with him. It's phenomenal that these cantankerous old paedophiles can't get along, although I'll admit the wildcard entry of Alwyn Baume has shaken everything up to a point where tensions have boiled over.

Alwyn continues his visits to Cameron and seeing him back in our own remote pod so often starts to wear on my patience. My own issues with Alwyn are raw enough that I tell him he's no longer welcome in our pod, and that if he wishes to see Cameron as the wing delegate, he can wait until Cameron leaves or send someone in to fetch him. He dismisses me and laughs a crooked and evil laugh, and I have to walk right up to him and confront him, telling him I'm not joking, and I don't want him in our pod under any circumstances. This leaves him silent and he retreats back to his room, and when I tell the others in my pod about it, they nod in bored acceptance of an issue that won't seem to die.

* * *

As summer encroaches and the days become hotter, if people want to do anything outside it has to be in the early morning or before we are locked in of an evening. For me this means the evening, and so a bounce of the basketball with Arthur and our hoop fills thirty minutes, or else I'll grab a book and walk to the small grassy knoll that teasingly overlooks the perimeter fence and try reading for an hour – or until someone comes and bothers me. There seems to be no unwritten rule or individual sense that people have to leave those happily engaged in solitary enjoyment alone. I've often been happily reading as Dave Cashin, Bill Scheeren or any of the other thirty-six paedophiles or rapists come and join me to start chatting about whatever is on their mind. I understand it: people are bored, or "time-rich" as Taylor (murderer; language student) tells me in the library, and so there is a complicit agreement that anyone will stop what they're doing to engage in a conversation.

And so, the grassy knoll is about as remote a place that one can find without sitting somewhere odd: perhaps tucked out of sight behind our greenhouse, or behind one of the pods, but it still draws someone in. As I'm comfortably seated and five minutes into the middle of *Atlas Shrugged* Kenny will approach me and talk incessantly about how serene it all is, missing the tidy irony that he's stripping me of the very serenity he's extrapolating in fulsome detail. I concede defeat and snap my book shut and tell Kenny about my conversation with Jason, and how I find it hard to process that he won't accept his own guilt. Kenny explains how everyone is on a different journey, and that no one can be expected to either understand or see the sense of justice in another's case: so why bother? It's the kind of sensible philosophical position Kenny lives by, and in some ways, I appreciate that he offers me a way out of having to weigh my conscience against Jason's earlier remarks. But I don't want a way out and I tell Kenny that Jason *is* wrong and that he *should* atone for what he's done. Simply serving the non-parole period of his sentence seems inadequate in his case. Kenny responds as he does: with silence. He can talk so much about so little, and then find himself speechless when asked to discuss something specific like this. But I don't know if his silence is contemplative or self-protective (it doesn't seem to be an empty silence), and when it's clear that he doesn't want to muse on the guilt and ownership of Jason raping a sixteen-year-old girl, the silence wafts along until Kenny starts up about preparations for Christmas, which is in a few days' time.

The next fifteen minutes is more lightly filled with recipes for barbecue sauce, cakes, pastries and speculation over who will come to our all-inclusive wing gathering, which is being organised by Navin Edwin (former Indian diplomat; long hair; child pornographer). The invitations that Navin produces and disseminates for each pod are printed in the most wonderful calligraphy, and I find myself staring at ours from point-blank range, trying to convince myself that it's actually some computer-printed script and not from the hand of a mere mortal. Such is its beauty that, from a few paces further back, I could almost be convinced I'm staring at a copy of the Magna Carta; but instead of any wafting late thirteenth-century Old English legalise, I'm being warmly invited to Christmas Day lunch in our wing's common area, and politely asked to bring along some treats or snacks for the others to share. Although I find myself in prison for this holiday season, it's beginning to feel a lot like Christmas.

CHAPTER 30

I've spent more than a few holiday seasons away from home. I've had Christmas in Timor Leste, the Middle East and Europe, and so Christmas away from home – away from Australia – is less the exception and more the rule for me in the past ten years. This is, however, my first holiday period in prison, and it's interesting to note the contrasts of extreme melancholy and indifferent apathy from various people here with me. Understandably, the parents of young children are quite flat; people like Cameron Tully, Craig Stevens (hand-sanitiser drinking; Ford Anglia back tattoo) and others. Then the Kenny Johnsons, Jason Dodds and some of the others seem immune to the fuss being made around the date, except to say they're happily anticipating a Christmas lunch of turkey provided by the prison kitchen. Most detainees are split into one of these two camps, but there are exceptions: Bill Scheeren (herb gardener; former scoutmaster) seems to resent the date and explains that his family has always made a large fuss, and being the only older member without children he's never enjoyed the family gatherings. He's told his extended family this, he tells me, and that he slowly withdrew from attending their gatherings each year. Once he was charged with sexually abusing a child, his family stopped trying to involve him.

On Christmas Eve after our pods are locked for the evening, I find myself sitting on our patio with my neighbours Cameron, Jason, Dave, Chappo and even the infirm Brian, and I listen in to the various conversations unfolding around me. Cameron has a guitar and is singing songs we all join in with – he spent years moonlighting as a pub singer and musician, and so he launches into these amazingly credible renditions of songs with ease. Between songs, Jason and Chappo recount their time in other jails, and how they are both still coming to terms with being a 'pest', or sexual offender. While Jason threw the same insults out that he now receives as a convicted rapist, Chappo admits to deliberately targeting sexual offenders for violence when he was in Goulburn jail; a time when that jail was known as the 'killing fields'. Dave, as someone who is not a sexual offender, jumps in and explains how he's not interested in anyone's crimes in this wing, and that a person would go crazy learning about the depravity people have been convicted of. "It's best not to know," he explains. It's a prescient comment and sound advice from the best friend of Ray Layton; someone who used his own children to produce child pornography.

It's pleasant on our patio singing and chatting away, and I try my best to steer the conversation to non-prison topics, which seems to only last a short two minutes, after which we're straight back to drugs, violence or something equally banal. Mostly, Dave and Chappo swap anecdotes and laugh at overlapping mutual friends, describing how they knew a certain person and wondering who is up to what these days. In some ways, it's nice to see these two connect on such a deep level, but then the world of drugs, violence and other ill-doings seems so foreign and unknown to me that I can only sit and stare out of the grilled patio windows and watch the congregation of rabbits and ducks that visit us each evening. I throw a few slices of bread to the ducks and try to tempt one of the bolder rabbits in with a carrot, and eventually, we all retire to our rooms for the remainder of Christmas Eve. Around midnight, just as it's turning over into Christmas proper, a car starts a lengthy burnout a couple of hundred metres away in the main prison parking lot and is soon followed by some horn blasts. It's hard not to smile and even laugh at this salute to a detained friend somewhere in the prison, who most likely knows who the driver is and was foretold of the noisy action and time of execution.

The following morning, we exchange handshakes and wish each other well, and I decide to go and find a quiet place to read before our mid-afternoon Christmas lunch. The grassy knoll is unoccupied, so I set myself up and lounge in the warm sun, reclining back into the soft grass and lazily watching the clouds float past, unsuccessfully trying to discern shapes from the fluffy cumuli. I would prefer to be with my family right now, watching the children rip open presents, shouting and yelling in their blissful youth, while I open another cold beer and look on, remembering what it was like as a child myself. Sitting down for Christmas lunch and being with the most important people in my life; sharing a meal; making jokes; openly giving my love and receiving theirs. I don't want to be in jail today, which sounds oddly juvenile to admit, yet I'm calm laying on my back outside enjoying the simple pleasures that are forgotten in a busy adult life. Simple pleasures like walking through grass barefooted, or deliberately through a *chut-chut-chutting* sprinkler, and enjoying the cold splashing water on a hot day.

Nearby birds are singing; today, they're not competing with the cacophony of a busy highway and the sounds are lovely and remind me of my childhood. There are little blue-headed superb fairy-wrens flitting about and chasing each other, their little vertical tails and vibrant colours on show. Smaller still are the brown white-browed scrubwrens, which are in larger numbers buzzing here and there around the garden. Then the others: common starlings, grey strike-thrushes, crows, wood ducks, magpies, galahs and cockatoos, and even after a while a solitary brown goshawk orbiting high above on a thermal. All here on Christmas Day. When I sit up and look at the perimeter fence perhaps seventy-five metres in front of me, I notice all of the kangaroos, never out of sight of prison, all congregating right up against it and trying to make use of the limited shade. There are about twenty or thirty either laying down or standing up. A few look in at me, and I wonder for the first time if these animals unknowingly enjoy a wicked irony: looking into a zoo of captive humans, held back from their natural habitat by fences and zookeepers. Poachers came for us, stripping away our liberty and putting us on display. Only two years ago in Asia, I mocked an orangutan for its captive state after it had picked up a clomp of dirt and hurled it at me, hitting me squarely in the back (a begrudgingly good shot – imagine my relief that it wasn't faeces!) With all of these free animals around me, surely my bad karma has returned?

Happily, no one interrupts my relaxing afternoon on the grassy knoll, and I start to notice the first few people bringing food into our wing's common room. Once it's clear that the majority of people are there, I stand up and brush off the grass, and head in myself. The room is perhaps half the size of a tennis court, with a low, angled roof that increases in height towards the other rooms and the guards' office for our wing. The walls are white brick and the doors all a vibrant orange with vertical viewing windows. A ping pong table is folded into a corner where two dozen encyclopaedias line a shelf, and stacks of grey chairs are being pulled apart for the thirty or so detainees that have come for the Christmas meal. Four tables are pushed together on one side with food, plates and cutlery busily lining its length, and around four or five single tables are each ringed by the same number of chairs around the remaining space in the room. Everyone is smiling and chatting, and Navin Edwin is chatting with Cameron and discussing their efforts to put this event together. Navin opens the lunch with a few words, not unlike Kenny Johnson two months earlier on Thanksgiving Day, and tells us that our detained status should not stop us from gathering and celebrating today. He receives a round of applause and then asks our disgraced priest John Aitchison to say a blessing. John is unprepared but quickly reaches into his bag of well-worn tricks and says something suitably non-denominational, smiling and welcoming people to start loading their plates.

As I'm the last to arrive, I stand by myself in the corner at the back of the room and observe this group of men interacting. I've now spent eight months here in this wing and have come to know many of the men here very well, and a few others less so but still well enough to say hello and share a few polite words. Here are the paedophiles and rapists of the Women and Child Chasers; reviled members of society and rejected by even their incarcerated others as not worthy of respect or status. John Aitchison is sitting cross-legged on the floor nearby and remarks that it's not a very dignified position for him to adopt, but he is reassured by Bill Scheeren that it's egalitarian and thus okay. The priest and the scoutmaster, chattering away. Bill is hovering over some pizzas he's made, but a few people are complaining about how spicy the base is, despite Cameron warning Bill about it that morning. The priest and the scoutmaster are joined by the university professor, as Arthur Hoyle sits down with his plate and enjoys his food. All three men are in their late-sixties and look like an odd trio of professionals who might gather together for a fishing trip.

There is MJ Stratford sitting with Dan Burman, Dave Cashin, Ray Layton and Jeffrey Lee, smiling as Ray tells some loud story which is making the others laugh, no doubt with some horrible racist or sexist angle to his punch line. They look so normal, and today are very much that, no matter that it's the worst of each of them that has brought them together for their meal today. Not one of these varied men would likely know each other outside of prison, and somehow that reality exacerbates the oddity of watching them sit and chat together. Then there is Kenny Johnson, Glen Vandavord, Jason Dodd, Tony Wyatt and Tom Johnstone all sitting at another table. A younger grouping, for sure, but still an odd group of men who share no obvious similar traits except a predilection for sexually preying on children. Tom and Glen, in particular, are making gluttons of themselves, filling their plates with cake, pastries and candy rather than anything more substantive; I overhear Kenny pointing out the fact to Glen, who seems embarrassed to be caught out.

Shaun Burke, Peter Middleton, Dave Adams, Rashid Abu'uh and Shane Williams share another table, but they seem to be eating silently and enjoying their food far more than each other's company. Arthur comments that Peter is having a particularly bad day, given his encroaching dementia and the fact his family has all but abandoned him to his fate here in the jail. It's sad watching this vague old man hunched over his paper plate of food, knowing that he's spending his first Christmas period like this, after what was presumably a life full of richer experiences with family and friends. I don't know what Peter Middleton's crimes are, but he seems better placed somewhere designed to care for the very old and infirm. Even the second most decrepit person here, my own pod's Brian Wilson, looks positively sprightly when compared to Peter. Brian himself sits and eats alone, his colostomy bag and history of antagonising others in the wing ensuring his enforced solitude. Owen Crockett and Brad Weir are standing and chatting over their food, and only a few metres away John Gould and Juan Cruz are doing the same.

Crafty and Thomo don't join in and can be seen outside pacing up and down the paved tennis court we have; they don't venture in because of their skittishness around some of the older detainees here who can't stand their petty criminal personalities. I pop my head outside and wish them a Merry Christmas, shaking their hands and telling them they are welcome inside if they want (they both decline). And so, I return to the common room and help myself to a plate full of food, enjoying a wonderful spread that nearly everyone has contributed to in some way, and I find a nook to sit and chat with Arthur. It's an odd but very merry gathering, and after about ten minutes John Aitchison starts up a solo rendition of 'We Wish you a Merry Christmas' and sings through three or four verses from memory, with a few others joining in the chorus.

I've spent eight months living with and around these men and seeing them all gathered and sharing each other's forced company today feels oddly like some church gathering, or perhaps even an exclusive club for men of high social ranking. But precisely the opposite is true: this is the club for the *lowest* socially ranked group of men in any society; not only criminals but sexual criminals who have committed the most abhorrent offending. As I squint through the smiles and jolly conversations, I notice it's hard to imperceptibly come to the conclusion that these men *are* all rapists and paedophiles; men who have preyed on others, including young children, for their own sexual gratification. But I know who they are. I want to be repulsed by each and every one of them, but I'm too overcome by the personalities and memories of recent interactions where I have seen the good side of them, and I no longer have an instinctive reaction like pulling away from an odorous smell. I could ignore all of these predators and retreat in seclusion like Alwyn Baume has done, but it's more realistic to face them as a fellow detainee.

I don't know how much longer I'll have to live in this wing, but I hope that I can continue with my life in five or six months' time. I want to process these experiences and reconcile these relationships to a finer absolute than I can now. I'm awash with humanity: both through the physical presence of these men and even the corrections staff, but there is also a metaphysical ether of their crimes and the victims that pervades the entire place, and no matter how hard I try to push that intangible ether away, it lingers and sticks to everything and every interaction. I live with paedophiles and rapists and I cannot escape this reality.

* * *

The Christmas lunch is winding down and I walk towards one of the orange doors linking the room to the main corridor and out past the guards' office, instead of the door opposite where all my neighbours are currently pouring out of and into the wide-open yard of the wing. Cameron is one of the last to leave the room, and he's smiling and carrying an armful of dirty dishes, happy that his flock has had a good afternoon together celebrating Christmas. When I get to the door, I grab the handle and twist it, but find it's unusually locked today.

This is not an exit.

EPILOGUE

Sir de pa lowara tega kegda,
Praday watan de paki nishta balakhtona.

O Wayfarer! Rest your head on the
stony cobblestone. It is a foreign land
– not the city of your kings.

Pashto couplet

A LEAP OF FAITH

In some ways, I feel the first thing I should do is offer an apology. I've been told that humanising the inhuman is deplorable in its own right, and even my own sister, whose female friend was brutally assaulted and raped while she slept soundly under the same roof, chastised me about discussing my experiences of being detained with her friend's attacker: Shaun Burke. It traumatised her so much that she woke up one morning from a troubled sleep and told me never to discuss Burke again, and that she would never read this book.

I respect her wishes.

If you read this and feel similarly about someone I've written about, either in how that person has victimised you or someone you know, or perhaps even how I've written judgementally about someone you care about, then I am sorry. I haven't approached this book in a premeditated manner, seeking out these men or this experience, and in some ways, I also feel like I've been subjected to a range of experiences and interactions that have been deeply confronting. I'm not a sexual offender, and I am not a victim. I am an unwilling prisoner among these men and have been subjected to my experiences in a way that I have had trouble processing at times. If you won't accept my apology for any offence I've caused or wounds I've re-opened, then perhaps you'll forgive me for the cathartic journey of documenting this experience; something I've needed to personally undertake for my own sanity.

I don't consider that who I am as a person has been important in this journey; I've not divulged a lot about myself to minimise distracting you from the men I live with. I do consider myself a perfectly ordinary person with the same sense of right and wrong as you. You'll recall that I'm a former military officer who served in Afghanistan; I have a sister, and I've travelled to certain parts of the world and speak a second language. Other than that, I am a visitor to another planet. Perhaps Dante's Pilgrim descending into the Inferno of Hell, but without a guiding Virgil to explain the journey and help me understand where I am. The opening lines of Dante Alighieri's *The Divine Comedy Volume 1: Inferno* (Translated by Mark Musa [1983]) feel familiar to my own story:

Midway along the journey of our life
I woke to find myself in a dark wood,
for I had wandered off from the straight path.

How I entered there I cannot say,
I had become so sleepy at the moment
when I first strayed, leaving the path of truth;

Midway along the journey of our life: In the Middle Ages, life was often thought of as a journey, a pilgrimage. Dante was thirty-five years old, which is one-half of man's Biblical life span of seventy years. I am not far off that, and I couldn't escape the comparison of The Pilgrim losing himself at this stage of his life.

How I entered there I cannot say: you'll also note that I haven't divulged what brought me to prison. If you are frustrated by this, you're not alone, and if I could have explained this aspect of my journey I would have, despite it being outside of my power and having little relevance to my observations. I am, without hyperbole or egotism, a special prisoner for reasons I cannot unravel. It may, therefore, be hard for you to trust my moral compass, and perhaps this is an unfair leap of faith I demand from the reader at the outset.

If I am comparable to The Pilgrim, then I believe Cameron Tully has come the closest to filling the role of my Virgil, but while the long-dead poet belongs in the first circle of limbo, Cameron cannot claim such innocence. I've often wondered about how much I've fallen under the spell of my super-charismatic neighbour, and if in some way I am a victim to a type of Stockholm-syndrome that's clouded my judgement. If anything, I feel that it's Cameron Tully who represents the best example of a person I've truly had trouble reconciling my feelings with, and I want to like him far more than I want to or care to like anyone else in this wing. But I also see him as an odd exception and don't feel that reconciling my conscience regarding him will carry over into an answer that fits anyone else. I'm guilty of this contradiction in my analysis, but I cannot condemn Cameron just as much as I cannot give him a moral pardon, and this leaves me wondering how I can so ruthlessly dislike the others with similar offences.

Thus, there is no tidy syllogism or solution to my ultimate conundrum: can one accept the humanity of these men and not lose oneself in the process? I'm sorry if you've arrived here without me falling decisively in one direction or the other, and I still feel like a spinning top when I search for something simple myself. However, what I've learned *has* changed how I view my situation and these men, and these may be illuminating in place of a more simple and desirable single truth.

Firstly, so many of these men are victims in their own right, and I've been shocked at how real the circular nature of sexual offending can be. It truly breaks my heart to think that there are victims today, coping so badly with the unforgivable wrongs visited on their innocence by abusers, that they will in time turn into predators themselves. It's not an unfair assertion to make; no more than it is wrong to forgive the men I live with simply *because* they have been abused themselves. The insidiousness of sexual predation is that it can be generations-deep in the harm it causes. The impact and compounding harm of institutionalised sexual abuse is an unforgivably worse evil – far worse than I realised before this journey began – and it's clear that Australia has much more work ahead of it on top of the symbolic 2018 apology.

Secondly, time is not an excuse or a healing elixir: historical crimes are as barbaric as the ones being perpetrated while you read this. There is a common premise among the men I live with that historical crimes are more forgivable, simply because the passage of five, ten, twenty or even fifty years means the perpetrator is a different person now. I wholly reject this premise: those that hide behind the banner of historical offences are inflicting an additional injury to their victims; victims who have also carried their burdens *without* justice for years.

Thirdly, evil exists. This may be the least revelatory point, but I have now seen it in the eyes of men here. Men who have lured children and women into premeditated sexual violence without a second of hesitation. This evil sits behind the eyes of both the cold and unfeeling shark-like predators, and the charismatic chameleons who hide their depravity through high-functioning sociability and emotional intelligence. In many ways, the latter category scares me more and makes me personally fearful for the vulnerable people in my life.

Fourthly, these men are as human as you and I, and some deserve to continue their own lives, having not only served their court-appointed sentences, but also atoned for their crimes through contrition and an acceptance of the evil they've wrought. This may be the hardest aspect for wider society to admit: that rapists and paedophiles who are released from prison deserve a place among us. They do, I believe, with the appropriate tight controls in place around how they can or cannot interact with the most vulnerable people in our society.

And lastly, on reflection, I believe I'm truly a better person for having undergone this journey. In some ways, this confronting exposure to the darkest of our own species has been illuminating, and my greatest fear has been unrealised: the fear that my morality would be pervaded or corrupted by an evil sickness, or that I would compromise my own integrity and excuse the severity of their heinous crimes. Instead, I feel a tempering and tightening of my moral armour has taken place, and an acknowledgement that insidious evil can hide behind warm humanity – and vice versa. For most of the men here, both exist in parallel, and it's impossible to accept one without acknowledging the other.

A SHORT STORY

In December 2018 our indefatigable prison librarian Belinda conceived of and ran a creative writing competition with the assistance of Australian author Julian Davies, and three months later I was informed my humble entry had taken out first prize. As this book captures my experiences in prison, I felt it appropriate to include this submission here for completeness (and perhaps to satisfy my own vanity). Thus herein is my short story titled *The Star of Gallantry*.

It is a work of fiction.

Witness J

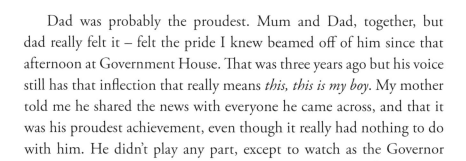

Dad was probably the proudest. Mum and Dad, together, but dad really felt it – felt the pride I knew beamed off of him since that afternoon at Government House. That was three years ago but his voice still has that inflection that really means *this, this is my boy*. My mother told me he shared the news with everyone he came across, and that it was his proudest achievement, even though it really had nothing to do with him. He didn't play any part, except to watch as the Governor

General pinned the Star of Gallantry on my chest that sunny afternoon in Yarralumla. It felt like I was receiving it for someone else, that I was a surrogate, and somehow not worthy; but no, it was my name on the citation. My war in Afghanistan.

I left the army after I got back from my deployment and worked for a few months doing odd jobs here and there. Nothing ever lasted long but I preferred to keep moving and doing new work, never really getting to know people long enough for them to want to know about my background, or ask me about Afghanistan. Over a bottle of whiskey in a rented apartment, I would convince myself I was scared of them wanting to know too much, and pry into a background that was a confusing knot of good and bad, but that wasn't it. I was scared they *wouldn't* care, that they wouldn't want to ask me, not because they didn't understand, or didn't feel they were allowed to, but that they simply thought it was boring. So I avoided people where I could, driving around just taking odd jobs where I found them, and settling into hovels that shamed some of the barracks rooms I'd occupied as a soldier.

'So, you were in the army?' people ask. 'Afghanistan? Wow, how was that?' I'd hear. Most people are tactful and know what to ask, but then some ask *that* question. 'So, did you kill anyone?' It is either asked with a wry grin by someone who doesn't understand how preciously fragile life is, or it was asked with a scorn by someone who thought you were the personification of evil, and that killing was a personal pleasure. It most certainly is not.

What do you say when someone asks you if you've killed someone? 'Yeah, sure – it's great to get a confirmed kill. A clean kill. The more the merrier!' someone might say, but I never find any words or just say 'no'. I could tell you that there aren't *clean kills*, and that all death in war is somehow tainted with the evil wrongness of warfare, but it's not true. Clean kills – good kills – do exist. Afghanistan is a land of big boy's rules: you pick up a weapon, you accept that you make yourself a target, and if you're killed, well, *big boy's rules*. If you're caught digging in an improvised explosive device and someone fires a missile at you, well then you played your hand and lost. All's fair in love and war.

But when the farmer who has toiled his rusty land for decades decides to escape the heat of the afternoon sun, and fixes an aqueduct at night when it's cooler, is then vaporised by a hellfire missile because someone thought he was digging in a road-side bomb, how do you make sense of that? When the patrol goes there the next day; when the viscous coppery metallic blood has already dried and blackened in the hot sun the farmer tried to escape, and it's clear he *was* fixing an aqueduct – is it our fault? Or is it just *the war*? At the site of this agricultural murder a stoic son comes up to the patrol, and tells us matter of factly his father told us not to harm him, and that he would be digging at night to escape the hot sun. Our captain explains *no one* told him this, and that he doesn't know what the son's talking about, but another patrol explains that he did tell them the day before, and they forget to put it in their patrol report. There are good kills, and there are bad kills.

I mostly drive around now in my spare time; just sitting in my car and aimlessly wandering around the town or city I find myself in. I'll pull up to a lake, or the ocean, and just sit there feeling both heavier and lighter than I ever have before in my life, and I'll picture having a conversation about Afghanistan with someone who asks me the right questions. Mostly they just listen, and allow me to unwind about the experience in a way that seems to firstly strip away the physical encumbrances of war. I'll talk about the rifle I carried, the ACOG-RMR sight on it, the *Night Aiming Device* attachment on top, and how I load tracer bullets into thirty-round magazines at the start and the end. The radios attached to my armour – both a smaller *Soldier Personal Radio*, and the *M-BITR* for encrypted longer distance communications. Maps: 1:25k for the bigger ones, and 1:5k for close in identification of the buildings we're raiding that day. Pens, grease pencils, hand grenades, smoke grenades, M72 rockets, M18 claymores, F3 minelabs, knives, spare batteries, night-vision goggles, biometric enrolment equipment, pistols, pen flares, patrol cameras, torches, zip-ties, tourniquets, ammonium nitrate test kits to detect fertiliser for bomb making, x-spray for detecting the same residue on the hands of the Afghans we come across, high value target cards, range cards, water, food, nomex gloves, multi-cam uniforms, ballistic glasses, helmets, and ceramic plates in our chest webbing.

It's heavy – all of it, and so are our tactics of walking through the lush green of the irrigated Afghan valleys, armed to the teeth and looking for a fight. We fool ourselves that we're experts in COIN: counter-insurgency tactics, and that we know the Afghans better than Alexander the Great, Genghis Khan, the British, or the Russians, who all came before us in this graveyard of empires. We can explain to you how the *pashtuni* tribal line splits one way into the *hotaki* and *tokhi ghilzai* branch, and another way into the convoluted *durrani* and *tareen* branch, but we can't listen to one farmer who specifically warned us he would be digging an aqueduct and would we please not vaporise him.

We don't listen. We wade through the flowering pomegranate and almond trees, or marvel at the shimmering rhubarb or pistachio orchards, smiling and waving as wary shepherds cajole their *markhor*, *urial* and *argali* sheep with long twisting horns and glutinous rumps. There are braying donkeys and fluttering green bulbuls, all living their lives peacefully around our patrol. We bring violence into this garden of Eden and expect the last word in any argument. Nothing our enemy can tell us about the inviolability of self-determination will send us home early from this patrol of death. We seek confrontation; we seek violence. We are Karl von Clausewitz's extension of diplomacy.

The village elders receive us warmly at a *shura*, a sit down meal where matters of importance to the village are discussed, and we explain why their friend and relative the farmer was killed. We apologise, and offer money and food as compensation for vaporising a man who personified the proud lineage of *pashtun* warriors, all because he dared to farm his own land. '*Inshallah*', they say – if god willed it. As we sit and eat rich *kabob*, *aushak*, *shomleh*, *bendei*, *shinwari tikka* and *doday* we shrug and tell them through our interpreter 'perhaps the farmer wouldn't have been killed if the taliban weren't in this village', all with a straight face, knowing we were told the day before of his innocent plans. 'Where are your sons? The ones of *fighting age*?' we ask the elders. 'Surely they're with the taliban?' 'No', they tell us, 'they're off earning money for their families in Tarin Kot, or Kandahar, but certainly *not* working with the *taliban, alhamdulellah*' – thanks to god. We nod and eat while a *tabla* and *harmonium* plays on a radio nearby, followed by the whine of a *dil-roba* stringed instrument. A fast jet roars in the distance as the toothless men wearing their flowing *shalwar kameez* outfits talk with us.

There are no women in sight – no women anywhere, but we feel their presence close by as the marvellous food is too accomplished to have been made by our hosts. The smells of fresh coriander, saffron, garlic and leather all mingle with the fetidness of animal droppings, bad breath and cheap soap. Young boys surround the sitting men, pouring us more chai from cheaply made aluminium pots, and clearing away the platters of food scraps. 'Why don't you fight the taliban?' our captain asks through the interpreter. The old men all look at each other and chatter, before the senior man gives their answer. 'Sometimes you must be a wolf, and sometimes you must be a lamb', the interpreter tells us, which everyone seems satisfied with. We thank them and leave and continue our patrol, noticing the complete absence of anyone now that we are retracing our route back. A young boy runs out and is quickly intercepted by a woman in a head to toe sky-blue burqa. It's the first woman we have seen on this patrol, but it won't be our last.

Suddenly great mounds of earth are thrown into the sky all around us and I feel stunned; dirt is falling around me and smoke is thick in the air. I'm standing and watching as my friends run around me, yelling and pointing, shooting, but there is no noise at all; nothing that I recognise except for a ringing that returns to my ears. I suddenly feel naked, and realise that I'm no longer holding my rifle, and spend what feels like an eternity staring at my hands wondering what is happening. I'm still standing but feel myself pulled to the ground and find my rifle lying at my feet, covered with slippery and sticky blood. I pick it up noticing I'm somehow hurt, and cannot hear anything except for the ringing in my ears. The late afternoon sun is shooting through the vibrant green almond trees in beautiful rays. The leaves of the almond tree are falling away in little puffs as angry bullets snap above our patrol, and it's these sounds that make me realise my hearing is returning. It sounds like a stockman is standing above me cracking a long whip, and each sound brings an involuntary flinch that embarrasses me. Occasionally a bullet will hit something and tumble past with a terrifying buzzing sound, or come close enough to sound like a sharp whistle. These sharp whistles are the most terrifying sounds of my life.

I can't see my friend in front of me, but hear on our radio that he has been shot, and is only fifty terrifying metres from where I am now. I get up and run, sloshing through an aqueduct that gives me cover from the angry volley of bullets in front, and reach my friend who is gurgling blood from an impossible wound on his neck. I don't know what to do, and look behind me to realise no one has followed me up the aqueduct, and that I'm alone and scared; exposed. I lift my rifle up and fire until the magazine empties, and then quickly put another in and empty that one too. I throw a hand grenade, and then a smoke grenade. When I start pulling my friend back through the aqueduct he is completely submerged, and so I have to pull him awkwardly braced against my leg, which makes me move slower than I thought possible in a situation like this. Every dream of running in slow motion has come true in a moment of desperate reality, but soon enough I'm back with our captain who is yelling into his radio.

The sounds of high-performance jet aircraft arrive and a calamitous and terrifying explosion occurs in front of us, and then the shooting stops. A helicopter comes and takes two injured but alive men from our patrol, and we move forward into the area where the bomb hit. Three young men lay lifeless on the ground near rifles: the sons of the village elders we ate with. A sky-blue burqa is there too, stained a dark red and with no signs of movement or life.

We move forward.

We return to our patrol base and slap each other on the back, and smile and recount actions and deeds and get news our injured friends are stable and will live. I have a bandage put on my hand that I didn't know was cut badly, and clean my rifle and equipment. My hands shake and don't stop for hours afterwards, and strangely I can't eat dinner that night, but I'm still full from our meal with the village elders before. The captain tells us we did well, and that he is proud of us, and thanks us for making a real contribution on today's patrol – that we 'gave it to the enemy', but I only feel a hollowness and oddness. It's not supposed to be like this, and there is no real elation or triumph in receiving and then delivering violence, but I sleep soundly, with no dreams. Only empty blackness.

The next morning a sky-blue burqa has walked up to our patrol base with a child in her arms, and explains to our interpreter he is injured. The boy is nine, ten, but who can really tell. He has no legs and is wrapped in a dirty shawl, and is limply handed over to our medic who arranges a helicopter for him and sends him away to the hospital in Kandahar where our two injured friends are. The child dies. We wake up the next day and have to go out on patrol again. And then the next day, and then the one after that.

Suddenly I'm back in Australia, and pushing my baggage through an airport to a group of waving and smiling families, and I quickly turn right to escape and find a taxi. Some Vietnam veterans from the local returned service club slap me on the back and tell me well done, and that they're proud of me, but they don't know anything about where I've been or what I've done. I sit in my room alone with a bottle of whiskey, wondering why I neither have the power to celebrate or cry. I only feel stunned, and proud, or ashamed? It's hard to tell, but I do feel that I'm alive and home. Family receive me warmly with hugs and tears and joy and I feel happy but hollow. I drive around a lot.

Three months later I open the letter, the one with the golden embossed crown and logo of the Governor General, and learn that she wants to give me our nation's second highest award for gallantry, the one right below the Victoria Cross. The captain told me it was for pulling my friend back through that aqueduct and to safety that day. He rings me that same afternoon and tells me how proud of me he is, and that this award is an important event for the unit. My invitation to the ceremony says I can bring five people, and on the day everything goes well: the Governor General pins the Star of Gallantry on me, with its orange and yellow triangular patterned ribbon, and I smile and have my photo taken. My dad shakes my hand, and my mother hugs me. They're proud of me, but I feel like a complete fraud and can't understand why I'm here, standing on manicured lawns and being called a hero, when I know how terrified I was that day. I drive around a lot after the ceremony, thinking and trying to make sense of it. I mostly think about a farmer trying to fix his aqueducts at night, a bloodied sky-blue burqa on the ground, and a legless child flown to hospital to die away from his family. *Inshallah*?

On television people say Afghanistan is not our war, and that it's time for everyone to come home, and that our mission is finished. The military holds parades, and people say 'thank you' and 'well done' and shake our hands and pat our backs. 'Well done digger', they say, and then that's it. Other veterans go on television and share their experience, and this feels odd and foreign and for some reason repulses me. I have to turn off the television, put down the newspaper, and drive around until anything makes sense, but it never does; nothing seems to fit into place, so I avoid everything about it and lose myself in driving until my fuel runs out, and then I drink until my whiskey runs out. The Star of Gallantry sits in a drawer safely out of the way and people stop asking about it.

The further I go the further I think I can escape this past, but every night my dreams return anew: running in slow motion under fire, the stockman's whip cracking at my ear and coppery metallic blood on my hands and in my nostrils. A man, a woman, a boy. There is no movie, or book or Anzac legend I can relate to. Let the months and years come, they can take nothing more. I am so alone, and so without hope that I can confront both without fear. I tell myself the life that has borne me through these years is still in my hands and my eyes, and as long as it's there I will find a way. I tell myself this as I stop on a quiet bridge, and sense the peace and quiet just on the other side of the railing.

Made in the USA
Monee, IL
28 September 2020